AF521688

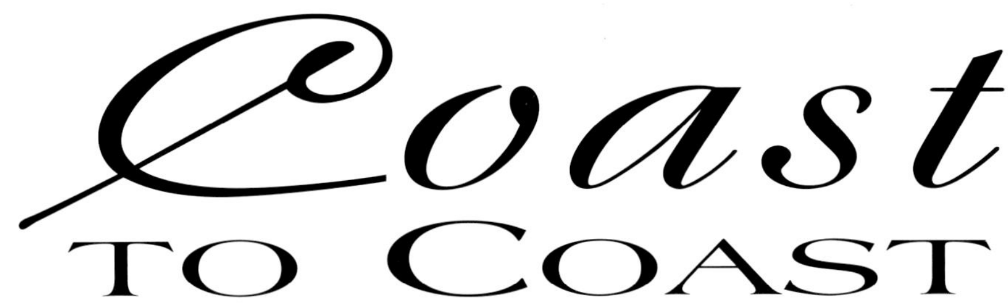

Coast to Coast

The Contemporary Landscape in Florida

from the

Geiger-Percy Collection

Gary R. Libby

With Essays by
Wendell Garrett
and
Nicolai Cikovsky Jr.

The Museum of Arts and Sciences
Daytona Beach, Florida

THE MUSEUM OF ARTS AND SCIENCES
1040 Museum Boulevard, Daytona Beach, Florida 32114

Library of Congress Catalog Card Number: 98-067011

ISBN Number: 0-933053-14-2

Second Edition

Author, Editor, and Project Director – Gary R. Libby

Assistant Project Editor – Cynthia Ryals

Word Processing – Robert J. Cruz

Book Design – Stacey G. Stivers

Photography – Ray Stanyard

Printed by Everbest Printing Company, China
through Four Colour Imports, Ltd.

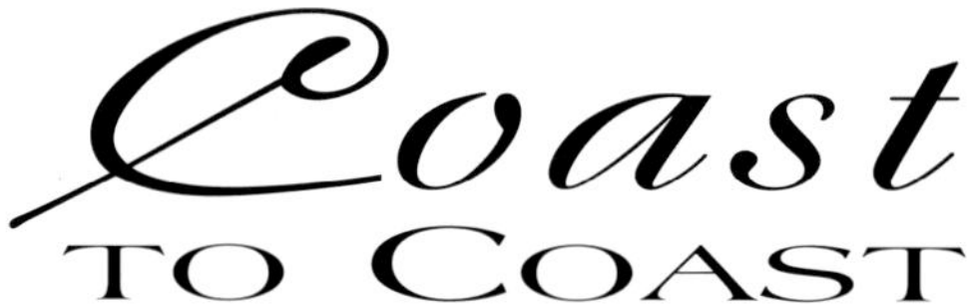

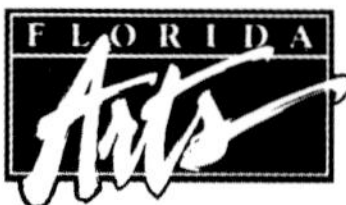

The Museum of Arts and Sciences is recognized by the State of Florida as a Major Cultural Institution
and receives funding from the State of Florida through the Florida Department of State,
the Florida Arts Council and Division of Cultural Affairs.

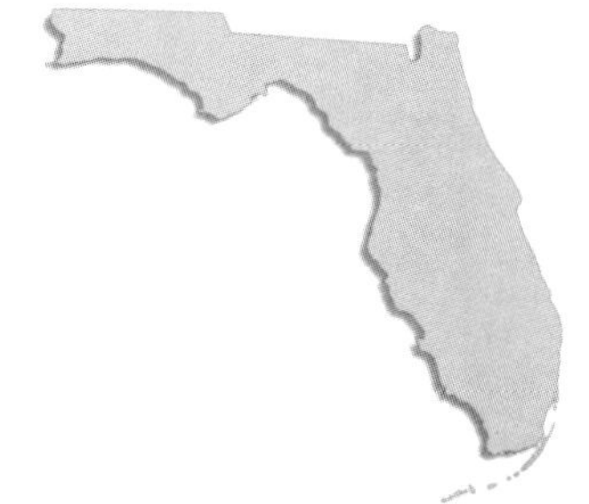

Table of Contents

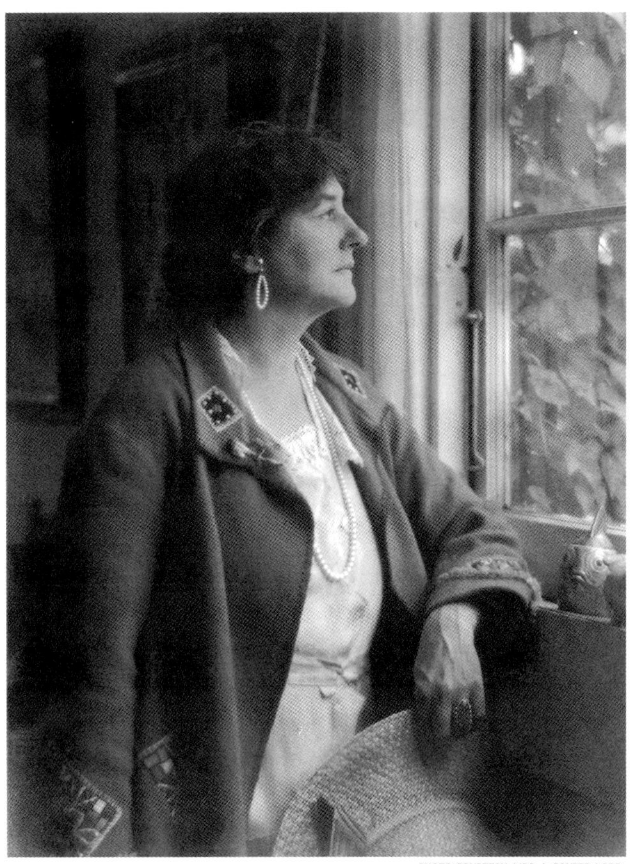

PHOTO COURTESY, MRS. J. COUPER LORD.

RACHEL HARTLEY, 1884-1959.

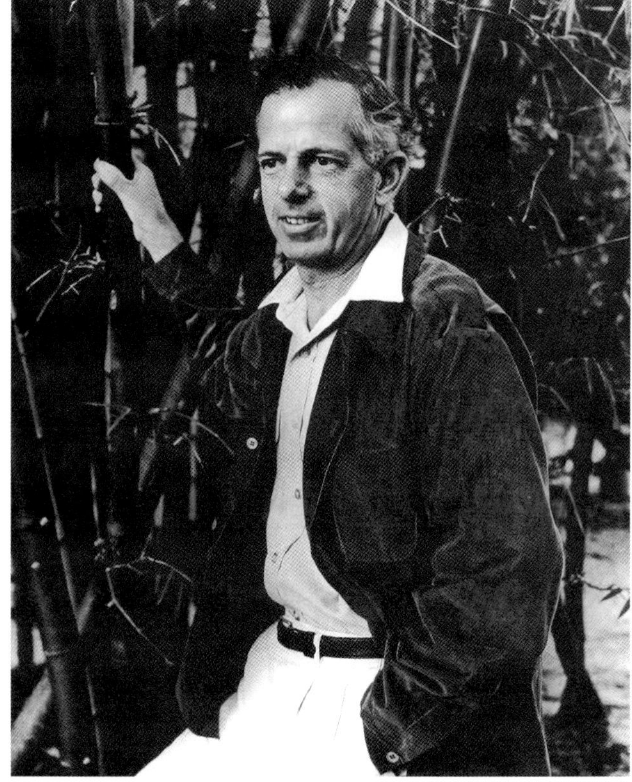

PHOTO COURTESY, CORBINO GALLERIES.

HILTON LEECH, 1906-1969.

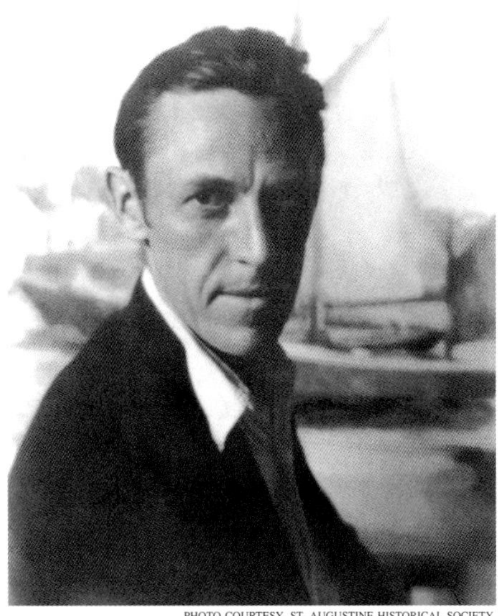

PHOTO COURTESY, ST. AUGUSTINE HISTORICAL SOCIETY

TOD LINDENMUTH, 1885-1976.

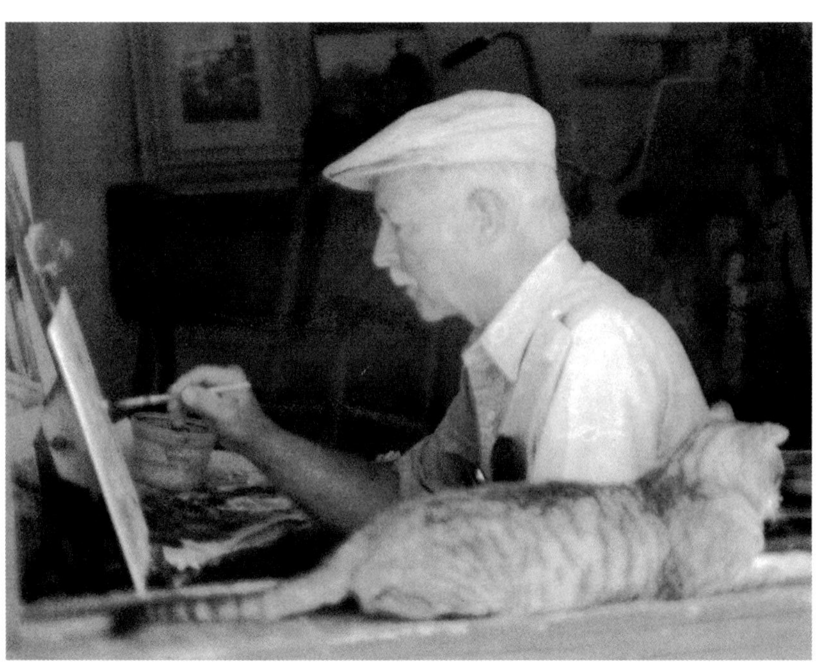

PHOTO COURTESY, ST. AUGUSTINE HISTORICAL SOCIETY

EMMETT FRITZ, 1917-1995.

Foreword and Acknowledgments

Gary R. Libby

Since World War II, Florida has been rediscovered yet again. And, with the exception of the most remote areas in the state, Florida has been a hospitable partner in the national migration to the South. This tremendous population shift, together with superhighways, new technologies like air conditioning, the desire and wherewithal to corner the market on international tourism and increased national political power, has brought abundant riches to the state and her citizens, both new and old. However, these riches have come with a price that is only now being fully understood by the Sunshine State and its people. For the last 10 years, Florida has been seriously assessing its resources and its ability to continue growing at current rates. State legislation and local initiatives in cities and counties throughout Florida now monitor and try to better control land use, water use, population densities and other ingredients of the Florida lifestyle. During this incredible period of change, visual artists in the state, individually and in groups, have responded to this dynamic with an increased sense of urgency and skill. Many openly discuss the gradual and often rapid loss of habitat in Florida in their work while others celebrate those protected, scenic areas saved and maintained by federal, state, and local efforts. Almost all attempt to capture the unique beauty of Florida terrain and atmosphere. Together, these artists are creating a Florida School of Art potentially as powerful and beautiful as similar movements in the Hudson River Valley of New York more than 150 years ago, or out west at the turn of this century in New Mexico and California. *Coast to Coast: The Contemporary Landscape in Florida* is a glimpse into the world of this developing art movement that started more than 60 years ago in the work of Rachel Hartley, Emmett Fritz, Tod Lindenmuth, Hilton Leech and other 20th century artists who recognized something extraordinary in the landscapes of Florida.

It is a pleasure for the Museum of Arts and Sciences to work with collectors Debbie Geiger and George W. Percy in presenting *Coast to Coast: The Contemporary Landscape in Florida*. The works presented here represent a selection of paintings, watercolors and pastels from the larger Geiger-Percy Collection. They are representative examples of the rise and flowering of the contemporary Florida landscape with particular emphasis on developments after 1990.

I would like to thank cultural historian Wendell Garrett for his perceptive essay that establishes a framework for appreciating the rise of modern and contemporary landscape painting in Florida. Garrett presents a panoramic look into the history of the state and some of the forces that came together to create a renascence in Florida and the South after World War II.

Additional thanks are extended to Nicolai Cikovsky Jr., curator of American and British painting at the National Gallery of Art in Washington, D.C., for his essay on the environmental and aesthetic dimensions reflected in the Geiger-Percy Collection, and their relationship to a broader concern for the preservation of the land in American art. Thanks to Tracy Ayers, the Institute of Science and Public Affairs at Florida State University, for her essay on the natural landscape of Florida, which discusses the state's topography and provides insight into the uniqueness of each region. Appreciation is also extended to Mr. Ray Stanyard, Tallahassee, Florida, who photographed all pieces in this publication; and Ms. Earline McCormick, Division of Historical Resources, Florida Department of State, who assisted with manuscript corrections.

I would like to acknowledge the Trustees of the Museum of Arts and Sciences for their support of this project. They are: President Thomas S. Hart, Past President Roger Lewis, M.D., Vice President Cici Brown, Vice President Antoinette Slick, Vice President Blaine Lansberry, Secretary Constance Yuschok, Assistant Secretary Marc Davidson, Assistant Treasurer Marilyn Chandler Ford, Ph.D., Special Representative Brop Kelly Burnett, Deborah B. Allen, Lonnie Brown, Sheila Crawford, Dr. Sylvester Covington, Pramila Desai, Sue Feibleman, Linda Freidus, John E. Graham Jr., Janice Griffin, Anne Higginbotham, Sherrie R. Hustedt, Thomas C. Kelly, Edith Lamb, Dr. Inez Marchand, David Neubauer, Neil Samuels, Julie Rand, Vicki E. Shultz, Lydia Simko, Stuart Sixma, Walter W. Snell, D. Glenn Vincent, and Allison Zacharias.

Additional thanks are extended to the artists whose works are represented here. A majority of the information on each artist is the result of personal correspondence and communication to George Percy, as well as interviews and discussions with me, all of which were often time consuming and demanding, but that yielded, I hope, a clearer view into each artist and some of the forces that helped to shape each work of art represented here.

Thanks are given to the following for their combined efforts: Mr. Michael Corbino and Mrs. Marcia Corbino, Corbino Galleries, Longboat Key, Florida, who obtained information from Robert Larsen and Craig Rubadoux, and who assisted in locating photographs of Hilton Leech.

Several people were instrumental in providing photographs, information or both for many of the artists who helped establish the Florida School, including: Mr. Page Edwards, executive director, St. Augustine Historical Society, regarding Emmett Fritz and Tod Lindenmuth; Ms. Ann Fisk, Rockport, Massachusetts, regarding her father, Tod Lindenmuth; Mr. Andrew Pocock, Pauline Pocock Antiques, Fort Lauderdale, Florida, regarding Rachel Hartley; and Katharine L. (Mrs. Elden) Rowland, Sarasota, Florida, regarding Hilton Leech.

Expertise and technical assistance for several essays and the topographical map on page 8 were provided by Dr. Edward Fernald, state geographer and director, Institute of Science and Public Affairs, Florida State University; Mr. Alan Nelson, Bureau of Archaeological Research, Florida Department of State, Tallahassee; and Dr. James J. Miller, chief, Bureau of Archaeological Research, Florida Department of State.

Thanks to Mr. Tyler Turkle of the Tallahassee/Leon County Cultural Resources Commission, for assistance in contacting several artists. Additional thanks to Ms. Katie Dempsey, Division of Cultural Affairs, Florida Department of State, for introductions to a number of the artists in the Collection.

Special thanks to Mr. Thomas Jacoby, Ms. Sally Ann Freeman, Mr. Lee Mainella, Mr. Joseph McFadden, Ms. Julie Bowland, and Mr. John Stanford for many hours of conversation with the collectors, and for inspiring their interest in collecting.

I would also like to thank Margaret and John J. Wilkinson, Cici and Hyatt Brown, Frank, Ruth and Joseph Larned, Julia Menard, Barbara and Thomas Staed, Blaine and Brian Lansberry and a Trustee of the Anderson C. Bouchelle Trust, for their support of this publication.

Final thanks are extended to my Administrative Assistant Robert Cruz, publications specialist Stacey Stivers, and Communications Manager Cynthia Ryals for their important contributions to this book.

This publication was edited according to the guidelines set forth in "The Associated Press Stylebook and Libel Manual," the Associated Press, New York, 1994; and "The Little, Brown Handbook," 2nd Edition, Little, Brown and Company. 1984.

— Gary R. Libby
Director
The Musuem of Arts and Sciences

The Natural Landscape of Florida

Tracy Ayers

"The miracle of light pours over the green and brown expanse of saw grass and of water, shining and slowly moving, the grass and water that is the meaning and the central fact of the Everglades."

— Marjory Stoneman Douglas

Many artists have attempted to capture the unique sense of Florida described by Marjory Stoneman Douglas. She was not the first, however, to recognize the natural beauty of the Sunshine State. Early explorers, like Juan Ponce de Leon, called it La Florida, "feast (land) of flowers," and were amazed at the richness and variety of the Florida landscape.

The land and water of Florida present a wonderful mosaic of environments. These are formed by the interaction of many natural features, like geology, soils, vegetation, drainage and climate. These factors combine to form the distinctive landscapes that are uniquely Florida. To aid the reader in appreciating the paintings illustrated in this collection, a brief overview of the physical characteristics of Florida is presented here. It is hoped that this will make it easier to appreciate the variety of the landscapes portrayed by the artists, as well as help locate the places shown.

Florida is divided into two general areas, one called the "peninsula," stretching south; and one called the "panhandle," extending east to west. It is bordered on the east by the Atlantic Ocean and on the south and west by the Gulf of Mexico. The climate is predominantly humid subtropical, ranging to tropical at the southern tip of the peninsula. Summers are long and hot; winters short and cool.

Geologically, Florida is made up of sands and clays resting on a base of limestone. These materials represent sediments deposited at different times over millions of years at the bottom of oceans when sea levels were higher. The present land surface of the state consists of uplands and lowlands. The former, shown on the map (see page 8) in shades of red and brown, represent much older surfaces laid down tens of millions of years ago. The lowlands, represented in green, were formed during the last ice age, or Pleistocene, within the last million years. As one moves from the present coast of the panhandle to the Georgia border, and from the Atlantic or Gulf Coast of the peninsula to its central ridge, the land rises in a series of rough steps or terraces that are the remnants of ancient sea-level stands.

The modern surface of Florida has been shaped largely by water. The uplands consists of well-drained plains and rolling hills formed by the action of ancient rivers and winds. They are no more than 345 feet above sea level and typically are between 50 and 150 feet in elevation. The lowlands, less than 50 feet, are flat and wet. Relief in the lowland coastal plain fringing all of the state is so slight that water is often trapped on the land in creeks, lakes, swamps, marshes and flatwoods, only slowly evaporating or making its way to the sea.

The southern half of the peninsula, being warmer and wetter, is characterized along the coastline by dense growths of mangroves. In the interior, there are extensive areas of freshwater marsh and wooded swamps. The former are dominated by grasslands; the Everglades, which is by far the largest of these grassy marshes, is dominated by saw grass. It is described as a "river of grass" because of the shallow, overflowing waters that seasonally cover the unbroken expanse of saw grass interspersed with sloughs, tree islands, marshes, pine-forested uplands, hardwood hammocks, and cypress swamps. The swamps, especially prominent in southwest Florida, are dominated by stands of cypress trees. Big Cypress Swamp is the best known of these.

The Atlantic coast from north to south is fronted by wide, sandy beaches and prominent dunes. On the Gulf, beaches and dunes are found in the western part of the panhandle; the farther west one goes, the wider the beaches become. From Tampa Bay north through the Big Bend, where the panhandle joins the peninsula, the coast is characterized by marshes instead of beaches. These northern coastal marshes are in contrast to the southern mangrove coasts. They generally occur behind the beaches and dunes, except in the Big Bend, where they extend right up to the Gulf shoreline. Similar marshes are found behind the dunes along the Atlantic coast.

About 500 years ago, longleaf pine forests covered much of the southeast United States, including the northern half of Florida. The original virgin timber was cut a century ago, but today's flatwoods preserve much of the character of this open pineland. The flatwoods, which cover much of the lowlands, in from the coast and north of the Lake Okeechobee region, are characterized by a mixture of longleaf or other pine, saw palmetto and wiregrass.

In the uplands, the vegetation is a mixture of longleaf pine, oaks and wiregrass on the hilltops; mixed forests of longleaf

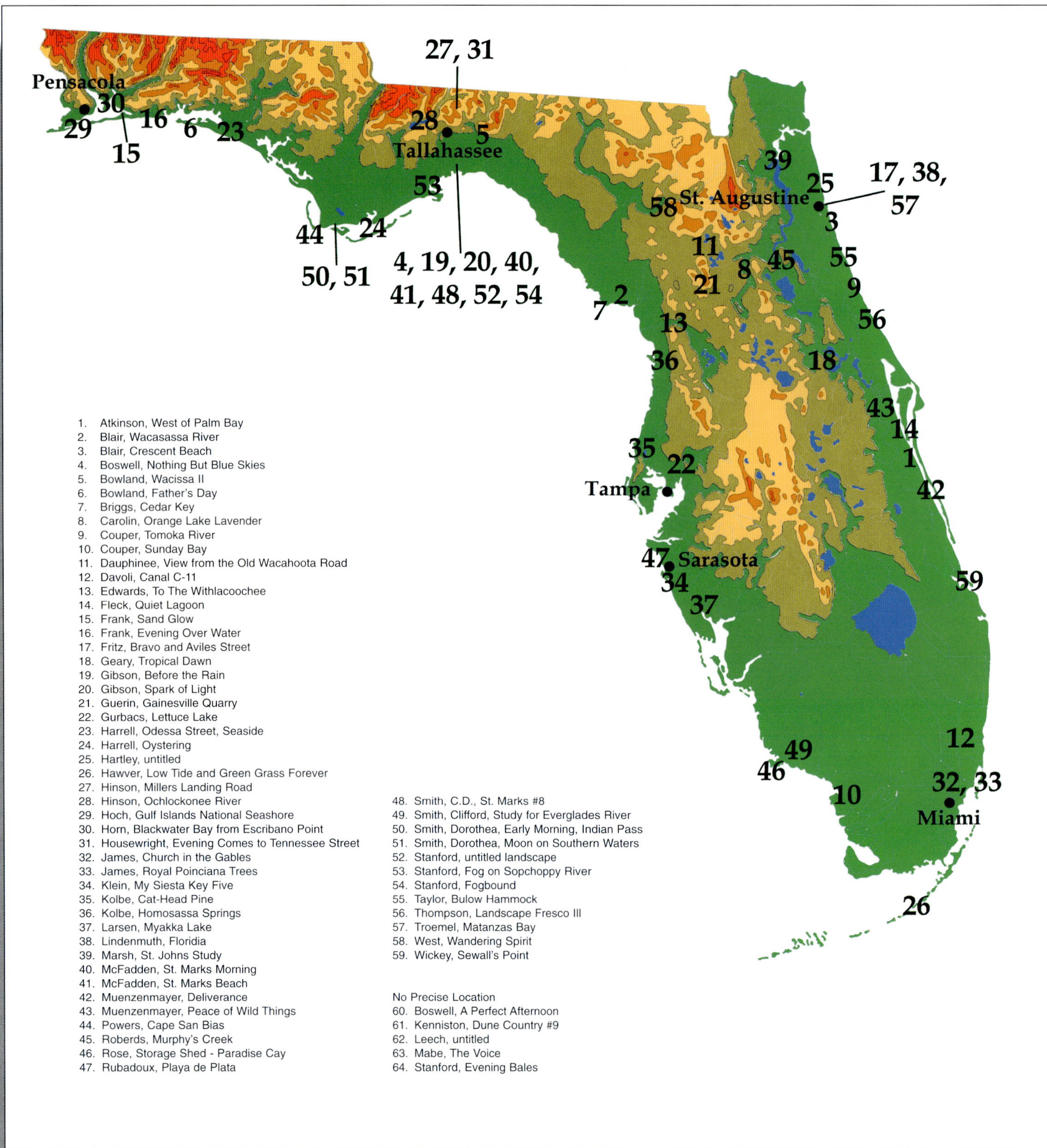

GRAPHIC COURTESY, INSTITUTE OF SCIENCE AND PUBLIC AFFAIRS, FLORIDA STATE UNIVERSITY.

A MAP OF FLORIDA IDENTIFYING THE LOCATION OF EACH PAINTING.

pine, oaks, hickories, beeches and magnolias on the hill slopes; and hardwood swamps in river floodplains and lake margins.

Underlying Florida are several large, fresh water reservoirs called aquifers, which are a principal source of Florida's many rivers and creeks. The aquifers supply water to the surface through springs, like Homosassa Springs, illustrated in a painting by Mitchell Lee Kolbe in this publication. Florida streams are also fed by runoff from surrounding land surfaces, and larger rivers, like the Apalachicola, Ochlockonee and Suwannee, which flow into Florida from Georgia and Alabama. Florida streams flow in a southerly direction, emptying into the Gulf or the Atlantic, except the St. Johns River, which flows north through northeast Florida, emptying into the Atlantic near Jacksonville.

In the central part of the state, there are hundreds of small lakes with no outlets. They are fed by small streams and drain directly into the aquifer. Other lakes, those along the St. Johns for example, are more like wide places in the river. They reflect the very shallow slope of this drowned drainage basin. These lakes are bordered by hardwood swamps and hammocks.

For the painter, Florida's landscapes are represented not only by topography and vegetation, but more importantly by color and light. The Florida light is strong and presents the viewer with a kaleidoscope of colors at different times of day, different seasons of the year, and in different parts of the state. In summer at midday, the light is so intense that the landscape appears almost washed out. At sunset or sunrise, however, the sky glows in shades of red, orange, yellow, purple and blue, and the landscape takes on those tints. In late afternoon, dramatic clouds appear in Florida skies bringing cooling, afternoon thunderstorms.

Florida is wet with very lush vegetation. Over the surface of the uplands, the predominant shades are green. This is also true of the flatwoods, river bottoms, lake margins and spring runs. The Everglades, cypress swamps, and mangrove fringes of South Florida are green as well, with brown and gold tones in the grasslands. The coastal marshes of North Florida present brown and gold tones, while the beaches are crystalline white or a modulated palette of greens, blues, reds, browns and off whites, depending upon the time of day and the strength of the light.

The Sabal Palm, which is the state tree, is an icon of Florida for many painters. In fact, it is found all over the state, but is especially distinctive of the southern grassy marshes and drier, raised "hammock" areas in North Florida marshes along rivers and coasts.

Ultimately, it is the "miracle of light" described by Marjory Stoneman Douglas that has made Florida so interesting to the artists who have been painting here for nearly a century and a half. The light, clouds, colors, lush vegetation, abundant water and distinctive landforms give Florida a distinctive character and atmosphere that painters have sought to capture.

— Tracy Ayers
Institute of Science and Public Affairs
Florida State University

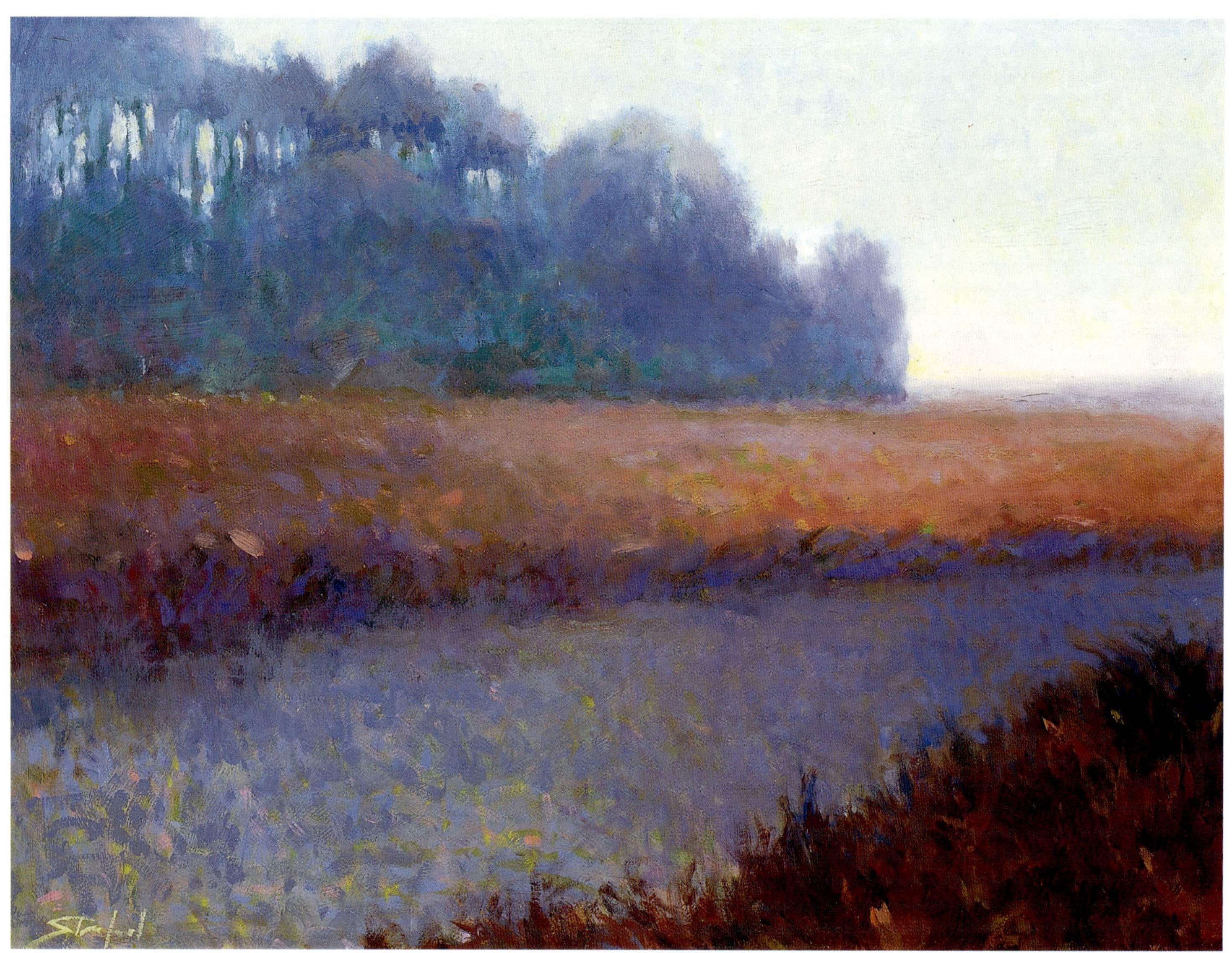

THE FIRST PAINTING THAT WAS ACQUIRED IN THE GEIGER-PERCY COLLECTION WAS *FOGBOUND,* BY JOHN STANFORD.

Debbie Geiger and George Percy
The Collectors and Their Collection

Born in Tallahassee, Florida, as a fourth generation Floridian, Debbie Geiger's roots are deep in the state. Her father was an officer in the United States Air Force and, when she was growing up, her family was stationed in various cities in Florida and California. Geiger completed a journalism degree at San Diego State University, then moved back to Tallahassee to take a public relations position with the Florida Division of Tourism. She was responsible for marketing Northwest Florida before becoming assistant bureau chief, and finally, bureau chief of the Division's Publicity Bureau. During her years with the state tourism office, she became familiar with Florida's lesser-known but most compelling places.

In 1985, she left state government to open her own public relations firm, Geiger & Associates, specializing solely in the representation of travel industry clients. Today, her firm represents United States destinations from the wine country of California to the coast of Maine, and international clients from castles in Ireland to remote parts of Australia. Geiger has lectured extensively on the economic impact of heritage, cultural and ecotourism, and the role that the media play in conveying messages about destinations. She believes that tourism, when correctly planned, holds the key to preserving many endangered places throughout the world. For her, sharing these landscape paintings of natural Florida is a way to remind people why the state is such a unique and remarkable place.

George Percy is not originally from Florida. He was born in New York, but at age one, spent the better part of a year stationed in Miami Beach with his mother and U.S. Navy father. Apart from this, he grew up in Westhampton Beach on Long Island. He graduated from Yale University with a degree in anthropology and did his graduate studies in archaeology at Tulane University in New Orleans. He came to Florida in 1967 to work on the excavation of a prehistoric Indian site near Panacea, on the coast south of Tallahassee. He returned in 1970 to teach archaeology at Florida State University in Tallahassee and has lived there since.

Beginning in 1974, he went to work for the Florida Department of State. Since 1987, he has been director of the department's Division of Historical Resources. Concern for Florida's rapidly changing environment and the loss of its historical and natural resources have been central to his professional life during this period. He has traveled extensively throughout Florida and, for more than two decades, has been involved in many state programs concerned with protecting and preserving the historical and natural heritage of the state. In the course of his work, he has acquired a broad knowledge and deep appreciation for the natural beauty of Florida, as well as its history, folk culture, art and architectural traditions. For him, an interest in landscape paintings has been a way of touching his emotional ties to Florida that lie beneath the more objective routine of his professional activities.

Our Collection

Both of us love Florida. We have traveled and worked extensively throughout the state, and we are captivated by its beauty and uniqueness, and made nostalgic by changing lifestyles. At the same time, we are distressed by the gradual (and not-so-gradual) disappearance of natural places.

Florida landscape art captures the sense of place that is so important to us. Collecting these paintings is a way we have found of sharing our experiences and remembering details, feelings and happenings at different times in our lives. Less selfishly, we think landscape art is a way of communicating the essential qualities of Florida, sharing them with many people. Art is meant to be seen. It communicates ideas and values. We are glad for others to learn more about Florida through our collection, and to take time to appreciate its beauty and the importance of preserving its individuality. Even if Florida no longer seems charged with the promise that anything is possible, there is still something extremely fulfilling about it—a thrill of connecting with unspoiled places, and the beauty and bounty of nature.

We have been collecting Florida landscape paintings for more than a decade. We began casually, purchasing pieces that gave us pleasure. The first piece we acquired is illustrated in Page 10. It forcefully reminded George Percy of his summer in Florida in 1967, which he spent working at a prehistoric Indian archaeological site near Panacea, on the coast south of Tallahassee. Each day, the archaeologists started very early in the morning to get as much work in as possible before the day got too hot. John Stanford's painting perfectly captures the feel of early summer mornings over the coastal marshes of the Northwest Florida Gulf Coast.

As the collection grew, pleasure became passion and combined with a developing sense of mission to gather examples of the best in contemporary Florida landscape painting. At its present stage, our Florida collection includes more than 200 works. Our interests have broadened, of course, and we have collected many landscapes from other states, especially the Southwest, and other countries, and Florida art other than landscape. But, the core of the collection remains the Florida landscape.

We also must confess that our principal motive is still the pursuit of art for the personal pleasure it brings. We rarely sacrifice this priority to the greater sense of mission. Our collection is not, and probably never will be, an objective survey of the history of landscape painting in Florida in any period. It has emerged from the heart—from a process of looking and responding—rather than from any kind of academic framework. We believe this is its greatest strength. Often, serious collectors of contemporary art of whatever type lack sufficient historical perspective on their field of interest to know which works are more important, so they are thrown back on their own responses as the principal guide to assembling a collection. We recognize, however, that in our enthusiasm for what we like, it would be easy to try to claim more for the collection than it is. It is very much a collection still in process.

Even so, as we have gotten deeper into collection, we have come to realize that the history of Florida art (specifically landscape painting, but the same could be said about Florida art in general) is largely unorganized, underappreciated and underrepresented in serious public and private collections. Indeed, there is no authoritative survey of the development of landscape art in the South that covers very much of the 20th century. Even on a state-by-state basis, the landscape art of the South has not been well explored. Scholars simply have not taken the time to inform themselves about much of the area, particularly for the period after World War II.

Happily, in the past several years, Southern painting has received more exposure—it would be interesting to learn what forces in the cultural life of the South have been responsible for this—and several important private collections have been shown. These include the Roger Ogden Collection, emphasizing Louisiana art; the Sam and Robbie Vickers Collection of Florida art; the Robert Coggins Collection, with fine examples of Georgia painting; and the Collection of the Greenville Museum of Art with its South Carolina works.

There is still, however, very little information on landscape art in many parts of the South. In Florida, few books or articles have been written. Few institutions are collecting Florida landscapes as a principal focus of their holdings, and few are making their collections, extensive or not, available to the general public on a frequent basis.

We have educated ourselves about Florida art mostly by visiting private collections and private galleries throughout the state, and by talking to the artists themselves or their friends and families. Of course, this is one of the special privileges of collecting contemporary art. If one is less concerned with buying for investment or historic value than with simply acquiring something one likes, the whole process of seeking art is made much more satisfying by being able to talk with the artists about the way they see Florida.

In our Collection, we include any work we believe has artistic merit and relates to Florida in its content. In regard to merit, while we always review the artist's background and learn as much as we can from secondary sources, we primarily look for work that is skillfully done and deepens or corresponds to our sense of the qualities of the Florida environment. It does not matter if an artist was born in Florida, is a resident of Florida, or simply visits Florida even on a very casual basis. Any work that represents or is explicitly inspired by the Florida landscape we include in our definition of Florida landscape art.

We have tried to include works that express the tremendous variety of Florida landscapes, and the diverse ways of seeing and representing these places. Thus, the works in our Collection range from highly realistic to very abstract, expressing a mood or quality rather than depicting an actual place. We include widely different styles of painting in different mediums, including oil, acrylic, watercolor, pastel, and mixed media; works on paper, as well as on canvas and board. We think that a broad range of styles and mediums is a distinctive feature of Florida landscape art after World War II.

We have been very conscious of searching out artists who represent different parts of Florida. In our own experience, many people, especially those who haven't spent much time in Florida, have an overly simplified view of the natural landscape—a stereotyped view based upon tourist advertising. To them, Florida is sun, sand, the ocean, tropical plants, golf courses, orange groves, Mediterranean-style architecture, St. Augustine, Miami, and the Everglades (and, of course, Disney World and other theme parks). Somehow Florida is more a state of mind than anything physically connected to the rest of the South.

This mythical view of Florida, in our opinion, has deflected an objective exploration of Florida art. So, we have taken pains to collect works representing not only well-known areas, but less familiar parts of the state that are more typical of its environment as a whole, and that relate it to landscapes across the lower South.

Rather than concentrate on a few painters or those in a particular area of the state, we have tried to include a wide sample of the many fine painters working in Florida today and over the past several decades. The Florida art scene has been populated for more than a century by year-round and seasonal residents who have been busily painting the Florida landscape. They have tended to congregate in some places more than others, particularly in and around St. Augustine, Vero Beach and Fort Pierce, Miami, Key West, Sarasota, Tampa, Gainesville and Tallahassee.

While there are certainly many artists who come to Florida from other places, a significant number of contemporary artists were born here and trained at schools in the state, or returned to live here after attending art schools elsewhere. Others came from out of state to attend school here and chose to remain. This is another significant characteristic of the contemporary Florida artists population compared, for example, to artists in Florida at the end of the 19th or early 20th century. For much of the 20th century, art departments at a number of Florida colleges and universities, as well as private art schools, have been started by well-known artists who came to live in Florida. Perhaps the best known of the latter is that established by Jerry Farnsworth and Helen Sawyer in Sarasota, as well as the Ringling School of Art, also established in Sarasota. We have tried to include in our Collection many works by these indigenous artists on the grounds that there may be an indigenous quality to their painting not found from artists who were working in other regional traditions before turning their hand to Florida.

There is a deep and complicated tradition of landscape painting in Florida, and a great opportunity for serious scholarship in seeking the history of this tradition and its connections to the broader picture of American painting. It is our hope that, in a small way, in addition to deriving personal pleasure from the art we collect, we are helping to lay the groundwork for a stronger scholarly and popular appreciation of Florida art, as well as a better understanding of the natural beauty of this unique area of the United States. We also hope that increased exposure to Florida landscape painting will lead to better collections of Florida artists by public institutions.

Florida is often said to be a place where almost everyone is from some place else. It seems to us that landscape art is a potentially important force in the cultural life of our state for bringing about a better sense of community and a better understanding of a place many now call home.

Our collection is not complete. We look forward to many years of discovering new artists who choose the Florida landscape—urban or rural, realistic or expressive, past or present—as their subject.

— Debbie Geiger and George Percy

Calling Florida Home

Wendell Garrett

Florida does beguile and gratify me—giving me my first and last (evidently) sense of the tropics, or à peu près, the subtropics, and revealing to me a blandness in nature of which I had no idea.

— Henry James to Edmund Gosse, February 16, 1905

"In the beginning," wrote John Locke in the *Second Treatise on Civil Government*, "all the world was America." Locke intended only a metaphor for the state of nature that preceded the establishment of civil society. But, his metaphor evokes much more. It implies a way America was first seen from Europe—as a new beginning, a break in the long, sad continuities of history. A second chance for fallen humanity. The North American Indians, the Native Americans, lived in something close to Locke's state of nature. Even the European whites in America were liberated, in part at least, from the deadweights of the past. They brought certain ideas and institutions from the older civilization, but transformed these in the hard experience of subduing a wilderness and pushing on to ever-receding frontiers. Other ideas and institutions, like feudalism, they simply left behind; and the absence of feudalism assured a separate political evolution in the New World. "The great advantage of the Americans," as Alexis de Tocqueville said in *Democracy in America*, "is that they have arrived at a state of democracy without having to endure a democratic revolution, and they are born equal without becoming so."

Although the United States began with the Declaration of Independence in 1776, the actual origins of the American people go much further back in time—to at least the 16th century, when the Spanish, under Juan Ponce de Leon, sailed from Puerto Rico in search of gold and silver, spices and pearls, and discovered a distinctive, jutting peninsula (believing it to be another island) while searching for Bimini, of which he was promised the governorship. The date was early April 1513, six days after the crew had celebrated Easter's Pascua Florida (Feast of Flowers), for which the new land, Florida, was named. America thus began as an outpost of Europe, as the Spanish set up posts in Florida and in the western parts of the North American continent. Columbus' discovery of the New World on behalf of the Spanish crown in 1492 and the subsequent exploration and settlement of the Western Hemisphere by Spain and other European states were all aspects of the great explosion of Western energies that took place at the beginning of modern times. Over a period of 500 years, from the age of Columbus to the sudden collapse of the European empires in our own time, the states of Europe extended their influence—their languages, their economies, and their peoples—over the globe. The United States was only the most important and most dramatic product of this outward thrust during the past half-millennium of world history.

It was not until 1565 that Pedro Menéndez de Avilés, arriving with a thousand settlers and a priest, established St. Augustine, the first permanent European settlement in North America. Though their colony survived, life was difficult for the Spanish settlers who were beset by the combination of harsh climate (Florida hurricanes), hostile natives, famine, fire, and disease. St. Augustine was attacked time and again by pirates and armies of the rival French and British empires. Florida gained importance in the defense of Spain's commercial coastal route, but it never produced bounteous wealth for Spain as settlements in Mexico, the Caribbean, and South America had done. When the British captured the important Spanish port of Havana, Cuba, in the French and Indian War (1754-1763), they offered to exchange Havana for the rights to Florida. Forced to choose, the Spanish reluctantly agreed.

During their two decades as stewards of Florida (1763-1783), the British brought zeal and resources to the territory's development that far exceeded Spanish efforts. England split Florida into two parts: East Florida, with its capital at St. Augustine, and West Florida, with its capital at Pensacola. The British began establishing Florida as a major agricultural center. Stately plantations producing indigo, rice, and oranges rose up along the Atlantic coast and the St. Johns River. They offered port subsidies and land grants to attract new settlers, and mapped out most of the inhabited areas of the state. St. Augustine bustled with activity; East Florida British Governor James Grant captured the confident tenor of the times in a letter to a friend: "There is not so gay a Town in America as this is at present, the People are Musick and Dancing mad." Bolstered by stipends from the British Parliament, Florida remained loyal to King George III during the American Revolution and, in fact, became a haven for Loyalists from the northern colonies. But, British domination did not last long. In 1783, Spain avenged her loss of Florida by capturing the British colony of Bahamas. To regain the islands, England returned Florida to Spanish control in the Treaty of Paris, and once again the Spanish flag flew over Florida.

Florida remained in Spanish hands for the next four decades (1783-1821), but Spain's second attempt to develop Florida was a failure from the start. British plantation owners left. To attract settlers, the Spanish offered land grants to anyone willing to immigrate to the colony, and as English-speaking homesteaders from the United States began to stream into the region, its Spanish character underwent a subtle shift. In 1791, Secretary of State Thomas Jefferson wrote to President George Washington: "I wish 10,000 of our inhabitants would accept the invitation. It would be a means of delivering to us peaceably what must otherwise cost us a war. In the meantime, we may complain of the seduction of our inhabitants just enough to make the Spanish believe it is a very wise policy." This maneuvering over control of Florida between the two nations broke into open conflict with the War of 1812 and the First Seminole War of 1818. Andrew Jackson's unopposed marches through Florida during these two conflicts convinced Spain that it had no choice but to negotiate a graceful departure. In 1821 Spain ceded Florida to the United States.

The new territorial government aggressively set about encouraging the growth of its charge. Tallahassee was chosen in 1824 as the capital, streets were laid in Cowford, a cattle crossing on the St. Johns River, and the village was renamed Jacksonville in honor of Old Hickory. Florida's population of 8,000 in 1821 quadrupled to 34,000 by 1830. But, one obstacle to settlement yet remained—the Seminole Indians. The Seminoles had migrated into the peninsula from Georgia toward the end of the 18th century and, by the 1820s, much of Florida's richest farmland, which the territorial government was eager to open to white homesteaders, lay in their hands. After a series of compromise treaties, the Removal Law, passed in 1830, ordered all of the country's Indians east of the Mississippi removed west to reservations in an uninhabited portion of the Arkansas Territory. When the Seminoles refused to leave their homes, the white settlers tried to move the Indians by force, igniting the Second Seminole War, which lasted seven years (1835-1842) and took a terrible toll on both Indian and white lives. With the Seminoles decimated and out of the war, the territorial General Legislature petitioned Congress for statehood, and on March 3, 1845, President John Tyler signed a bill making Florida the 27th state in the Union. Florida grew rapidly over the next 15 years; cotton, cattle ranching and forest industries thrived; railroads began to appear, and visitors from the North arrived to enjoy the Sunshine State. By 1860, Florida's population had grown to 140,000; then came the Civil War.

In 1861 Florida withdrew from the Union and, during the next four years, the state furnished 15,000 troops for the Confederate Army, plus salt, beef, bacon and cotton. When General Robert E. Lee surrendered at Appomattox, Tallahassee was the only southern capital still in Confederate hands. Florida's fledgling cities and industries escaped from the Civil War relatively unscathed. The state emerged from the turmoil and rigors of Reconstruction to rebuild its economy and usher in an era of rapid growth and development. The last years of the century brought intensive development throughout Florida. St. Augustine was a peaceful fishing village that began to attract tourists. Key West, the largest city with 18,000 people, was a prosperous naval base, and the center of the sponge and cigar industries. Jacksonville owed its prosperity to lumber resources and naval ports. Pensacola was an important Gulf port and Tampa took off when cigar manufacturers moved from Key West to Ybor City. Plantations in the north and west produced cotton, corn and tobacco, orange groves in the northeastern area increased in commercial importance, and vast phosphate deposits were discovered in the center of the state.

State planners recognized that the expansion of railroads was the requisite catalyst for economic growth. Industrialists Henry Plant and William Chipley built railroads that connected Tampa and Pensacola to the developed regions in Florida's northeast. To ensure the profitability of their new railroads, both men invested heavily in the isolated cities at the end of the line. But, the man who revolutionized Florida tourism was the flamboyant Henry Morrison Flagler, a partner in John D. Rockefeller's Standard Oil Company. In the 1880s Flagler envisioned the sunny, Atlantic coast state as a vast playground for millionaires—a southern Newport. He bought up and knit together the short rail lines that extended south from Jacksonville and laid track as far as West Palm Beach, incorporating it all under the Florida East Coast Railway Company. In 1896, Flagler's trains reached the infant hamlet of Miami, and by 1912 the rail line extended south to Key West. In Palm Beach, Flagler built his own mansion, Whitehall, as well as two palatial hotels.

Florida entered the 20th century with a diversified economy centered on ranching, citrus, timber and tourism; prosperity was everywhere. The expanded rail system vastly improved mail service around the state; telephones and electricity reached most rural areas; and an extensive road system accommodated the rapid growth of the automobile. After World War I, real estate was going through the roof as millions of immigrants, speculators and builders descended on the state, and new communities sprang up seemingly overnight. Between 1920 and 1925, the population increased four times faster than in any other state. But, in the spring of 1926, the bubble burst, with banks failing and millionaires turning into paupers overnight. Two hurricanes, the first to hit the state in more than a decade, pummeled the Gold Coast in 1926 and 1928, catastrophically damaging both the resort areas and the interior farmlands of the southern peninsula. The Mediterranean fruit fly invaded Florida, destroying 60 percent of the citrus groves. The 1929 stock market crash that precipitated the Great Depression seemed almost an afterthought to Florida's ruined economy. Trying valiantly to recover from those years of crisis, Florida entrepreneurs turned to the development of tangible resources, such as paper mills, cooperative farms, port improvements and commercial real estate. President Franklin D. Roosevelt's New Deal programs helped the state begin to climb back on its feet. But, the event that finally lifted Florida, and the nation, out of the Depression was World War II. The Sunshine State became a training center for troops, sailors and airmen as scores of army bases and training facilities for other services were opened and expanded all over Florida. When the war ended, many servicemen returned to settle there and in the 1940s the state's population nearly doubled. During the bullish economy of the 1950s, Florida became America's 10th most populous state. Tourists and retirees came in droves, making Florida "the state where everyone is from somewhere else." Florida is a living testament to the American belief that there will always be a tomorrow, the clouds will roll away, and a stunning sun will shine.

In the 20th century, as in the 19th, the South has been the region most sharply at odds with the rest of nation. No other part of the United States has projected such a clear-cut, sectional image. Although the most spectacular period of sectional conflict came to an end with the close of Reconstruction, sectionalism has been a powerful and recurring force in the national experience. The South remains the nation's most distinctive region, most notably in a cultural sense. In fiction, the dominant mode of the South has been local color, an attachment to place and community, a variety of writing that focused on regional landscape and speech patterns, and localized characters and attitudes, and was characterized by a generally sentimental approach to southern life. In painting, regionalist artists have celebrated the countryside and modes of life in their native locality. The dominant aura of nostalgia and ghostly stillness provide an ambiguous overlay of past and present—an art seen as expressions of a charming and innocent realism; an art of sympathetic observation and pungent social criticism. These southern regionalist paintings convey an aura of loneliness, mystery and melancholy through luminous lighting and the absence of figures.

The state of southern letters, and art as a whole, was still so undistinguished in 1920 that the nation's reigning social and cultural critic, H.L. Mencken of Baltimore, felt compelled to write a lengthy essay in which he proclaimed the South "the Sahara of the Bozart"—a desert of the fine arts. Mencken charged that a much earlier southern civilization—the age of Washington and Jefferson, which, he contended, was the finest civilization the Western Hemisphere had seen—after the Civil War had become a sham and a fraud, and such it remained in the early 20th century. Never had a single essay written about Dixie created such controversy. In conservative southern circles, The Sahara was met with a withering counterattack; an impassioned defense of the South. But, for many young southerners of literary and artistic ambition and an iconoclastic disposition, it served as a call to arms; indeed it served to embolden those creative, kindred spirits who would themselves become part of that movement of the 1920s, 1930s, and 1940s known as the Southern Renascence. Whatever its causes—the birth of a new, bold critical spirit, the opening of the South in World War I, the southern migration of industry on a large scale, or the response of those who took a "backward glance" at what was slipping away—the Southern Renascence remains one of the greatest outbursts of literary and artistic excellence the nation has witnessed. Indeed, it has been compared in many respects to the New England Renaissance, which had occurred a century before. And, it had come for many of the same reasons—a transition from a largely agrarian economy to an emerging industrial one, thus the threat to an older way of life and seeing the obsession with the past with a mixture of pride and shame. Seeing the universal in the particular and the regional, these artists painted haunting landscapes as their fellow writers composed a searching literature that is as marked by difference as by similarity, by disjuncture as by continuity. These southerners went in search of a colloquial voice and found a great measure of it. But, this was soon submerged, at least in Florida, by still more dramatic changes in local culture.

Following World War II, Florida entered another extended period of growth, which has continued to the present time. In the 1950s and 1960s, businesses from out of state were actively recruited, and an impressive flow of industry entered the state. People followed the jobs that were created.

By 1980, Florida was the eighth largest state in the nation with well over nine million residents, up from a million and a half in 1930. By 1990, three million additional residents raised Florida's rank to fourth in the United States. Retirees accounted for half the population growth in the decade.

Beginning in the 1930s, Florida's ethnic composition also changed dramatically. At least 30 different ethnic groups, apart from Anglo-Americans and Afro-Americans, became part of Florida society. By far the largest concentration of immigrants was the Cuban exile community, which came in several principal waves between 1959 and 1980 to escape Fidel Castro's revolutionary society. By 1990, Haitians displaced

Cubans as the second largest immigrant category.

Post-World War II Florida has become a very different place from the Florida that young southern artists were seeking to describe in the years between the World Wars. Florida, at the end of the 20th century, is a place where a significant number of residents is "from somewhere else." The local color and sense of place and community that writers and other artists of the Southern Renascence sought to express were profoundly changed in Florida, perhaps more than in any other part of the South in the post-war years. Tremendous growth and development led to extensive alteration of the natural landscape, the razing of thousands of older buildings and other structures, fundamental change in the size and composition of social communities and the appearance of many new cultural traditions. The population of Florida at the end of the 20th century includes a large number of people with no attachment to place and community in Florida, and no sentimental feelings about southern life.

Since the end of the 1960s, another cultural renascence has been gradually making itself felt in Florida, fueled by the work of artists and others who have been deeply distressed by the massive destruction of natural and cultural environments, and the sense of rootlessness on the part of so many new residents. Environmental, historic and cultural preservation movements, among the strongest in the nation, have focused on protecting what remains of Florida's natural and cultural resources to create a new sense of place and community on the basis of renewed appreciation for the natural beauty and cultural richness of the state as it now exists.

The arts, especially literature and painting, have been stimulated by this broad-based environmental movement and have tended to fill very important roles. First, as a moral voice, artists have documented, graphically and popularly, how Florida has been overwhelmed by its destiny—what has been lost and the consequences for the quality of life here. More positively, as a creative force, artists have been searching for a new vision of Florida, trying to articulate the elements of a new sense of place and community. The strong tendency to realism in Florida arts is not accidental. Realism is an approach that appeals to broad audiences and communicates its concerns with the least amount of ambiguity. Florida has reached a point in its history where it needs an easily communicated sense of identity that blends the many colloquial voices that now call Florida home.

— Wendell Garrett
Editor at Large
The Magazine Antiques

A High and Sacred Mission

Nicolai Cikovsky Jr.

The works in the Geiger-Percy Collection are tremendously varied in style, ranging from the abstract to the realistically representational. However, they clearly share—perhaps as a conscious, philosophical attitude or artistic program, but surely as a collective, artistic result—one thing: the preservation in paintings of the natural landscape that is being inexorably consumed by civilization. That has happened with alarmingly accelerated speed everywhere in America during the half century following the end of World War II, but in few places, as these artists have seen, has it happened as rapidly as in Florida. And, to the extent the contemporary painters of the Florida landscape in this period have as their purpose its preservation in pigment, this gives that purpose particular urgency. As a consequence, what results pictorially has particular force—all the more forceful, of course, because, for most of these artists, being Florida natives, Florida residents, or Florida-educated, the Florida landscape has deep and special meaning for them, and so does its loss. They cherish the landscape's beauty and lament its disappearance. That is seen and felt in their paintings, and it resounds in their words.

Just as important as an inherent conservationist ethic is the obvious fascination of the artists represented in this collection with the qualities of the Florida landscape and their desire to celebrate Florida's natural beauty, in and of itself, as a timeless thing. Earlier painters and writers who came to Florida in the 19th century thought of it as a kind of Eden, a tropical paradise with light and air, colors and foliage and an overall atmosphere different from anywhere else in the country. In their work, they tried to convey the special beauty of the place. The same concern with describing Florida and its moods is carried forward in the work of landscape artists throughout the 20th century.

Whereas painters in the 19th and early 20th centuries concentrated on describing parts of East Florida, especially the coastal areas around St. Augustine and Miami, painters in the late 20th century have explored much more of the state. One of the most striking aspects about the works in the Geiger-Percy Collection is the tremendous variety of places they record. Many are not ones we typically think of when we think of Florida. Beyond the beaches, palms and orange groves, there are cypress swamps, vast prairies, Spanish moss, great rivers. Florida is a whole state, not just a fantasy or a state of mind known from tourist brochures. It is even more beautiful than we thought, in ways we never imagined, and it is also more clearly part of a larger southern region with landscapes that can be found all across the Gulf Coastal Plain. Even the names are more interesting. We thought we knew Florida through knowing St. Augustine and Miami. As magical as these places are, it is even more exciting to find new places like the Sopchoppy and Apalachicola.

These two compelling themes—celebrating Florida's beauty and documenting a beauty that is threatened—are two focal points of an important regional tradition in American landscape art, which began in the middle of the 19th century. The early part of this tradition—from the middle of the 19th century to the early part of the 20th century, generally before World War II—is represented in the Sam and Robbie Vickers Collection, which was the subject of an earlier publication and exhibition titled *Celebrating Florida*. That this tradition continues through to the end of the 20th century is clear from the works in the Geiger-Percy Collection.

The strength, longevity and diversity of the Florida landscape tradition has not been properly appreciated in the literature on regional art in the United States. Perhaps this is because we have only recently become aware of collections like the Vickers and the Geiger-Percy, or because it is only in the last decade or two that such collections have come to be assembled.

While some regional traditions of American landscape painting (and associated schools of painters) are well known, the work of artists in other regions is less widely known or appreciated. There is also no sense of the amount or coherency of the body of work they have produced. This is especially true of paintings of the South, compared to works, for example, from the Hudson River Valley, the White Mountains, the coast of Maine, eastern Pennsylvania, California, or New Mexico.

The regional landscape tradition in Florida is nearly a century and a half old, but is not yet well recognized. Although there is some awareness of important painters who came to northeast Florida around the turn of the century at the behest of Henry Flagler, the study of Florida art is still limited. Nor has Florida art been satisfactorily related to broader movements in the art history of the United States. It deserves to be better studied. And, the importance of the Geiger-Percy Collection is to make us aware of the richness of a relatively undiscovered tradition in American landscape painting, and to stimulate us to connect it to the great themes and traditions in the art of our country.

America has been called "nature's nation." Nature, Americans saw early on, was the best, most available and most fitting, expression of their nationality. "We have more of nature, pure and uncorrupt as she came from the hands of her Maker," someone wrote in 1854. That writer added that American nature was "as yet little injured by the hands of man." But, others saw that was not so. By the middle of the last century, many people saw that nature was already being lost to civilization—to the clearing of forests for agriculture, settlement, to logging, and to the railroad. Among them, American artists were particularly and painfully aware of the destruction and corruption of nature. The founder of the American landscape school, Thomas Cole, lamented the "meagre utilitarianism" and "what is sometimes called improvement" that were destroying natural beauty and purity beneath their "iron tramp. The ravages of the axe," Cole said without mincing words, "are daily increasing —the most noble scenes are made desolate, and oftentimes with a wantonness and barbarism scarcely credible."

American landscape artists were charged with the task, the "high and sacred mission," of saving in painted images what was being destroyed in reality. "The axe of civilization is busy with our old forests and artisan ingenuity is fast sweeping away the relics of our national infancy," a critic wrote in 1847, and it urgently "behooves our artists to rescue...the little that is left, before it is forever too late." They may use different language and other terminology—conservation, preservation, and ecology—but the landscape painters of Florida represented in this collection feel as strongly today—as it was felt a century and a half ago—the mission of recording the vanishing beauty of that part of the American landscape—a part largely unknown a century and a half ago— that they know and love. Like the American landscape painters who preceded them and whose footsteps they follow, they have the mission of rescuing the little that is left, before it is forever too late.

—Nicolai Cikovsky Jr.
Curator of American and British Painting
National Gallery of Art

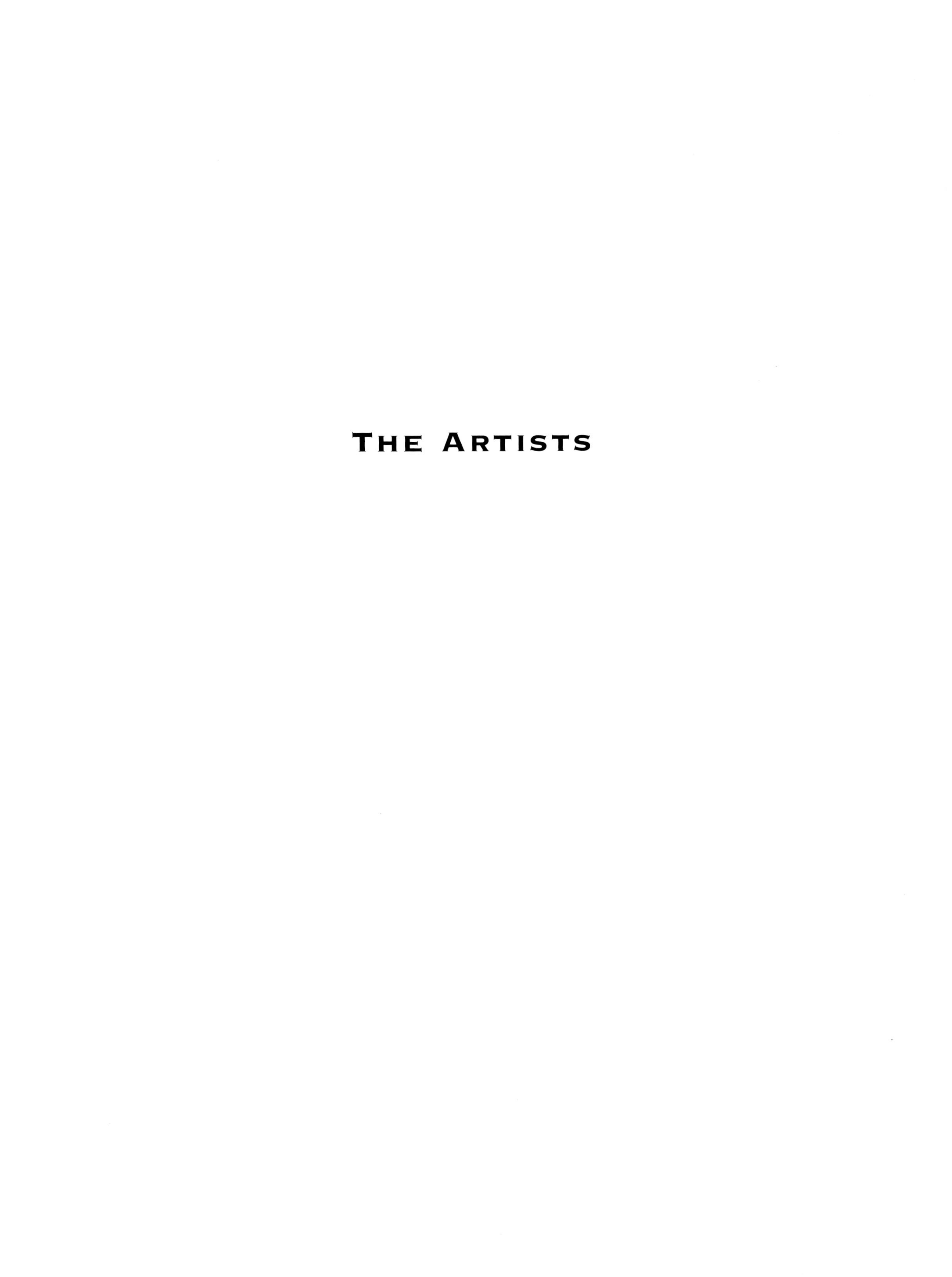

THE ARTISTS

George Atkinson

West of Palm Bay

1992, Pastel on paper, 17" x 35"

George Atkinson is an Illinois painter. He was born in Springfield in 1949, and grew up there. He earned a bachelor's of fine arts degree in 1976 at the San Francisco Art Institute, and returned to Springfield where he has since lived and worked. He is employed in the art and architecture program of the Illinois Capital Development Board.

Atkinson has enjoyed participation in more than 40 selected group exhibitions at museums and galleries throughout the United States, including the Illinois State Museum, Springfield; the State of Illinois Art Gallery and the Struve Gallery, Chicago, Illinois; the Rahr-West Art Museum, Manitowa, Wisconsin; the Museum of the Southwest, Midland, Texas; Wichita Center for the Arts, Wichita, Kansas; Flint Institute of Art, Flint, Michigan; The University of Oklahoma Museum of Art, Norman, Oklahoma; The Knoxville Museum of Art, Knoxville, Tennessee; The Philharmonic Center for the Arts, Naples, Florida; and Sherry French Galleries, New York, New York, where he earned two one-person exhibitions.

Atkinson's work is included in the collections of more than 25 national businesses and institutions, including AT&T, Prudential Insurance Company of America, Hallmark Cards Incorporated and GTE Corporation. His work is also included in the permanent collections of the Arkansas Art Center, Little Rock, Arkansas; The Illinois State Museum, Springfield; The Sunrise Art Museum, Charleston, West Virginia; The United States Department of State, Washington, D.C.; and the Center for the Arts, Vero Beach, Florida.

Known for his highly detailed and specific landscapes, Atkinson works in pastel, using only the broken edges to produce his precisionist effects that are both lyrical and romantic in their ability to capture pure nature. Atkinson is a Midwestern artist. The Midwest sky is the focal point of much of his work—vast, overpowering, creating a deep recession of space as it extends to the horizon. Atkinson is part of a group of contemporary prairie painters who celebrate the enduring features of land and sky that are characteristic of the American prairies. In her book *Plain Pictures: Images of the American Prairie*, Smithsonian Institution Press, 1996, Joni L. Kinsey discusses the contributions to American art of this group of contemporary landscape painters.

Atkinson and his family are regular summer visitors to Florida, spending most of their time in the Central East Coast region of the state. The artist has painted many views of the East Coast Region, as well as views of the Everglades, which he completed for the Sherry French exhibition titled *Expedition: Everglades River of Grass.* The latter was shown at the Sherry French Galleries in New York; the Henry Morrison Flagler Museum, Palm Beach, Florida; DeLand Museum of Art, DeLand, Florida; Edison Community College Gallery of Fine Art, Fort Myers, Florida; Center for the Arts, Vero Beach, Florida; and the Alexander Brest Gallery and Museum, Jacksonville University, Jacksonville, Florida.

His Florida works bring the unique perspective of the contemporary prairie painters to the representation of Florida landscapes—a composite view, conceived from photographs, synthesizing several angles of vision, vast scale and a sense of the extraordinary in the midst of the unremarkable.

West of Palm Bay was completed in 1992 during a brief automobile tour of the state. Atkinson describes the scene as an "unplanned occurrence" between two points of civilization on the road west from Melbourne to Kissimmee, Florida, where the "out of the way scene seemed at peace to have survived man's encroachment for another day." This mental and visual oasis represents, for Atkinson, a small victory in the natural world's struggle for survival. The view is looking west across the marshes of the upper St. Johns River.

The large pastel is designed to capture a broad expanse of Florida wetland and sky on a late afternoon where falling light animates the pastoral scene with a vibrant and colorful glow. Overhead, large and dramatic gray clouds reflect the light as they define the landscape below, interrupted only by water-filled ruts and tire tracks; a lingering sign of the presence of man in the boundless beauty of nature.

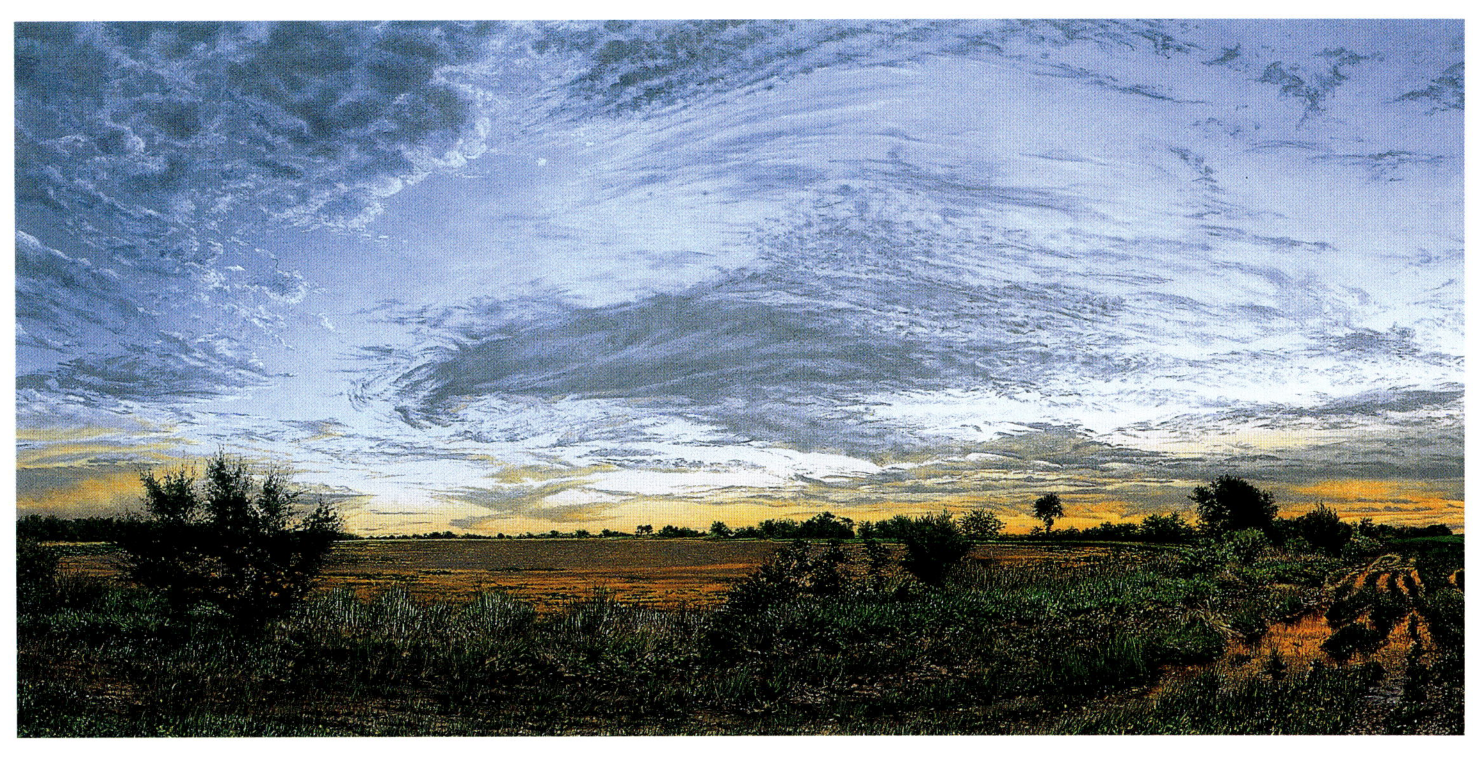

ELEANOR BLAIR

WACASASSA RIVER
1996, OIL ON WOOD PANEL, 8" X 8"

CRESCENT BEACH
1996, ACRYLIC ON PAPER, 17½" X 23¾"

Eleanor Blair was born in New Jersey, June 7, 1947, and attended the Art Students League in New York as a high school scholarship student. After graduating from high school, she attended New York's Cooper Union School of Art in 1969, where she studied drawing under Stefano Cusumano and color theory with Hannes Beckman.

Blair began her career as an abstract painter specializing in hard-edged, geometric shapes painted in acrylic and preconceived around scientific color relationships and optical effects. During this cerebral period, Blair perfected her understanding of color and its important role in painting.

After a move to Gainesville, Florida, in 1971, Blair taught courses in art at Santa Fe Community College from 1973 to 1975. Since the early 1970s, she has painted full time, given private art classes at her studio, and participated in the local Alachua County Artists in the Schools program. At Santa Fe Community College, she was given an assignment to teach a studio course in landscape painting that was to have a profound effect on her development as an artist. Working outdoors with her students, Blair discovered Florida and began to take extended hiking trips throughout the backwoods of north Florida. Her meticulously constructed geometric abstract paintings gave way to looser landscapes, which gained in popularity as Blair explored the blending of her substantial academic training and her new fascination with the beauty of rural Florida. "My whole attitude began to change. I gradually came to realize that a palm tree had more to offer visually than all of my concepts about color."

While she insists there is no substitute for the intense visual experience of painting outdoors, Blair usually begins by taking photographs of her landscape subjects to capture them before the Florida light changes. She then reviews the photos in her studio before starting a painting. Her mature style has been described as a distinctive and unmistakable "synthesis of Romanticism, Mysticism and Impressionism." Blair, herself, is less elliptic in describing her love of Florida and her attachment to landscape painting. She says, "I want to convey what it feels like to be out there in the wild. I feel that my job is to witness the changing Florida environment, and that my paintings are a souvenir I bring back to people."

Eleanor Blair exhibits widely and has been included in more than 40 exhibitions, including in Florida at the Museum of Arts and Sciences, Daytona Beach; The Capitol, Tallahassee; The Tampa Museum of Art, Tampa; The LeMoyne Art Foundation, Tallahassee; the Lowe Art Museum, Miami; and The Huntsville Museum of Art, Huntsville, Alabama. Her work is included in the collections of Holland and Knight, Jacksonville; Sun Banks, Florida; the Barnett Banks of Florida; the City of Coral Gables, Florida; the City of Winter Park, Florida; Florida International University, Miami; Shell Oil Company, the University of Florida, Gainesville; the University of Tampa; of The Museum of Arts and Sciences, Daytona Beach; and the Polk Museum of Art in Lakeland. Her work was featured in a 1981 article by Steve Hodges in *American Artist* magazine.

Blair's *Wacasassa River* is a small oil on board that captures the basin of this tidal river as it enters the Gulf of Mexico south of Cedar Key on the west coast. Blair's overcast atmosphere clearly delineates the landscape in horizontal bands of water, marsh and upland accentuated by tall sabal palms. In this oil, Blair works on a toned ground. She underpaints with dark transparent oils, then works opaque, lighter colors into the wet paint to create both brushstrokes of texture and contrasts that clarify shapes with areas of negative space. The result is a jewel-like, painterly celebration of this unique Northwest Florida scene actually completed in the studio from a photograph taken several years earlier by the artist. The Wacasassa has been one of Blair's favorite places to paint. Unfortunately, many of the palm trees captured in her canvases are now dead along the river.

In her larger acrylic on paper, *Crescent Beach*, Blair is preoccupied with capturing this Atlantic shore beach south of St. Augustine on a cool and crisp morning with soft and constant light from a low sun. Here Blair covers her weighty paper with a heavy coat of mid-value gray acrylic paint that is left to dry. Then, dark transparent colors are washed in, followed by light, opaque pigments painted into the dark underpaint. The effect of her acrylic painting is much more minimalist than her oils and closer in feeling to the monotype landscapes of other contemporary masters like Milton Avery.

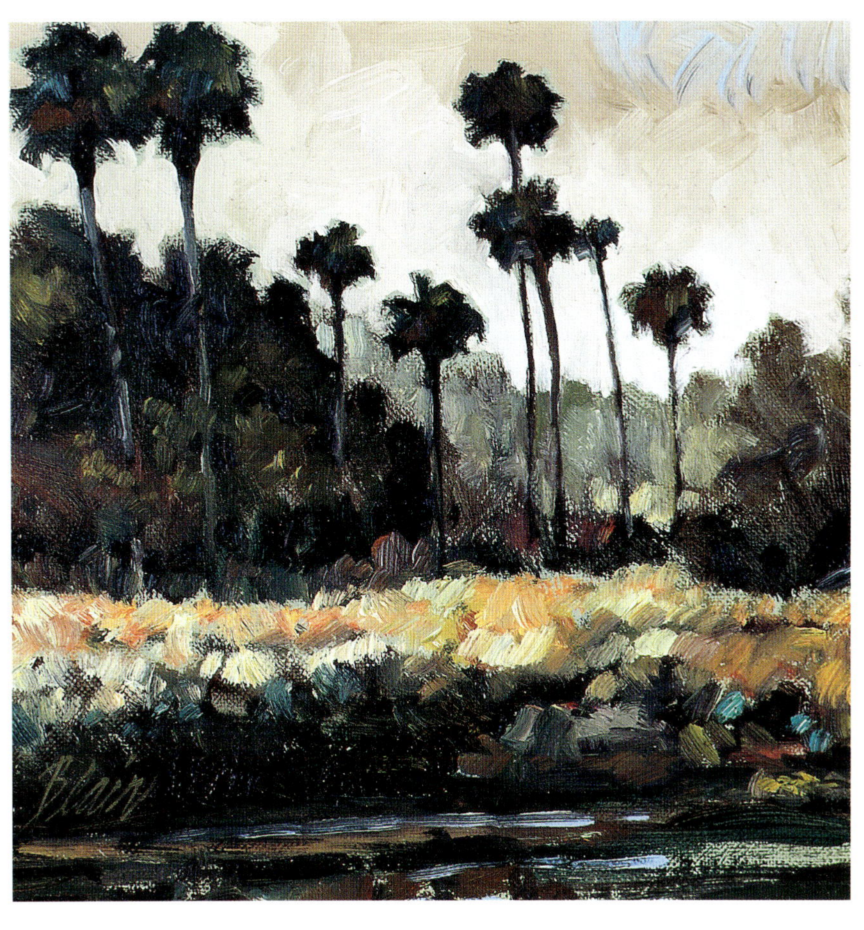
Blair

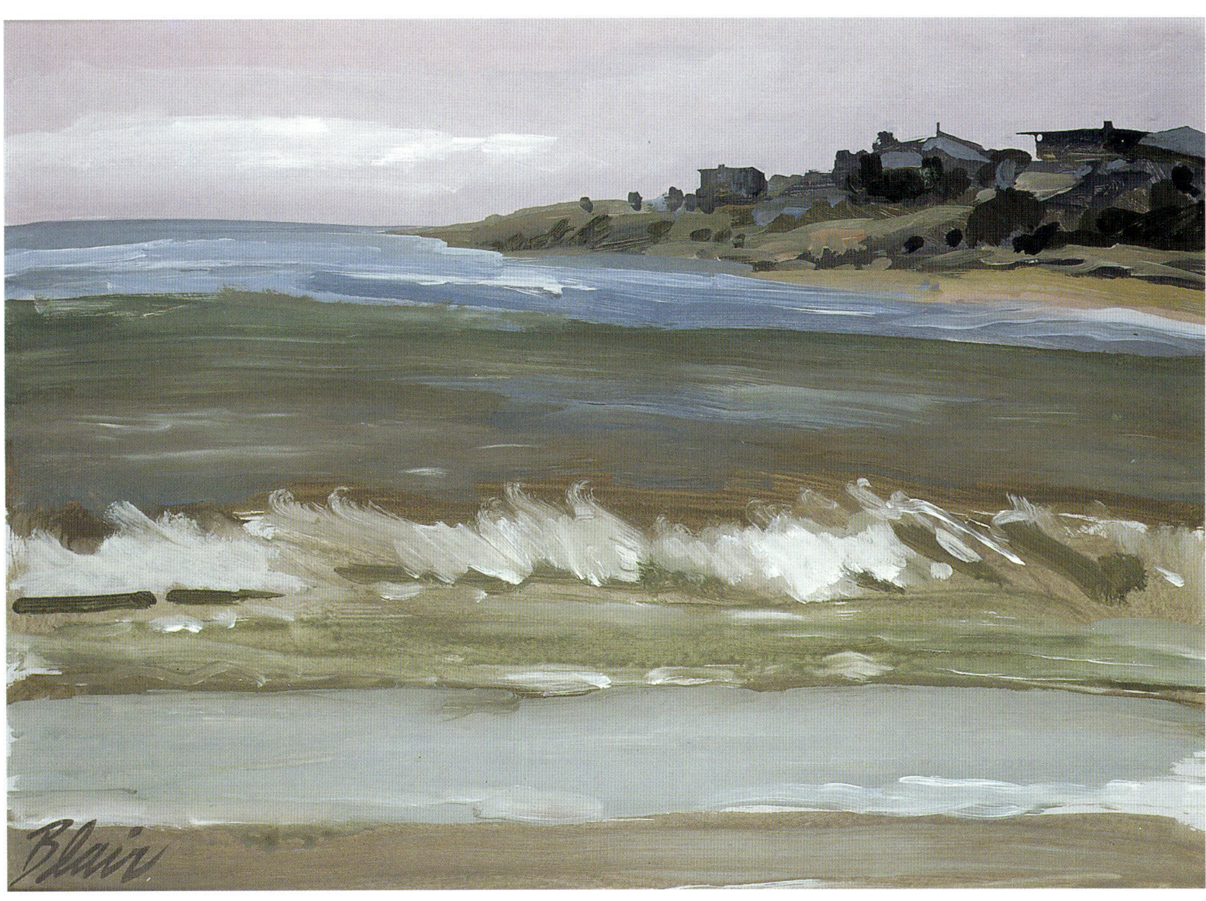
Blair

Sally Boswell

A Perfect Afternoon
1991, Oil on canvas, 18" x 30"

Nothing But Blue Skies
1994, Oil on masonite, 11⅛" x 11¼"

Born in 1948, Sally Boswell was raised in southwestern Missouri on the Ozark plateau near Joplin on a family dairy farm. Both of her parents were part-time artists—her father made jewelry and furniture, her mother was a painter, weaver and quiltmaker. Boswell finds it hard to remember a time when she wasn't drawing, coloring or painting. In public school, she was befriended and encouraged by her art and music teacher, Lenola Hodge, who created a special curriculum for her exceptionally talented and motivated student.

After finishing high school, Boswell attended Southwest Missouri State University in Springfield. After a move to Florida in 1971, Boswell began to concentrate on her painting while studying with Daniel Green in Tallahassee. In 1986, after successfully raising a family, she was hired as staff artist in residence at the Museum of Florida History.

Boswell considers herself primarily self taught. She is a fine craftsman. Her paintings are meticulously done and very realistic. They generally reflect everyday scenes. Cows are a favorite subject; also gardens and intimate views of the Northwest Florida coast. She finds exquisite beauty in the most typical places. Her colors and compositions are literal, but very rich. She is able to seek out and capture the "good vibrations" of places, which make her feel good. Her paintings seem uncomplicated, but they have a strong emotional content and appeal to a universal desire to find beauty and romance in the most common places.

Boswell believes that her father, an accomplished carpenter, taught her to both observe and absorb her surroundings while her mother taught her the value of craftsmanship and the importance of a finely finished product.

Boswell hopes that her work affects viewers in nostalgic and personal ways giving them "a chance to linger, to notice a beautiful image or savor a sweet memory." Her realistic paintings of meadows, cows, flowers and beautiful landscapes reflect her own personal pleasure as an artist.

In her oil on canvas *A Perfect Afternoon*, 1991, Boswell invites the viewer to a closer, more realistic look at nature and her bounty. Here, a typical hot, North Florida afternoon sees accurately rendered domestic cattle enjoying a cool dip in a pond. The location is one of hundreds of small farms that dot Northwest Florida, and contribute to its pastoral and classically arcadian quality so accurately captured in this large and impressive oil painting.

An oil on masonite, *Nothing But Blue Skies*, 1994, captures a cool, clear day and bright, blue sky at the St. Marks Wildlife Refuge, south of Tallahassee on the Gulf Coast of Florida. Boswell accurately captures this broad panorama of both fresh- and saltwater marsh, pine and palm forest in a painting of great clarity and detail. The viewer is invited to see miles deep into this real and metaphorical "refuge" as foreground, midground and background march toward a horizon of billowy clouds in an ultramarine Florida sky.

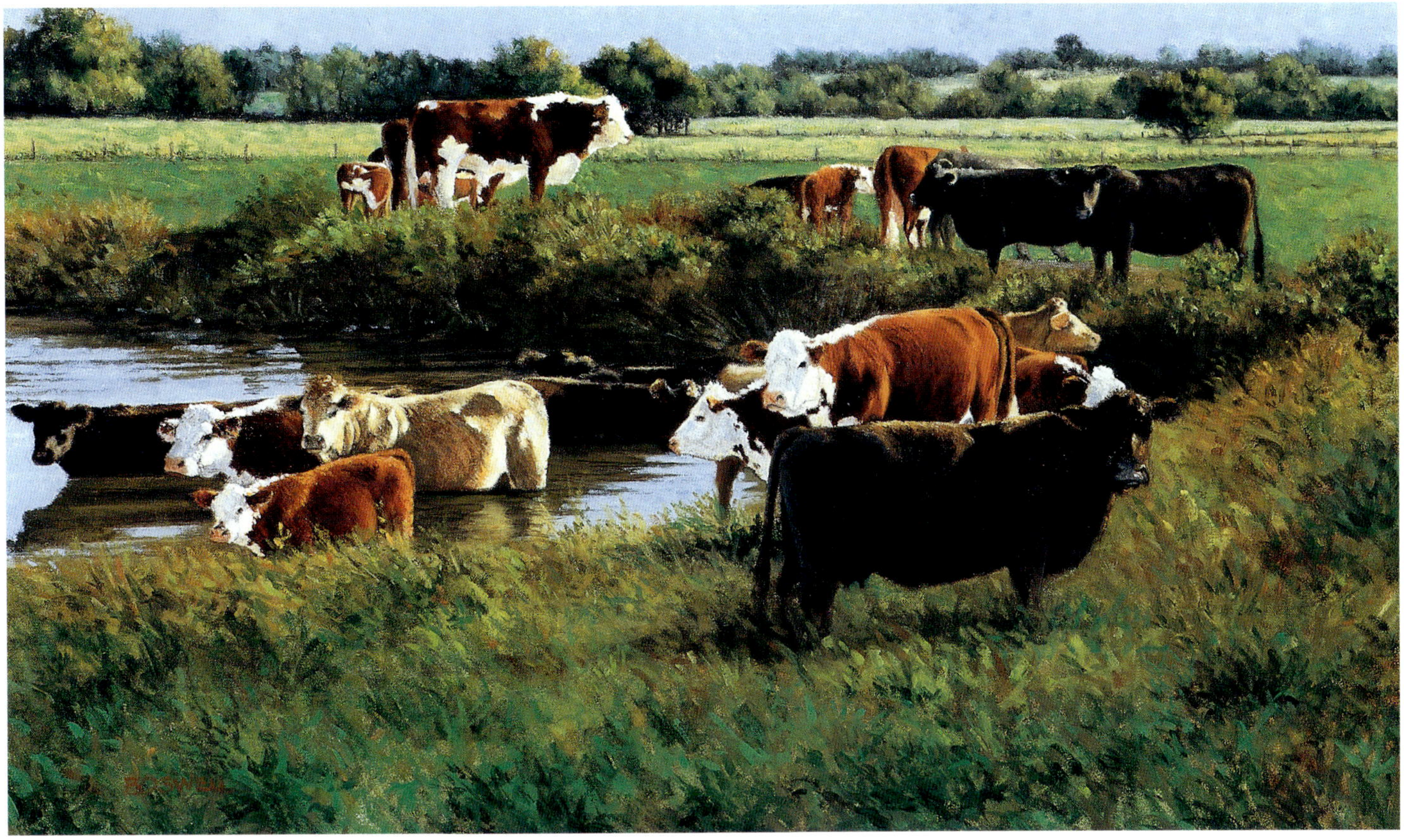

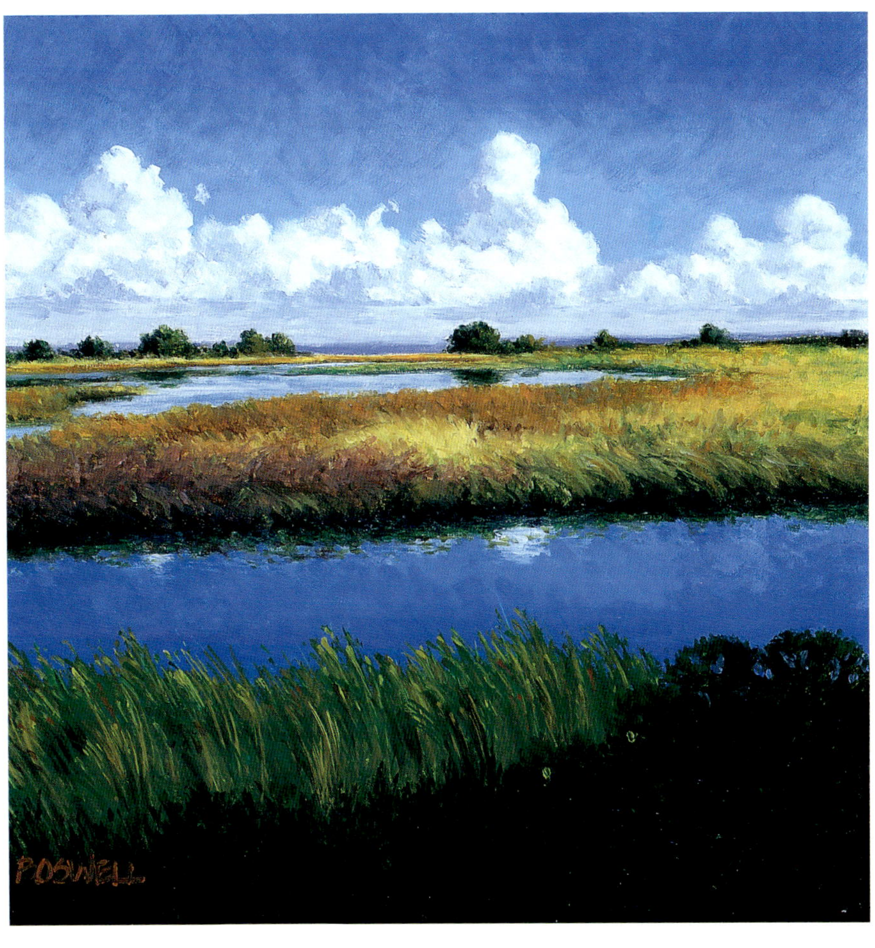
BOSWELL

Julie Bowland

Wacissa II
1991, Oil on canvas, 17¾" x 36"

Father's Day
1991, Oil on canvas, 24" x 48"

Julie Bowland is a Florida native. Born in Miami in 1957, she graduated from high school in Michigan and attended Florida State University where she earned a bachelor's degree of fine arts in painting in 1989. She earned a master's degree of fine arts in painting from Arizona State University in 1991.

Bowland is primarily a plein aire landscape painter in love with the Florida outback. She is widely known for highly expressionistic and Fauve-like colorful impasto paintings of great energy and vitality. She is an interpreter rather than a describer, and is interested in capturing what a specific place "means" to her in personal and direct terms.

Bowland feels that the wild and untouched Florida landscape provides a refuge for her that she hopes is shared by viewers of her work. She is uncomfortable with much of the modern world and its growing disregard for the integrity of the environment and human spiritual values. A colorist at heart, she is committed to "exploring and pushing oil paint and color into new realms."

Bowland has enjoyed solo exhibitions at more than 10 locations in Florida and Georgia, including Broward Community College, Pembroke Pines, Florida; The Museum of Art, Tallahassee, Florida; and North Florida Junior College, Madison, Florida. She has participated in a number of group exhibitions, including Florida State University Fine Arts Museum, Tallahassee, Florida; Thomas Center Gallery, Gainesville, Florida; the Cultural Arts Center, Valdosta, Georgia; the Albany Museum of Art, Albany, Georgia; and the Chattahoochee Valley Art Museum, La Grange, Georgia.

Her work is included in the collections of the Barnett Banks, Jacksonville, Florida; the City of Tallahassee, Florida; Florida Community College, Jacksonville, Florida; and The Museum of Arts and Sciences, Daytona Beach, Florida.

Wacissa II is an energetic oil painted on location near the headwaters of the Wacissa River near the small town of Wacissa, Jefferson County, Florida. This painting, dated 1991, is part of a series of this locale begun by Bowland in 1989. Bowland is interested in this location because of its abundant wildlife, natural beauty and serenity. She places the viewer overlooking a small island and the adjacent marsh and cypress-lined river. The heavy brushstroke and thick impasto energize the scene painted in full light on a hot July day. The artist has tried to convey a sense of real space as she expresses what the place felt like to her that day.

Father's Day was completed in 1991, and painted on location on Father's Day at Grayton Beach in Walton County on the northwest coast of Florida. The artist (and her father) are looking west as a thunderstorm is moving in rapidly from the north. The painting was done quickly in one sitting and conveys the energy of the approaching storm so typical of summer afternoons at the beach in North Florida.

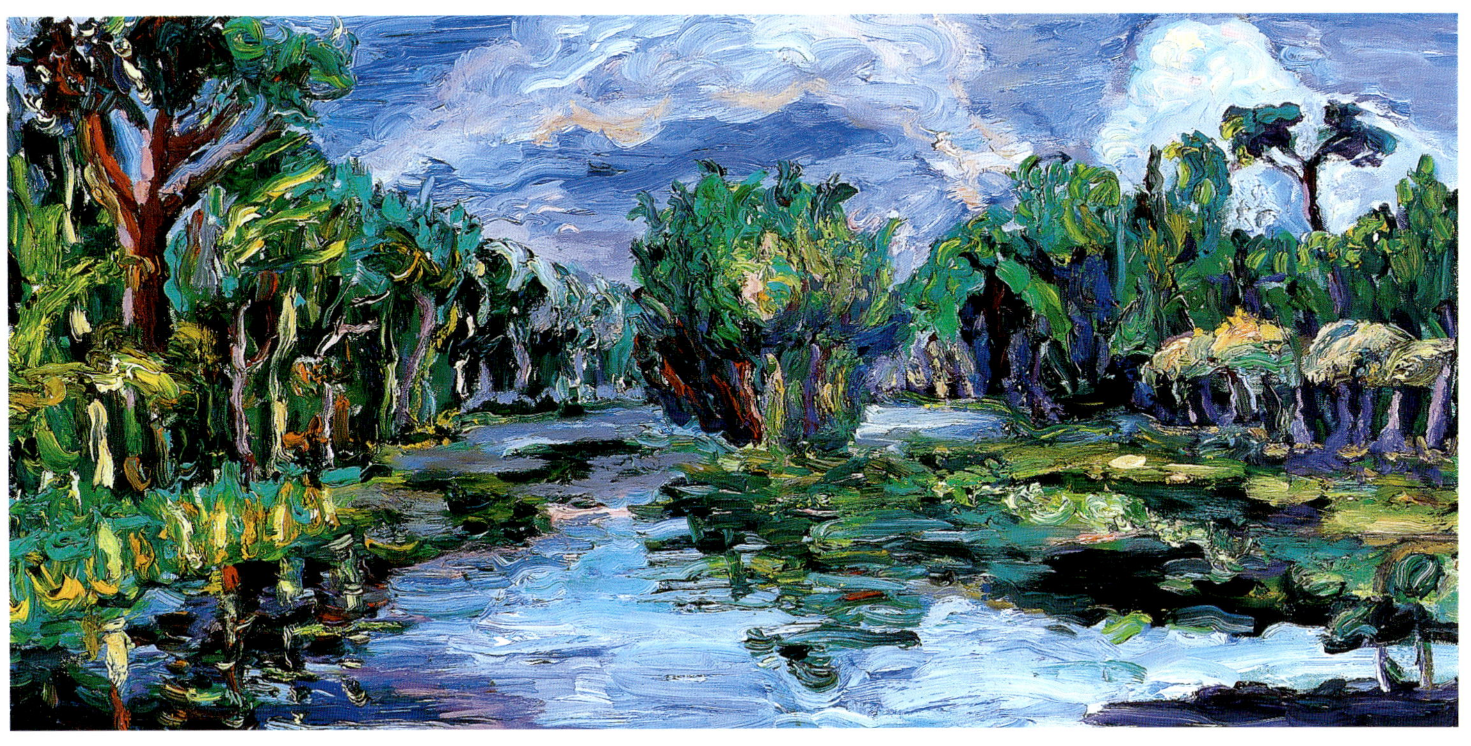

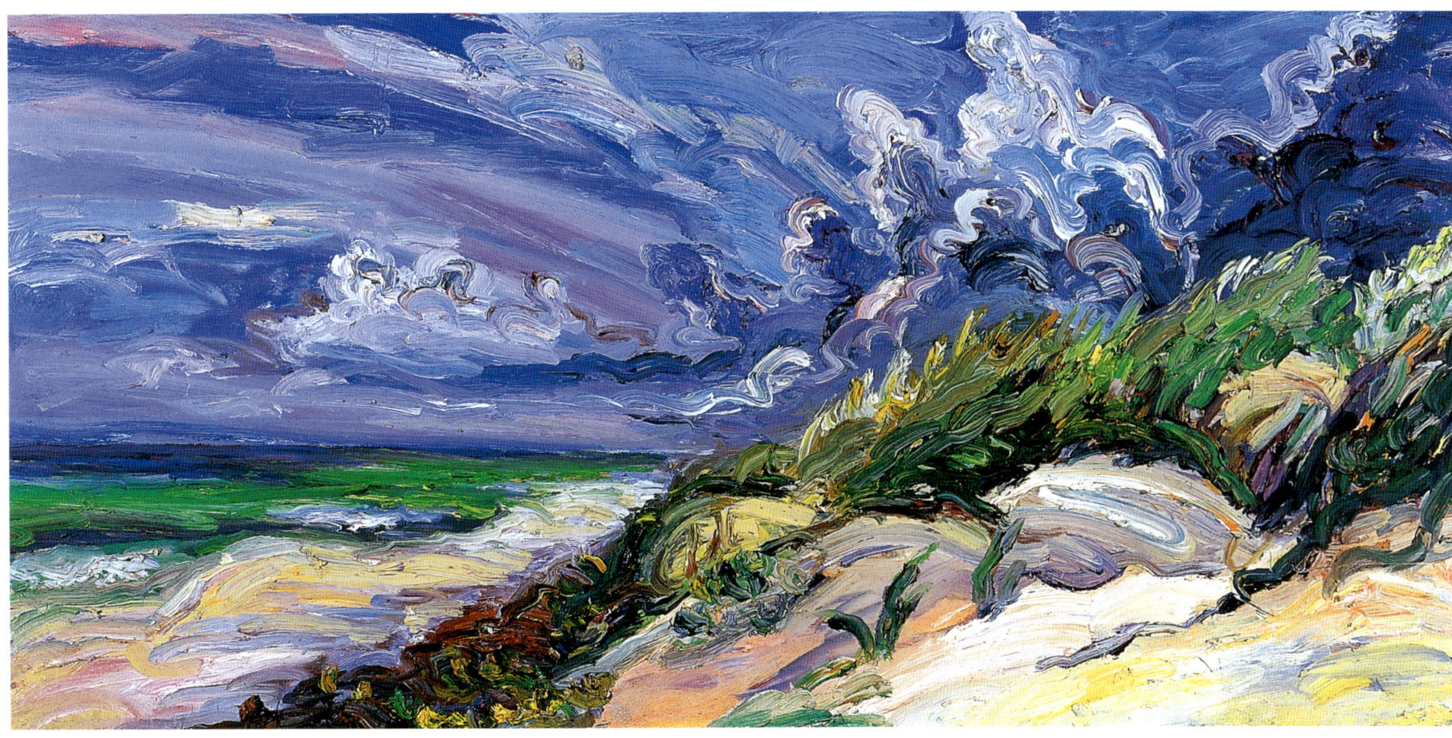

John Briggs

Cedar Key

1993, Oil on Masonite, 21" x 28"

John Briggs was born in Hamilton, Ohio, in 1948, but he has lived most of his life in south central Florida. In 1976, he earned a master's of fine arts degree from Florida State University in Tallahassee, followed by a National Endowment for the Arts artist-in-residence appointment in both Bradenton and Plant City. He continues to live and work in Plant City.

Briggs is a realist painter whose highly detailed and carefully crafted oil on canvas works document the contemporary Florida landscape in all of its unique incarnations. On another conscious level, his work reminds the viewer of Florida "in the balance" as much of the wild parts of the state are destroyed or degraded on a daily basis.

Briggs is a plein aire painter who often records the topographical locations he chooses in a series of oil sketches completed on site over a period of days. Once he has selected a site, he returns day after day searching for the right quality of light to capture. His output includes easel paintings, large murals, and mural-like works completed for public buildings and private museums. His public murals were featured in a May article in *American Artist* magazine, 1982.

Briggs has enjoyed 10 one-person exhibitions since 1990, including shows at the Florida House of Representatives, Tallahassee, Florida; the Florida Gulf Coast Art Center, Belleair, Florida; the Cultural Art Center, DeLand, Florida; the Appleton Museum of Art, Ocala, Florida; the Fort Lauderdale Museum of Art, Fort Lauderdale, Florida; the Polk Museum of Art, Lakeland, Florida; the Brevard Art Center, Melbourne, Florida; and the Pensacola Museum of Art, Pensacola, Florida. He has been included in more than 30 group exhibitions since 1990, including shows at the Flint Institute of Art, Flint, Michigan; the National Parks Academy for the Arts, Jackson Hole, Wyoming; the Ringling School of Art and Design, Sarasota, Florida; the Center for the Arts, Vero Beach, Florida; the Fort Lauderdale Museum of Art, Fort Lauderdale, Florida; the Miami Center of Contemporary Art, Miami, Florida; and the Russell Rotunda, Capital Hill, Washington, D.C. In 1996, John Briggs received his third Individual Artist Fellowship from the state of Florida and completed four paintings for the King Federal Justice Center, Miami, as part of the Art in Architecture Program of the General Services Administration, Washington, D.C. His work is included in numerous corporate, public and private collections, including the Joseph Hirshhorn Estate Collection, Naples, Florida; the Jacksonville Museum of Art, Jacksonville, Florida; the Fort Lauderdale Museum of Art, Fort Lauderdale, Florida; the Florida Gulf Coast Art Center, Belleair, Florida; the Polk Museum of Art, Lakeland, Florida; The Barnett Banks of Florida; Tropicana Corporation, Bradenton, Florida; the City of Orlando, Florida; and the City of St. Petersburg, Florida. Between 1991 and 1996, he served as artist-in-residence at the Appleton Museum and Central Florida Community College, Ocala, Florida.

Briggs' *Cedar Key* is an accurately rendered oil on masonite completed in 1993. It captures a scene near the bridges outside Cedar Key, Florida, west of Gainesville, on a Florida winter afternoon of clear and cool declining light. Briggs feels that his use of abandoned, single-room masonry shelters suggests a transitory quality to Florida in the 1990s—a one-room shelter for someone who won't be staying long and a scene that won't last long either. Briggs places the viewer on the adjacent highway to emphasize this poignant symbol of contemporary Florida. And, while the shelters so carefully rendered in the painting are now gone, the lone palm continues to mark the spot chosen by Briggs to represent his conflict between natural and man-built objects in the Florida landscape.

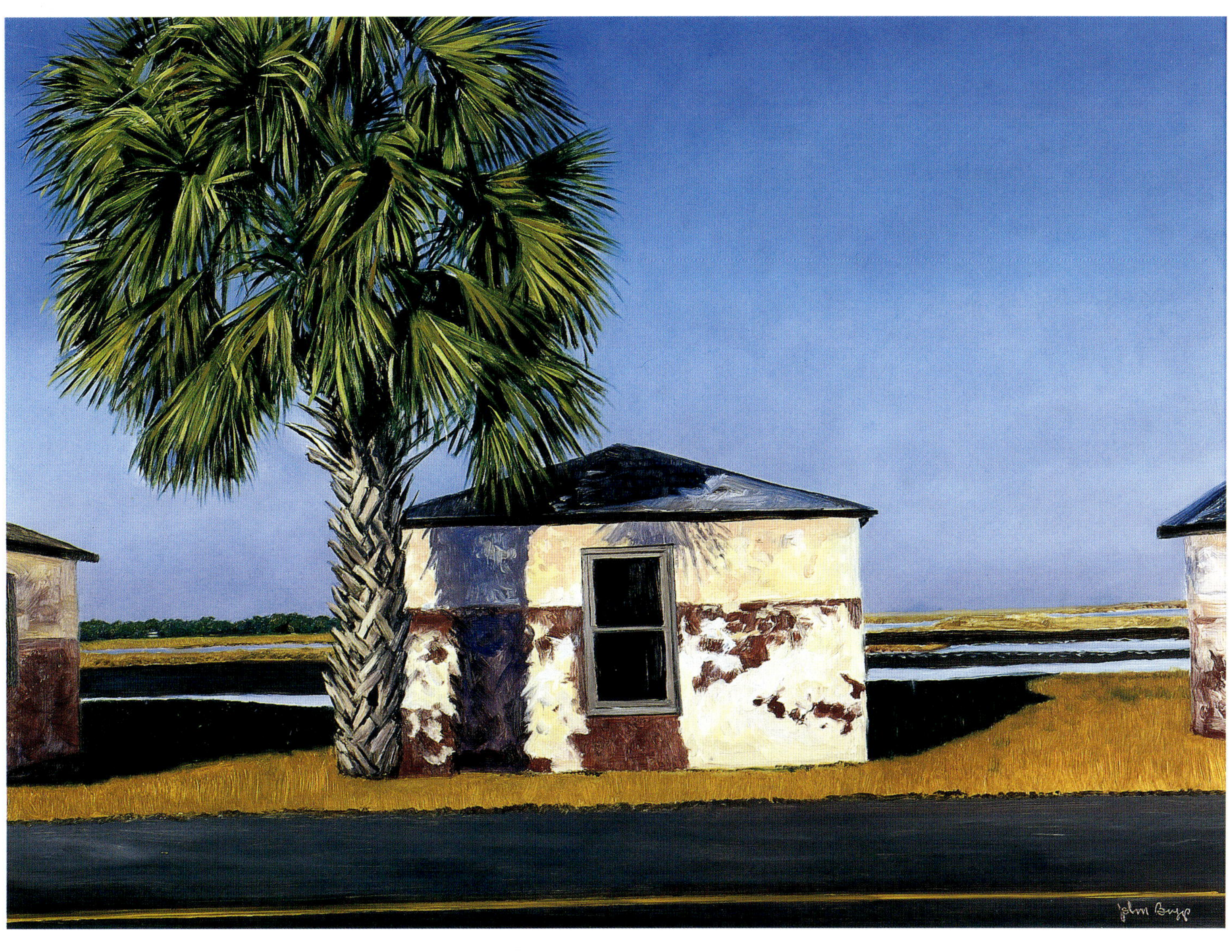

Peter Carolin

Orange Lake Lavender
1994, Oil on canvas, 31½" x 51½"

Peter Carolin was born in 1963 and raised in Detroit, Michigan. His earliest memories include visits to the Art Institute and a yearly pilgrimage to Fort Walton Beach, Florida, to visit his grandparents. These early trips to Florida and the tropical colors of the Gulf Coast were an important influence on Carolin, who was also affected by a sophomore year of undergraduate school spent in Angers, France, where he studied French language and culture by day, and figure drawing at the Beaux Arts Academy by night.

After finishing a bachelor's of fine arts degree at the University of Notre Dame, he chose the University of Florida in Gainesville for graduate work where he completed a master's of fine arts degree in 1988. Carolin came to the university because of his early love for Florida colors and the reputation of Professor Jerry Cutler, known as an important regional colorist. Carolin was also influenced by the work of expressionist Florida painter Hiram Williams and inspired by the same places as other Gainesville painters, notably Eleanor Blair and Margaret Ross Tolbert. Carolin developed his own integration of impressionistic and expressionistic styles while at the University of Florida.

Since coming to Gainesville in 1985, in addition to his graduate studies, Carolin has taught drawing, painting and computer graphics, as well as sculpture and art appreciation at the University of Florida and in public schools. He has worked as both a painter and a sculptor. Carolin feels deeply about the Florida landscape and the effect of Florida light on color, which is a critical ingredient in his style. And, while his life has gone through many changes since 1990, the one constant for him has been the land and painting the Florida landscape.

Carolin paints on site and often discovers a location by pure happenstance. His supplies are always kept in the trunk of his automobile and he is constantly searching for the right scene and atmosphere to create paintings that reflect a "Florida mood."

Carolin exhibits widely and has been included in exhibitions at Santa Fe Community College, Gainesville, Florida; Atlantic Center for the Arts, New Smyrna Beach, Florida; the Chateau de La Napoule, France; and the Gallery at the University of Notre Dame, South Bend, Indiana.

Carolin's large and atmospheric *Orange Lake Lavender* was completed in 1994. Carolin captures a view of Orange Lake looking east, off Highway 441, between the rural North Central Florida communities of McIntosh and Orange Lake. The painting includes 10 palms set between the viewer and the lake, which dominates the background of the painting. Above it all floats a lavender sky lit gently by an invisible sun that highlights large, floating clouds in this tribute to tropical, falling light and its ability to transform objects in the landscape. While this is a view of a particular place, it is also a painting of what Carolin thinks of as the "Florida mood" conveyed through balancing colors—quiet, subdued grass and trees; hopeful, clear, blue sky; and a brooding, melancholy lavender that precedes the end of another day. Of special note in many of Carolin's paintings are palm trees, an indigenous symbol for Florida. Moreover, Carolin also associates the palm with the "Tree of Life" first seen by Carolin in a Mesopotamian seal in a museum. To him, the palm is a constant metaphor for the rejuvenative powers of nature and its ability to create perspective in life and art.

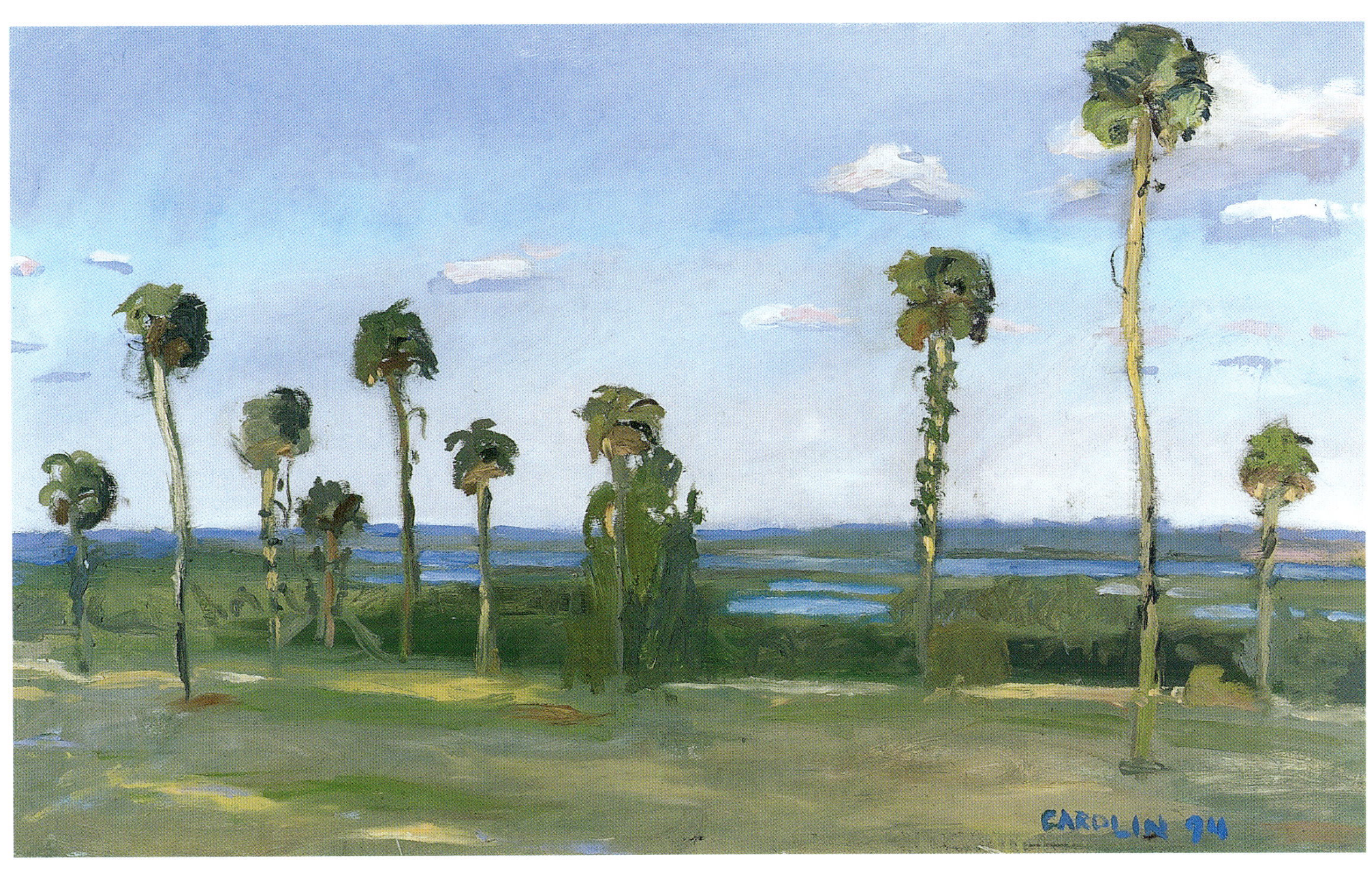
CAROLIN 94

James Couper

Tomoka River
1994, Oil on canvas, 12" x 20"

Sunday Bay
1993, Oil on canvas, 8" x 20"

James Couper was born in 1937, in Atlanta, Georgia, where he received his early education. In 1961, he received a bachelor's of arts degree from Georgia State University while also attending the Atlanta Art Institute. In 1963, he received a master's of arts degree from Florida State University in Tallahassee, where he studied with Karl Zerbe, the noted late German expressionist painter at Florida State University after World War II. Couper has been a member of the Visual Arts Faculty at Florida International University in Miami since 1972. He continues to live, teach and paint in Dade County, Florida.

A southern painter with a very strong conservationist ethic, Couper calls himself an expressionist who "interprets" Florida's vanishing wilderness. Not interested in politics, Couper creates images that contain an "implicit regard for the integrity of natural systems." Searching out places as undisturbed as possible, often in his canoe, allows him the opportunity to celebrate pure nature at her best.

After discovering the Everglades in the early 1980s, Couper turned from figurative to landscape painting. More than celebrating Florida's natural beauty, he sees his role as conveying the experience of wilderness and helping people understand what they are losing as wild places like the Everglades are destroyed. His pictures have no trace of people and, to heighten the sense of experience, he often emphasizes the more ephemeral qualities of nature—clouds, wind and light conditions. Couper's landscapes connect Florida to the landscape tradition elsewhere in the Southeast. Far from portraying Florida as a mythical Eden, he chooses ordinary places like cypress swamps, and relates the transitory qualities of an experience of once-common wild places to the concern for the disappearance of typical southern ecosystems. He is committed to providing what he calls "an eye to see, and an experience of the wild landscape, not just a picture of it." In this way, he relates Florida and its endangered wild places to many other environments of the South that are threatened in the same way. And, in doing so, he has expanded the subject matter of Florida landscape painting after World War II, when interest in landscape painting became a reflection of concern for the rapid destruction of American environments.

Since 1990, Couper has enjoyed more than 20 one-person exhibitions, including the Florida Gulf Coast Art Center, Belleair, Florida; the Lenox-Phoenix Center, Atlanta, Georgia; The Valdosta Art Center, Valdosta, Georgia; the Ormond Memorial Art Museum, Ormond Beach, Florida; the Miami Beach Convention Center, Miami, Florida; the Art Museum at Florida International University, Miami, Florida; and the Hambidge Center, Rabun Gap, Georgia. He has participated in two-person and group exhibitions, including The Tampa Museum of Art, Tampa, Florida; the Cummer Art Museum and Gardens, Jacksonville, Florida; The Center For the Arts, Vero Beach, Florida; the Polk Museum of Art, Lakeland, Florida; Center for Contemporary Art, North Miami, Florida; Gulf Coast Art Center, Mobile, Alabama; and the Wichita Art Association, Wichita, Kansas. Couper has been the recipient of several Individual Artists Awards from the Florida Department of State and has won both a Yaddo Saratoga Springs, New York, and a Hand Hallow Fellowship, East Chatham, New York. His work is included in the permanent collections of a number of institutions, including the John and Mable Ringling Museum of Art, Sarasota, Florida; the Center for the Arts, Vero Beach, Florida; the Museum of Art, Fort Lauderdale, Florida; Florida State University, Tallahassee, Florida; IBM Corporation, Raleigh, North Carolina; E.F. Hutton Company, New York, New York; Dade County Art in Public Places, Dade County, Florida; Broward County Art in Public Places, Broward County, Florida; and Alabama Power Company, Birmingham, Alabama.

Tomoka River is an oil on canvas completed in 1994. The painting is the result of investigations made by the artist from his canoe as he traveled down this small river north of Ormond Beach in Volusia County near the north Atlantic coast of the state. The banks of the Tomoka River are extremely overgrown with thick vegetation of palm, palmetto, cypress and oaks producing a dense undergrowth and canopy, which creates a dark and verdant interior captured in the painting. Couper adds turpentine to his oil paint giving it an increased fluidity and silkiness. He also mixes in a gel that maintains the richness of the oil but speeds the drying time of his formula. The result is a dazzling expressionist study of a typical, wild, romantic, North Florida jungle reflected in the quiet and still waters of a black-water creek.

In his *Sunday Bay*, 1993, Couper captures the open water and unobstructed light found in much of the western Everglades in South Florida. Using late afternoon, bright falling light to magically transform this isolated bay, Couper presents a narrow strip of green land wedged between a large and dramatic sky reflected in an exuberantly painted section of open Everglades water. The result is a canvas that salutes the airy, open spaces and unobstructed, transforming light of Florida.

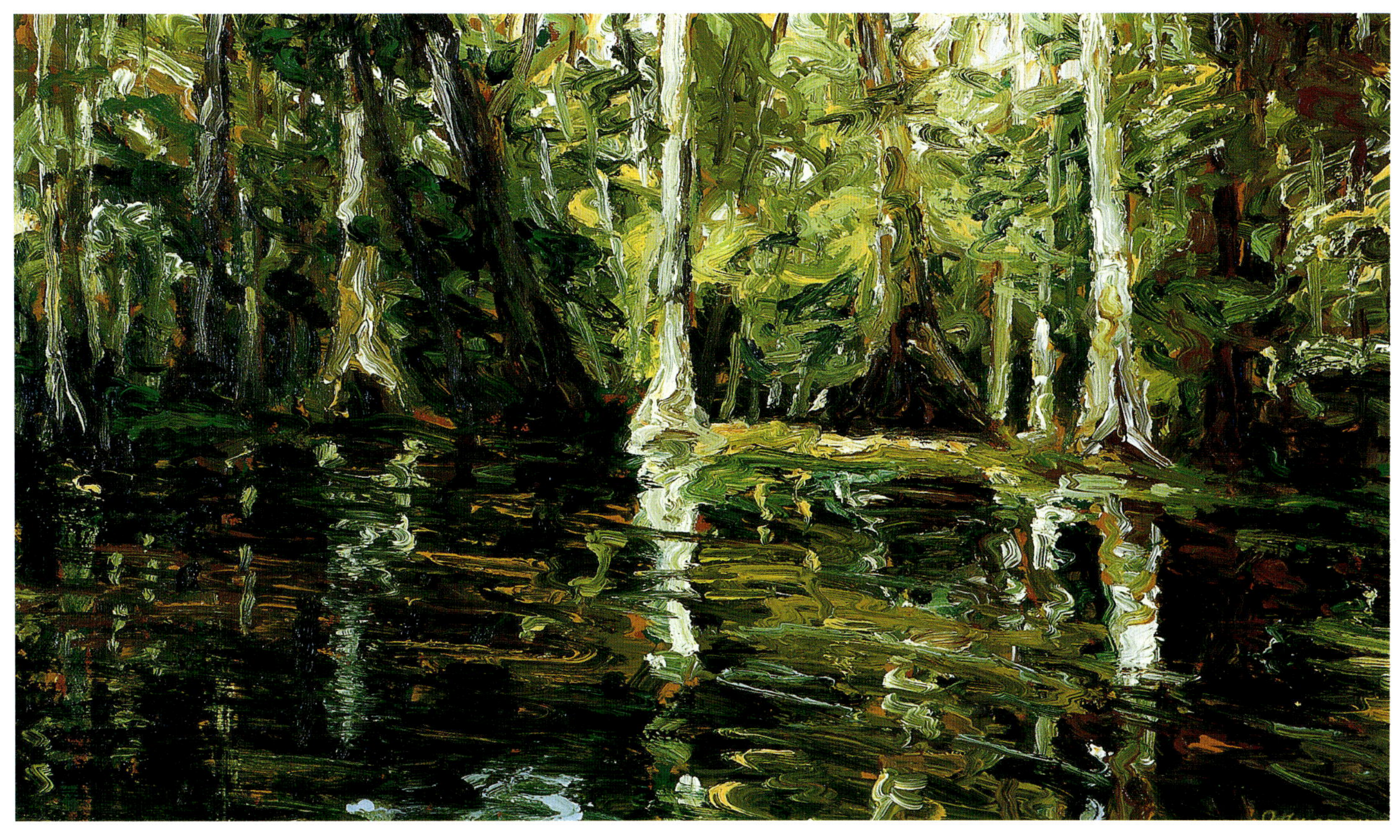

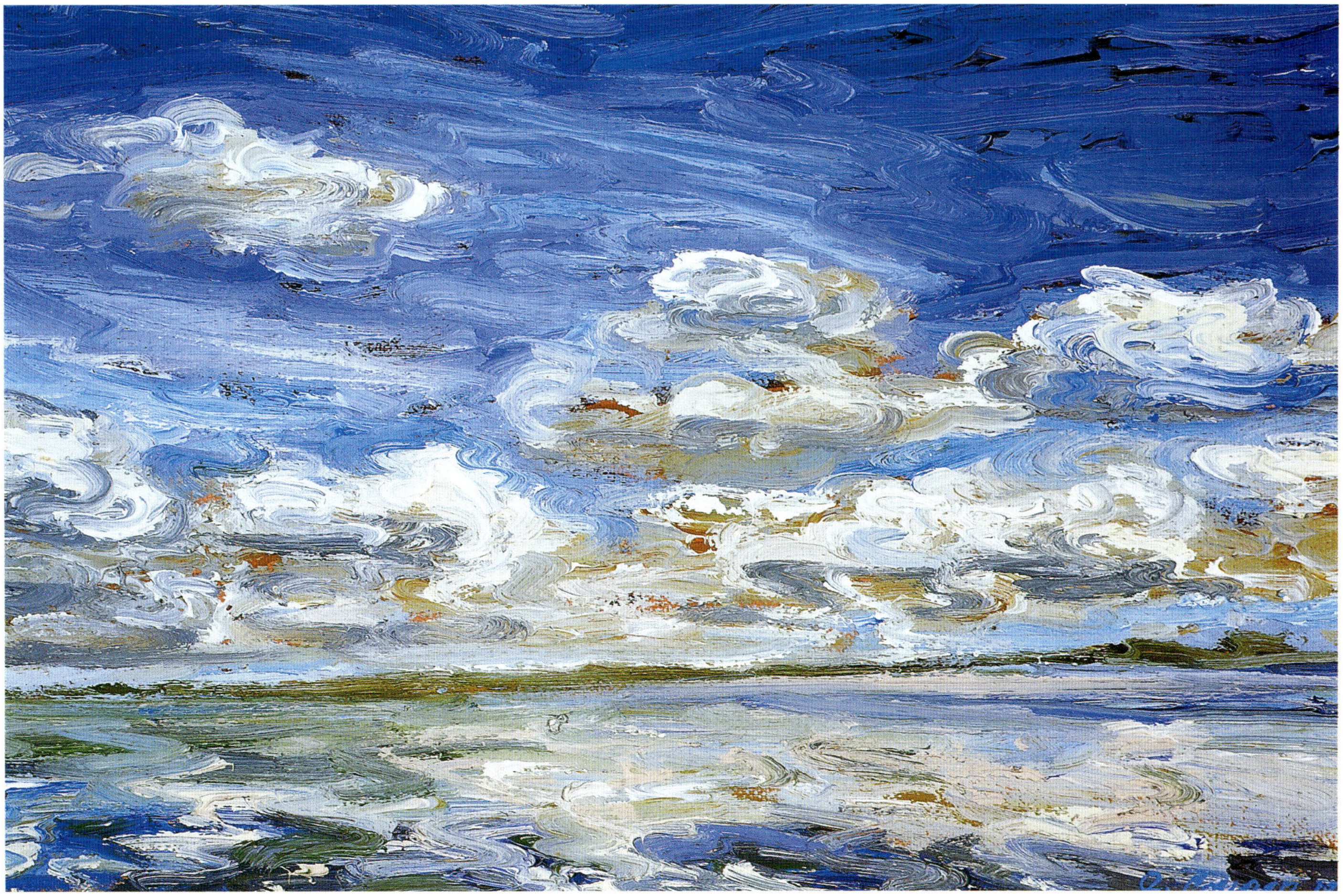

SUSAN DAUPHINEE

VIEW FROM THE OLD WACAHOOTA ROAD

1996, ACRYLIC ON PAPER, 16" X 26½"

Susan Dauphinee was born in 1952, in Gainesville, Florida, where she attended P.K. Yonge School, known for its advanced courses for talented students. She attended the Ringling School of Art in Sarasota in 1970 where she pursued her interest in art education and studio work. She now lives in Cedar Key, Florida, west of Gainesville on Florida's Gulf Coast. Dauphinee has exhibited widely in North Florida, including one-person and group exhibitions and demonstrations at The Appleton Museum, Ocala; Sante Fe Gallery, Gainesville; The Florida Department of State Capitol Complex Exhibition Program, Tallahassee; and the Florida School of the Arts, Palatka. Her work is included in the collections of the Walt Disney Corporation, Orlando, Florida; The Orlando Airport, Orlando, Florida; the Sun Banks of South Florida, Miami; the Barnett Banks of Florida, Jacksonville; and the Ocala Judicial Building, Ocala, Florida.

Susan Dauphinee is known for her colorful, impressionist acrylic paintings on paper of the North Central Florida area. Her chief subjects are coastal landscapes, especially coastal marshes, lakes and rivers. Less typically, she also paints inland scenes, including the prairie scene illustrated here. In all of her work, her overriding goal is to capture what she describes as the essence of Florida for the viewer. "I would like my paintings to be an extension of what I see and feel about the Florida landscape," she says. "I try to evoke an emotion of what I see and feel about the natural beauty and tranquility of our environment in Florida."

Dauphinee is an uninhibited observer of the landscape, spending countless hours looking at potential sites for her colorful and sophisticated works, whose style is influenced, somewhat, by the works of the great French Impressionists of the 19th century, Camille Pissarro, Mary Cassatt and Alfred Sisley, whom she has studied over the last 20 years. Like first generation impressionists, Dauphinee's work is colorful. "Art," she says, "allows me to see more color in my surroundings than most people would notice."

Typical procedures for the artist involve priming mounted paper and tinting it in a light terra-cotta, red-colored wash prior to scrubbing in both warm and cool hues. It is upon this base that she then defines her primary subjects. Dauphinee paints directly in her studio. Although she often uses color photographs and field sketches of ideas on four-inch sheets of paper, she prefers to paint without a preliminary sketch or charcoal outline. Dauphinee is preoccupied with exploring contrast and often uses light and dark—positive and negative—forms to that end.

In *View from the Old Wacahoota Road*, 1996, a wide, panoramic band of orange and golden grasses help frame a dark, single live oak tree seen against a background of dense foliage. Above, a mauve-tinted, milky sky reinforces this late afternoon on the north reaches of Paynes Prairie, in Alachua County, near Gainesville, Florida, on a clear, fall afternoon. It is a typical view of the prairie lands of this section of Florida and a prime example of a characteristic Florida landscape that is not yet widely known.

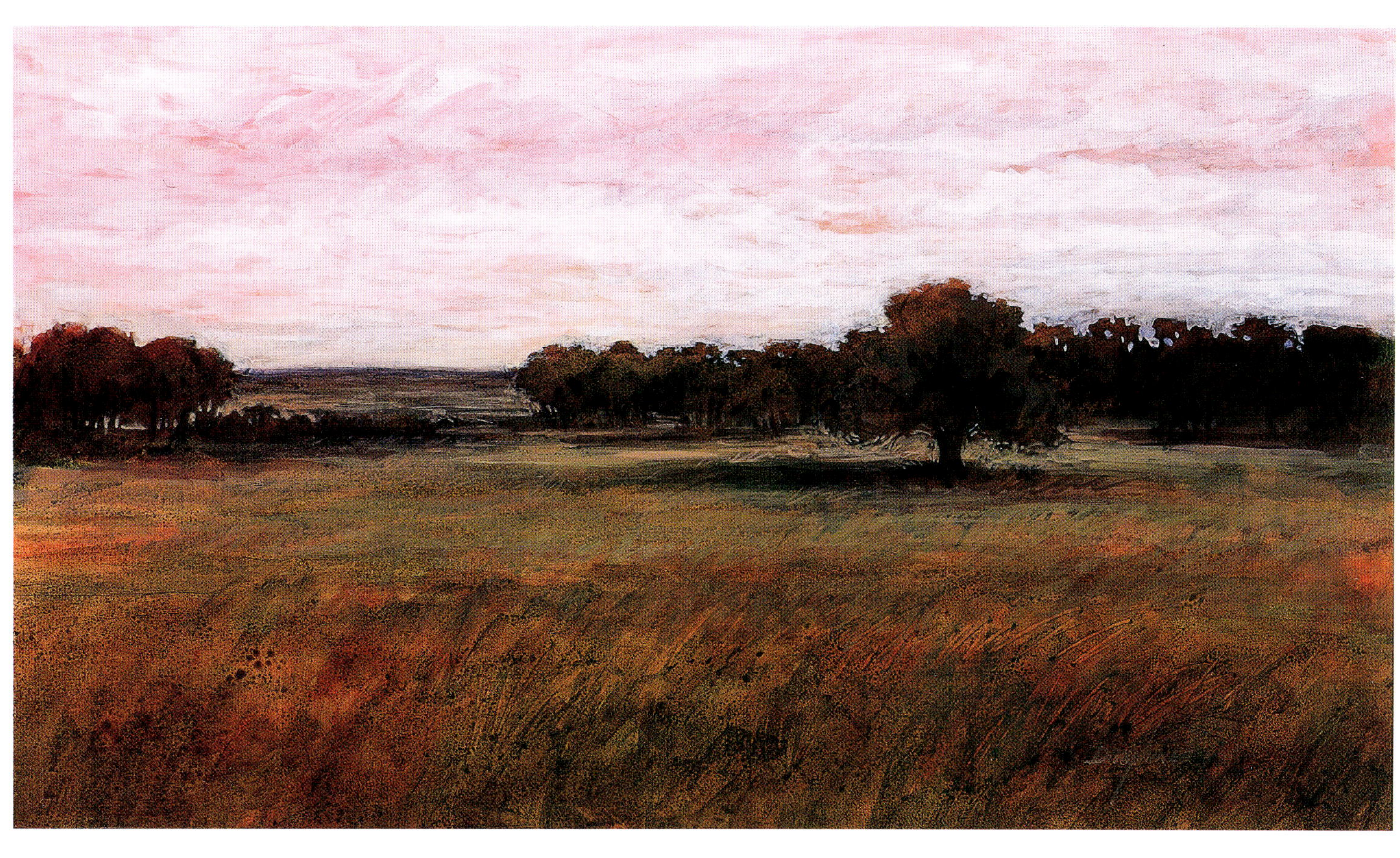

JOSEPH DAVOLI

CANAL C-11
1992, ACRYLIC ON PAPER, 30" X 22"

Joseph Davoli was born January 7, 1949, in Syracuse, New York, where he attended the Everson Museum School from 1964 to 1967. In 1967, Davoli also won a scholarship to attend the Boston Museum School, Massachusetts. From 1970 to 1973 he attended Syracuse University, New York, and from 1978 to 1982, he attended the South Florida Art Institute in Hollywood, Florida, as a scholarship winner. He continues an association with the South Florida Art Institute as an instructor of painting and design, a position he has held since 1982. In 1991, Davoli also became an instructor in painting and drawing at both Miami Dade Community College and the Miami Art League, Miami, Florida.

Davoli exhibits widely at commercial and public galleries. He has shown at the Fort Lauderdale Museum of Art, Fort Lauderdale, Florida; the Gallery at Nova University, Davie, Florida; The Society of the Four Arts, Palm Beach, Florida; The Center for Contemporary Art, North Miami, Florida; the Hollywood Art and Culture Center, Miami, Florida; Broward Community College, Fort Lauderdale, Florida; The Historical Museum of Southern Florida, Miami, Florida; The South Florida Art Institute, Hollywood, Florida; and Broward Community College, Davie, Florida. Davoli's work is included in the collections of The Southeast Bank, Miami, Florida; The Barnett Bank, Fort Lauderdale, Florida; Continental Corporation, Miami, Florida; The Royal Bank of Canada, Toronto, Canada; and Burdines, Miami, Florida. Davoli has received commissions from Art in Public Places programs in Dade County, Broward County, Orlando and Metro-Dade, Florida. He has also received an Individual Artist Fellowship from The Division of Cultural Affairs of the Florida Department of State. Davoli lives and works in Davie, Florida, in Broward County, near Fort Lauderdale.

Davoli's style is contemporary yet drawn from impressionism. His paintings tend to be large, his palette is brightly colored, and his images are somewhat abstract. Extraneous detail is often eliminated in favor of interpreting a few primary areas of visual interest within a larger scene. Davoli is very interested in the process of perception that leads to art. "Initially, I am attracted by something sensed by sight, a small spark connecting with my eyes. I try to find the source of this interest by observation and translate the initial spark into form. A dialogue develops between myself, the subject, and the painting until the painting becomes an image of a moment of perception."

Davoli's *Canal C-11* is an acrylic painting on paper completed in 1992. The physical subject for the painting is a site near Davie, Florida, known as the South New River Canal, or Canal C-11, which runs east and west, parallel to Griffin Road and Orange Drive. West of Davie Road, a footbridge crosses the canal, allowing for a long axis view down the body of water as it changes in appearance with the east-to-west movement of the sun. The painting captures a moment at dusk, facing west from the center of the bridge.

While not part of a series, Davoli has painted this scene many times over a period of 15 years. "This canal typifies the things that interest me about the South Florida landscape. The land here often appears as a 'floating world' suspended between a vast, moving sky, and water beneath, with the land being temporary and transient. The light here is always moving, reflecting back and forth between sky and water, causing the land to change color and appear almost like a mirage. The weather also causes this suspended, watery world to move and change form. Man-made forms, such as roads, levees, etc., impose a contrasting geometry that results in great visual tension in this landscape."

Canal C-11 is a very simple composition with a very limited color palette arranged in broad fields of color. Masses of green vegetation brightly highlighted by the low sun are reflected in the still, mirror-like waters of the canal. A blue sky mottled with red is also reflected in the water. Davoli has given special attention to colorful undergrowth seen only as reflections in the canal.

The canal is part of a system crisscrossing South Florida that helps to regulate flooding and permits agriculture and development in areas that would otherwise be too wet. These changes to the natural environment of the area have threatened the survival of South Florida's distinctive ecosystems, most notably the Everglades. Even though it has all the elements of a tranquil, South Florida landscape, Davoli's view of Eden in *Canal C-11*, ironically, is the result of man-made alterations that have created serious threats to the vitality of the Florida landscape.

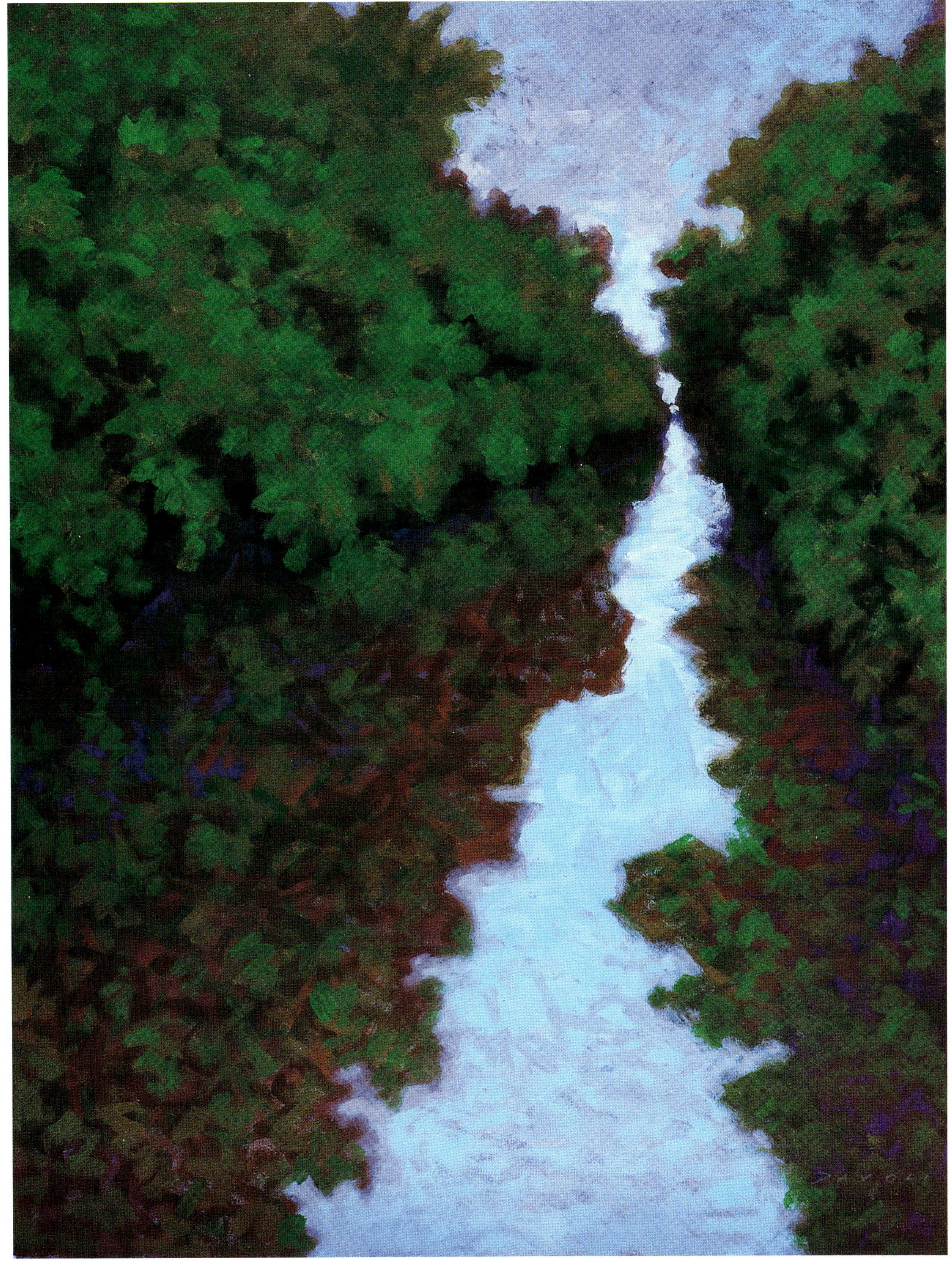
DAVOLI

Heidi Edwards

To The Withlacoochee

1995, Oil on canvas, 46" x 78"

Heidi Edwards was born in Chicago, Illinois, in 1947. She attended schools there and, as a child, remembers her weekly visits to the Chicago Art Institute located near the office of her architect father and grandfather. Edwards received a bachelor's of fine arts degree in 1970 from the University of Illinois, Champaign-Urbana. In 1971, she continued post-graduate studies at the School of the Chicago Art Institute.

Edwards has exhibited her work widely, including The Thomas Center, Gainesville, Florida; Office of The Mayor, Jacksonville, Florida; The Atlantic Center for the Arts, New Smyrna Beach, Florida; Sante Fe Community College, Gainesville, Florida; and The 22nd Floor Capitol Gallery, Tallahassee, Florida. Her work is included in numerous public and private collections, including: Amelia Island Plantation, Amelia Island, Florida; Florida Rock Industries, Jacksonville, Florida; The University of Florida College of Law and The Academic Advisement Center, both in Gainesville, Florida; Winn-Dixie Corporation, Jacksonville, Florida; Illinois Industrial Properties, Chicago, Illinois; and the City of Orlando, Orlando, Florida.

Edwards came to Florida in 1974 to be married, first living and painting in Williston, Florida, near Gainesville, in the north central region of the state. In 1995, she moved to nearby Irvine, Florida, south of Gainesville, where she continues to paint the Florida landscape in colorful and expressive canvases. "The landscape is the catalyst for my work. Imagery is only a point of departure for me, however. My primary subject is color, and the manner in which it becomes atmospheric space. My palette, which juxtaposes low-key and high-key colors, serves not realistic but emotional and decorative ends. The emphasis on the liquidity of pigment is a constant in my work, as is an active, gestural surface. The contrast between the graphic and painterly also interests me; I like playing off the simplicity of large, planar forms against sharp, staccato movements. My paintings are not intended as social commentary; instead, they are lyrical abstractions—places of the imagination—self portraits of respite and tranquility."

She describes her approach to painting as both traditional and highly experimental. She likes to experiment by building up layer upon layer of thin glazes as she creates the rich surface of each painting. Often the use of varnishes, in traditional ways, complements her more experimental approaches to painting. Edwards uses a variety of brushes from bristle in the early stages of each painting, to sable as she completes each piece. She is currently using an oil bar medium that substitutes wax for linseed oil in her constant search for a more pleasing surface.

To The Withlacoochee is a large and expansive oil on canvas completed in 1995. Edwards feels that this painting was a key piece in stimulating a body of her work that discusses the relationship between color, sky and water in the Florida landscape.

The painting was based on photos and sketches made by Edwards on site in the spring of 1995. Edwards uses a small boat to explore locations that might stimulate her imagination. She creates her paintings in her studio where she consolidates her research, imagination and experience into a finished object. *To The Withlacoochee* was completed in July 1995, and is based on a majestic section of the headwaters of the spring-fed Rainbow River in Marion County at sunset as it flows to the Withlacoochee River, then to the Gulf of Mexico.

A large, cerulean and robin's-egg blue sky frames huge, billowy clouds rendered in ochre and shades of yellow and cream. A sinuous line of riverbank holds vegetation rendered in lush greens, reds, yellows and colorful combinations that suggest, in loose and elegant brushstrokes, the richness of the wetland and marsh that borders the river. Edwards has placed the viewer directly in the flow of the slow and smooth stream as it makes its way westward through the breathtaking and undeveloped beauty of Rainbow Springs State Park. While Edwards is preoccupied with the aesthetics of the Florida landscape in her loose, colorful and expressive paintings, she is aware of an ever-tightening grip as development continues to nibble at the Florida she eloquently captures in her painterly explorations of color, water and sky. Recently, this location near Rainbow Spring was closed to the public.

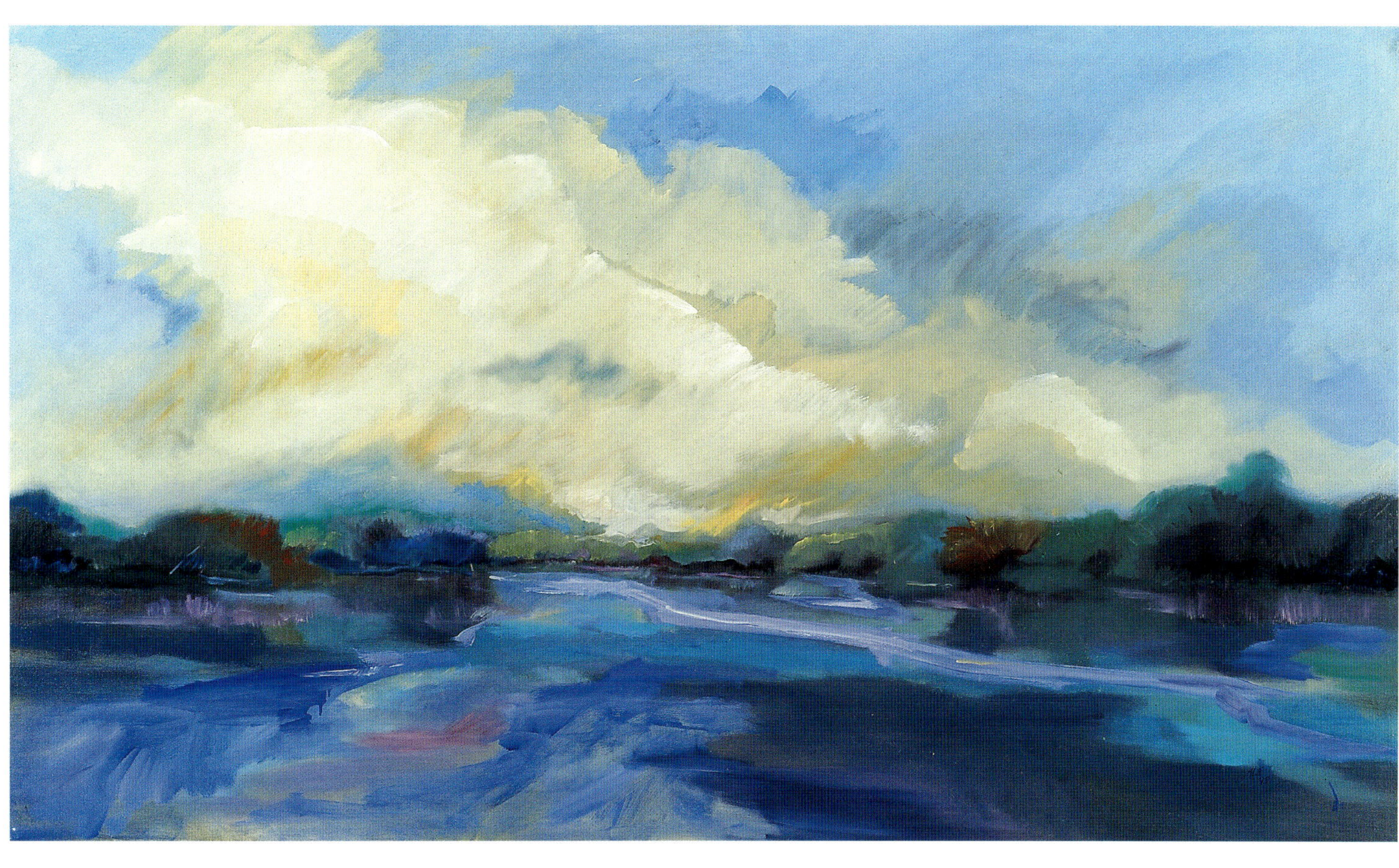

Hank Fleck

Quiet Lagoon

1990, Pastel on paper, 22" x 28"

Florida pastel artist Hank Fleck was born January 11, 1928, in the small, rural Pennsylvania town of Tarentuma, near Pittsburgh, where he received his education in parochial schools. While he always had "a desire to do art," he had no formal fine art training. He has learned on his own and from a number of influential, private teachers and workshop leaders, including William Schultz, Daniel Greene, Albert Handell and Foster Caddell. However, he did take a correspondence course in commercial art in the 1950s that convinced him he didn't want to pursue a career in that field.

Fleck left Pennsylvania for Oregon in 1949, where he and Mrs. Fleck began a family and where he found work. In 1959, the large Fleck family decided to move to Melbourne, Florida, on the north Atlantic side of the state. While Fleck continued to work in the private sector to support his growing family of 13 children, he continued to study and practice his art. In 1972, he began to concentrate on pastel. He was greatly influenced by a charismatic art instructor at the old Melbourne Art League who came to Florida each year for a two- to three-week workshop with aspiring artists. William Schultz was an accomplished, Massachusetts artist and Art Students League instructor who "fired up us Melbourne artists to work for another year until he returned," said Fleck. In the years following his work with Schultz, who now lives full time in Vero Beach, Fleck continued to read and visit museums where he fell under the strong influence of French Impressionism, which he "tempered by his own instincts." Gradually Fleck developed a deep attraction for the tropical Florida landscape that reminded him of his childhood romps in the deep forests of Pennsylvania but is now brightly illuminated by the special quality of Florida light and color. Fleck prefers to work in pastel because "it allows me to draw a lot." He also works in watercolor, oil and mixed media to keep "a fresh eye."

Now living in Tallahassee, Florida, Fleck is a signature artist with the Pastel Society of North Florida. His work has been included in juried and invitational exhibitions nationally, and is represented in the permanent collections of Southern Bell Corporation, Jacksonville, Florida; Florida State University Tallahassee; Tallahassee City Hall, Tallahassee, Florida; and the Philomath Art Museum, Salem, Oregon. At age 70, Fleck continues an active career and still travels each year to the areas around Salem to work with the Vistas and Vinyard Group of Artists. In 1997, Fleck's work was featured in an exhibition at the Oregon State Capitol.

Quiet Lagoon, a pastel on paper, 1990, explores a small body of water off the Banana River on south Merritt Island, Florida, in Brevard County, near the intersection of Pineda Causeway and South Tropical Trail. In a colorful, impressionistic style, Fleck captures a still lagoon that reflects tropical foliage, Australian pine trees and colorful wetland grasses. Fleck felt the scene "irresistible to me. I experienced great pleasure in my attempt to capture, in an impressionistic manner, the intense light and color of this beautiful, unspoiled refuge."

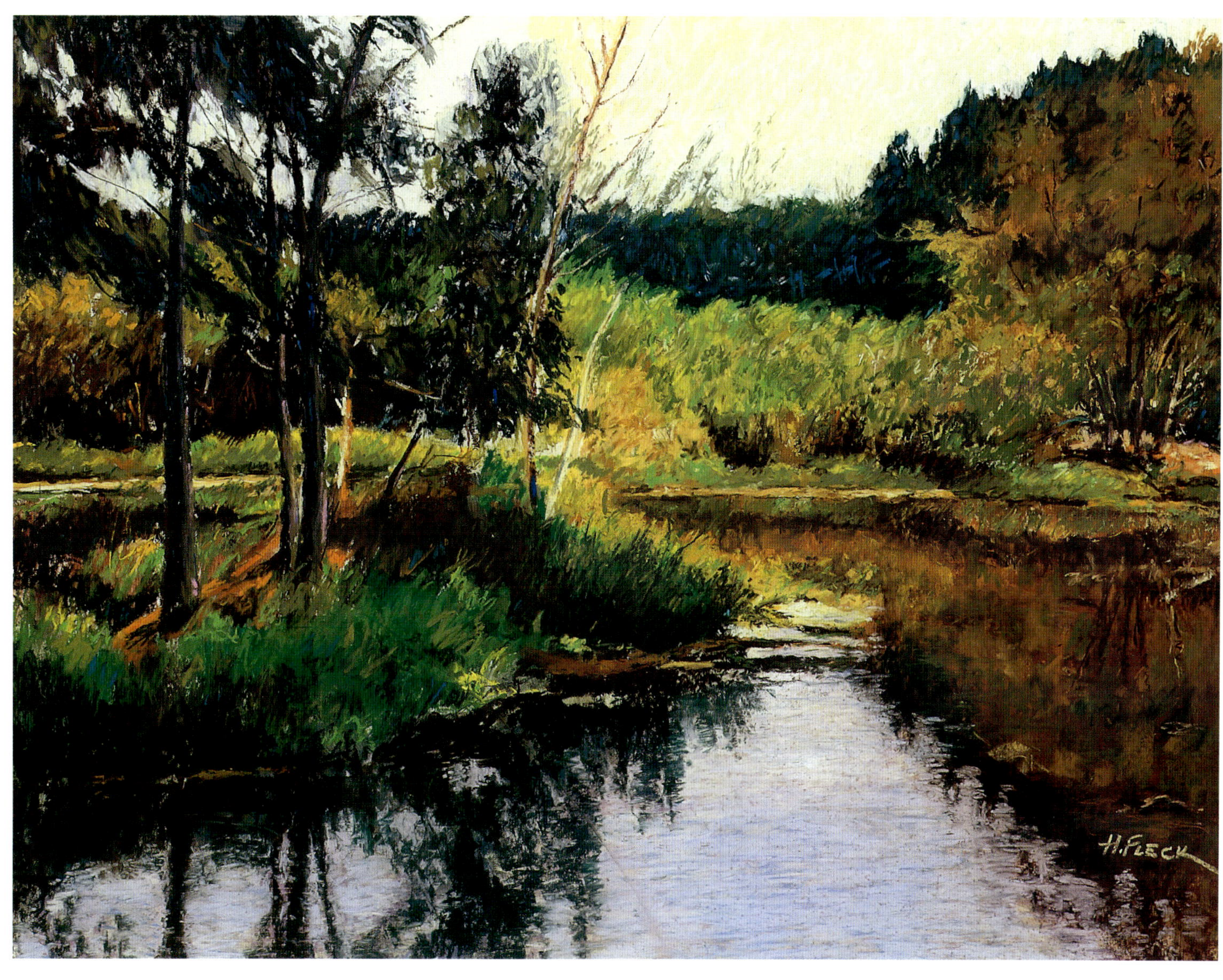
H.FLECK

ROBERT FRANK

SAND GLOW
1992, PASTEL ON PAPER, 7½" X 10½"

EVENING OVER WATER
1992, PASTEL ON PAPER, 7½" X 10½"

Robert Frank was born in Dayton, Ohio, in 1931. He attended schools there and took studio art classes at the Dayton Art Institute. After high school, Frank attended the University of Miami, Ohio, but transferred to the University of Cincinnati where he graduated with a bachelor's of arts degree in 1956.

Frank retired as an illustrator-artist working for the United States government at Wright-Patterson Field in 1989. That year, he moved to Mary Esther, Florida, a small town on Santa Rosa Sound near Fort Walton Beach in the western panhandle of the state. From 1989 to 1995 Frank painted the unusual landscapes of Northwest Florida in bright and luminist pastels, where a simplified and elegant realism rendered in an impressionistic style captures the light-filled and moody world of the Florida landscape. Frank exhibits widely in commercial galleries throughout the United States. His work is included in the collections of The Sears Corporation, Chicago, Illinois; The Andrew Jergens Company, Cincinnati, Ohio; The Kemper Group, Chicago, Illinois; The Powers Crossroads Art Collection, Newnan, Georgia; The Farmers and Merchants Bank, Fairborn, Ohio; Northwest Mutual Life Corporation, Chicago, Illinois; and Allied Paper Companies, Tuscaloosa, Alabama.

A teacher of pastel art, Frank is frequently featured in books on the subject of art. He has co-authored a number of publications, including *Creative Painting with Pastel*, (North Light Books, 1990), *Dramatize Your Paintings with Tonal Values*, (North Light Books, 1993), *Painting with Light*, (North Light Books, 1993), and *Basic Landscape Techniques in All Mediums*, (North Light Books, 1993). His work has also been featured in articles in *Midwest Art Magazine*, (1988) and *The Artist's Magazine*, (1993). He is a member of the Pastel Society of America and the Pastel Society of the West Coast. He has painted landscapes in many different parts of the United States, especially Illinois, Ohio, Massachusetts, Florida and Alabama. In 1995, he moved his home and studio to Daphne, Alabama. He and his wife anticipate a full-time return to Florida sometime in 1999.

Sand Glow is a 1992 pastel on paper of the dunes at Navarre Beach, a little west of Mary Esther on Santa Rosa Island, in the early hours of an August morning. Frank was impressed by the "never ending kaleidoscope of purple undertones and reflective colors as each hourly change of sunlight created a new scenario of translucent hues." In the pastel, Frank creates a rich foreground of blue and purple as reflective, rising light transforms the darkness of the dunescape into a multicolored, shimmering mass of mica. The midground neatly reveals brighter, direct, white light captured between two dunes, both capped with thick, gnarly, verdant undergrowth. Unfortunately, the location of this exuberant dunescape was levelled in 1995 by Hurricane Opal.

In *Evening Over Wate*r, another pastel of 1992, Frank chooses the North Florida coastline of Santa Rosa Sound near Mary Esther, Florida, as his subject. "This pastel is a portrayal of magnificent clouds and wispy tones that form over the North Florida coastline during the months of April and May."

Using falling, early evening light, Frank expands his colorful vision as backlit clouds float over a distant skyline and pink-purple sea in this tonalist tribute to the transformational qualities created by changing light in the Florida landscape.

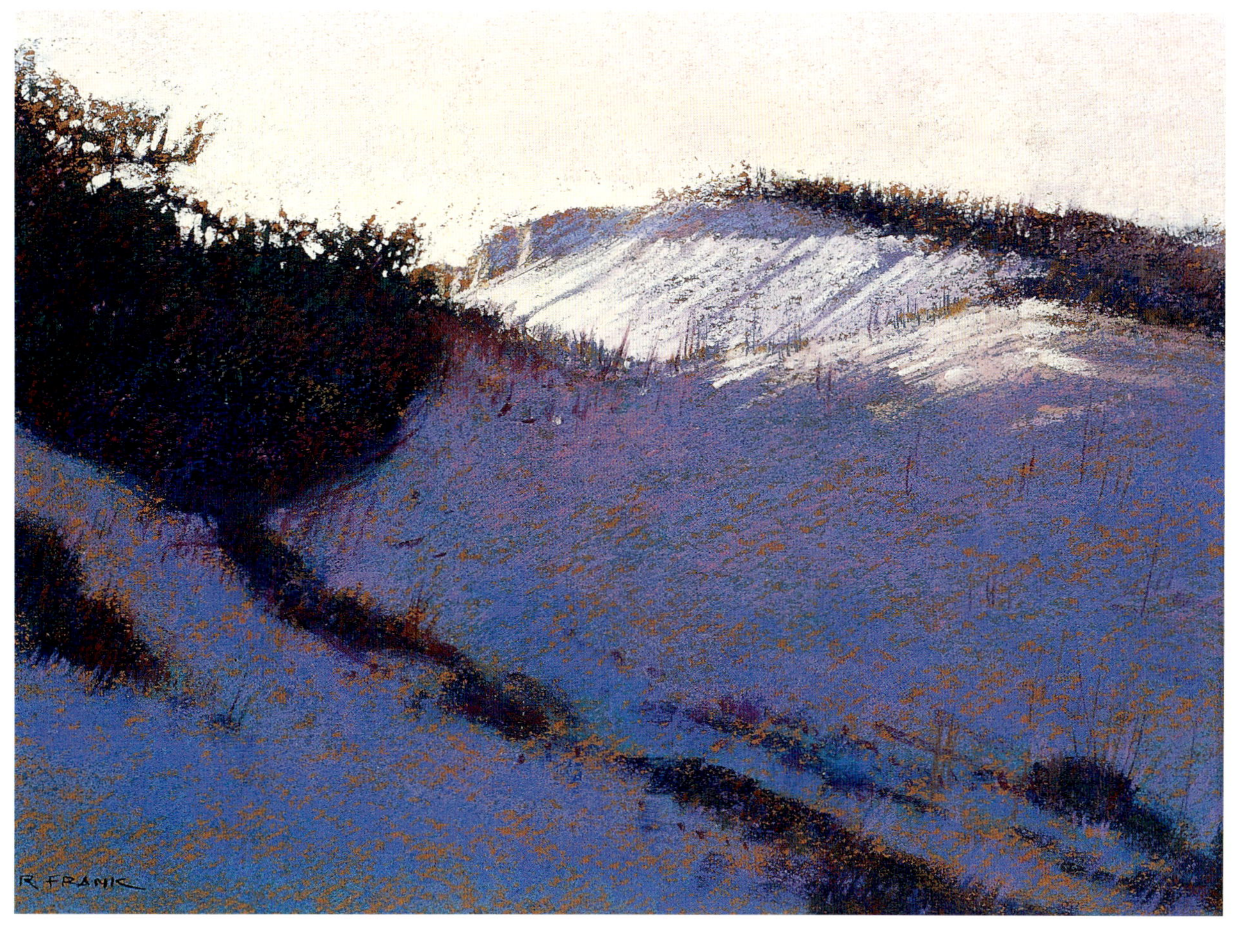
R. FRANK
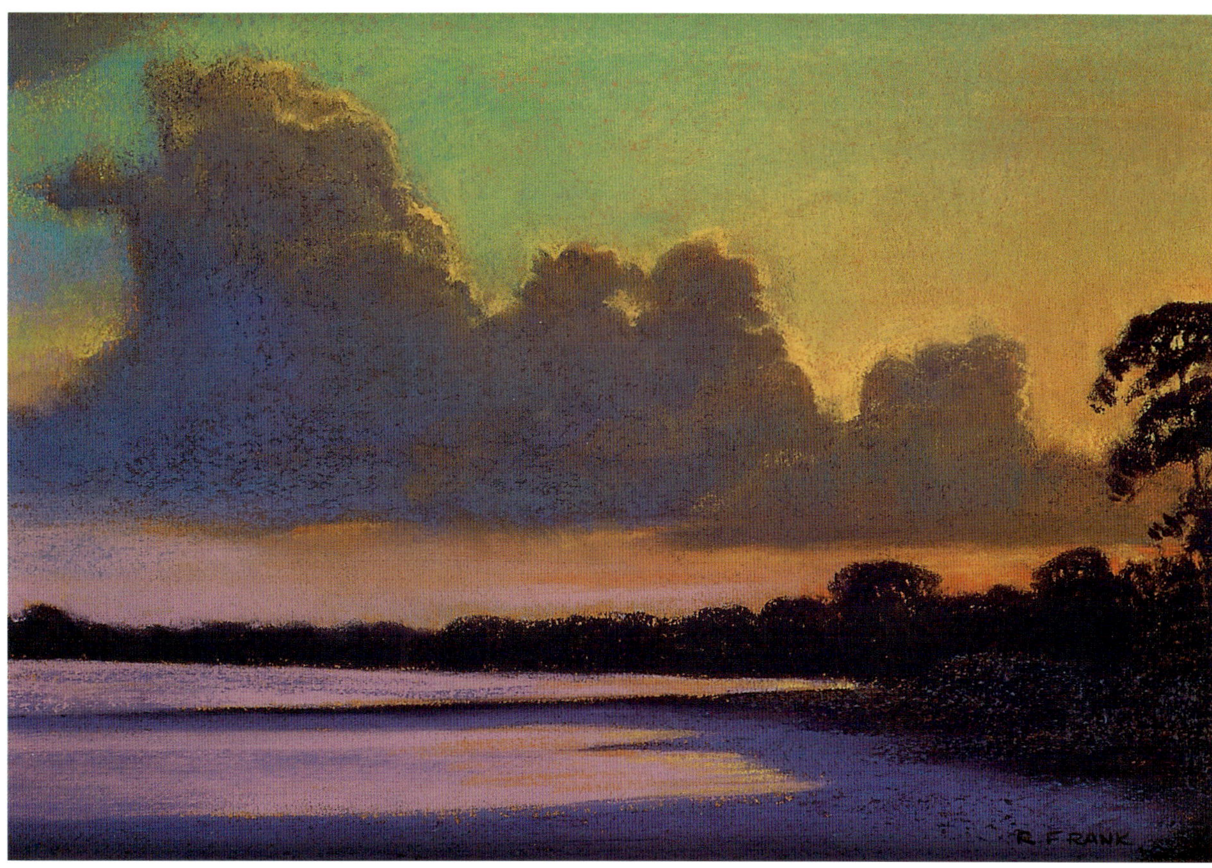
R. FRANK

Emmett John Fritz

1917 - 1995

Bravo and Aviles Street

Ca. 1957, Oil on canvas board, 16¾" x 29½"

Emmett John Fritz was born October 13, 1917, in Kansas City, Missouri. He was raised in New England and in New York City. He graduated from the Pratt Institute in 1937. Fritz began his artistic career after a tour of duty in the U.S. Army during World War II. After the war, Fritz was a cartoonist and caricaturist who drew for the comic strip "Roxie West" in the late 1940s. In 1950, Fritz moved to the historic Northeast Florida port city of St. Augustine, known as America's oldest city.

The town and its environs were to play a crucial role in his life until his death November 29, 1995. Like Frank Shapleigh and William Aiken Walker before him, Fritz painted the city in all of her moods, specializing in streetscapes of the old downtown districts. His first studio was located in the historic Arrivas House. He moved from there to the old Parks Hotel and then to the historic Gallegos House, both on north St. George Street. Later, he moved his studio to the Triay House and finally settled in a studio in the kitchen area of the Riberia House on St. George Street. The local historic preservation board had a window put in the wall to allow Fritz better natural light and a view of the street he so often captured in bright impressionist oil and acrylic paintings on heavy illustration board or canvas. Fritz exhibited widely in St. Augustine. His work is included in many local and regional museums. Travelers to St. Augustine, including King Juan Carlos of Spain, purchased hundreds of his paintings during this long and prolific career.

Bravo and Aviles Street is an oil on canvas board dating from 1957. The painting records a view looking west along Bravo Lane toward the intersection of Aviles Street. The cream-colored house in the far background is the O'Reilly House with the roof of the Convent of St. Joseph looming above it. The pink building to the right is the Oliver family store, remodeled into artist's studio spaces sometime in the 1930s. Until the late 1950s this area of the city was the artists' district of St. Augustine with Louis Vogt, Carl Martin and Fritz in residence at the Oliver building at the same time.

Fritz approaches his topographical view in a loose painterly fashion that suggests the bright light and cool shadows of this cityscape. Fritz emphasizes surface texture as he paints the aged and heavily patinated surfaces of masonry walls and the soft, lush green of banana and palm that also echo, in their yellowed, dying fronds, the temporal quality of the buildings, the street, and the city of St. Augustine. This work is very much in the tradition of the many late 19th and early 20th century views of St. Augustine, which portray Florida principally as an unusual and exotic place; a state of mind as well as an actual location.

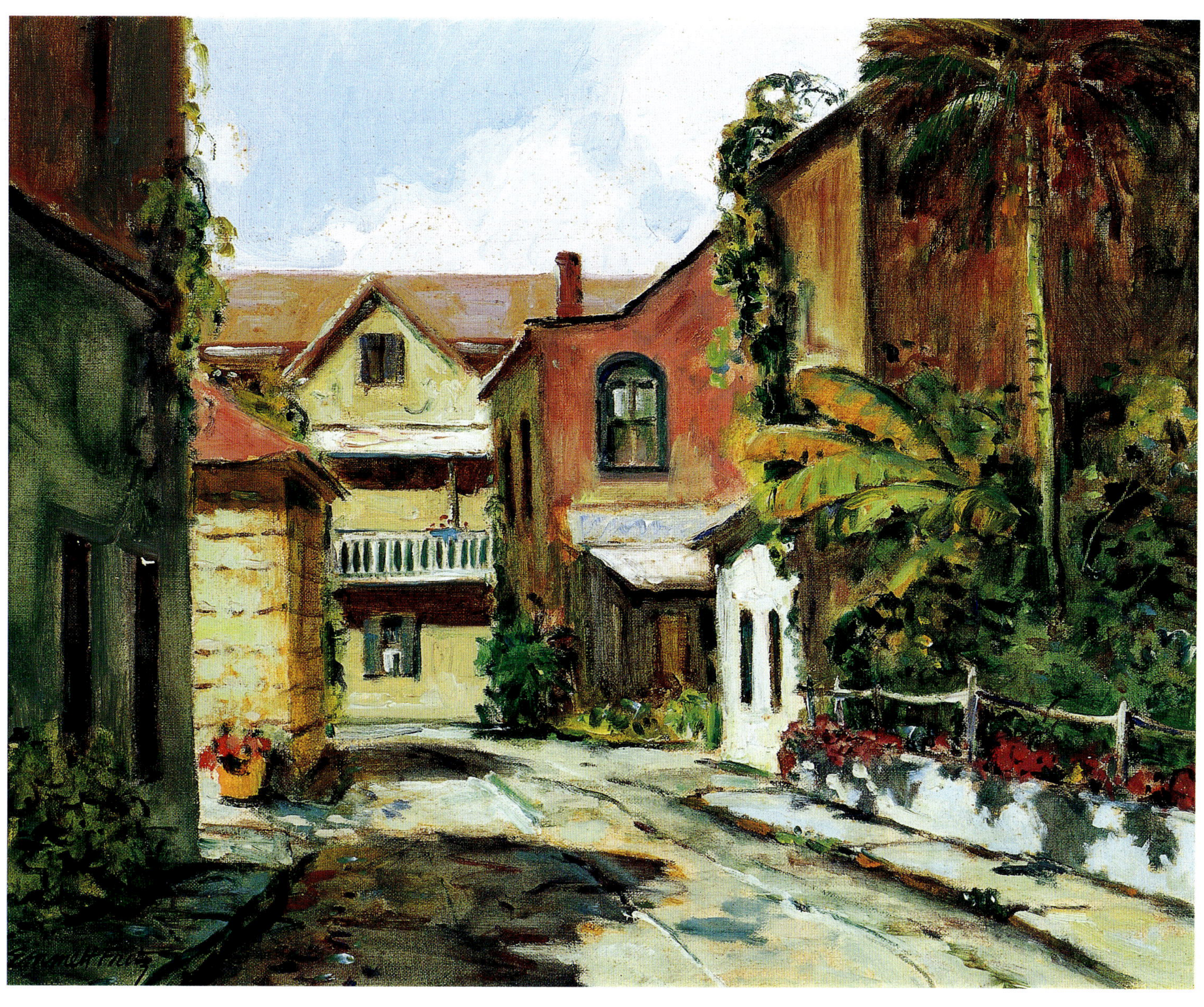

PATRICIA L. GEARY

TROPICAL DAWN

1995, ACRYLIC ON CANVAS, 37½" X 45¼"

Patricia Geary, an expressionist painter of colorful acrylic Florida landscapes, was born in 1939, in Saratoga Springs, New York, where she received her early education. She attended Skidmore College in Saratoga Springs, and received further training at the Elliott McMurrough School of Art, Indialantic, Florida, and the Brevard Museum of Arts and Sciences, Melbourne, Florida. She continues to study at the Penland School, North Carolina, the Crealde School of Art, Winter Park, Florida, and at Sebasco Estates, Maine, where she works with noted contemporary landscapist, Wolf Kahn. She first came to Florida in 1960 and now divides her time between Florida and North Carolina.

Geary participates in group exhibitions and has been included in exhibitions at the Brevard Museum of Arts and Sciences, Melbourne, Florida; the Maitland Art Center, Maitland, Florida; and Valencia Community College, Orlando, Florida. Her work is included in the collections of Florida Governor and Mrs. Lawton Chiles and the Brevard County School System, Brevard County, Florida.

Geary believes that her work is about her "wonderment at the fascinating world in which we live. They are not political or sociological statements." She has been painting the Florida landscape since 1965.

Her large acrylic on canvas *Tropical Dawn* was completed in 1995. It captures her emotional impression of a natural spring in Longwood, Florida, north of Orlando in the former Sanlando Springs Park, now a rural residential community of 800 families and a large number of Florida native animal and bird inhabitants. In *Tropical Dawn*, this spring takes on a timelessness and remoteness seen in implied contrast to the human development of Sanlando Spring Park.

Geary paints the dramatic scene in the early, cool, quiet morning as rising light begins to transform the scene with vivid oranges, purples and blues. A single heron stands guard over a sea of water hyacinth in this loose and painterly impression of the transformations in the Florida landscape caused by tropical light and color. Geary's objective is to capture the impact of atmospheric and reflected light in a nonliteral way as they create the lush, tropical beauty of the Eden-like spring, a sanctuary and symbol for rejuvenation and transformation in her personal visions of the Florida landscape.

In *Tropical Dawn*, Geary also conveys the emotional state of this unfolding display of light and color in the landscape. Her colors, rather than being impressionistic, become symbols for emotional reactions. Even though she professes no interest in sociological statements, this painting presents a very ironic view of Eden. Here is a quiet scene of natural beauty, almost a primeval dawn. But, on closer inspection, it is a remnant of a refuge in the midst of a large residential development that has dramatically diminished the metropolitan areas of Central Florida. This is a picture of a fragile Eden on the edge. Geary's work, like artist Julie Bowland, also represented in this publication, is aimed at distilling timeless, emotional states that offer a sanctuary next door to the real world, which has undergone unfortunate transformations and no longer looks very much like Eden.

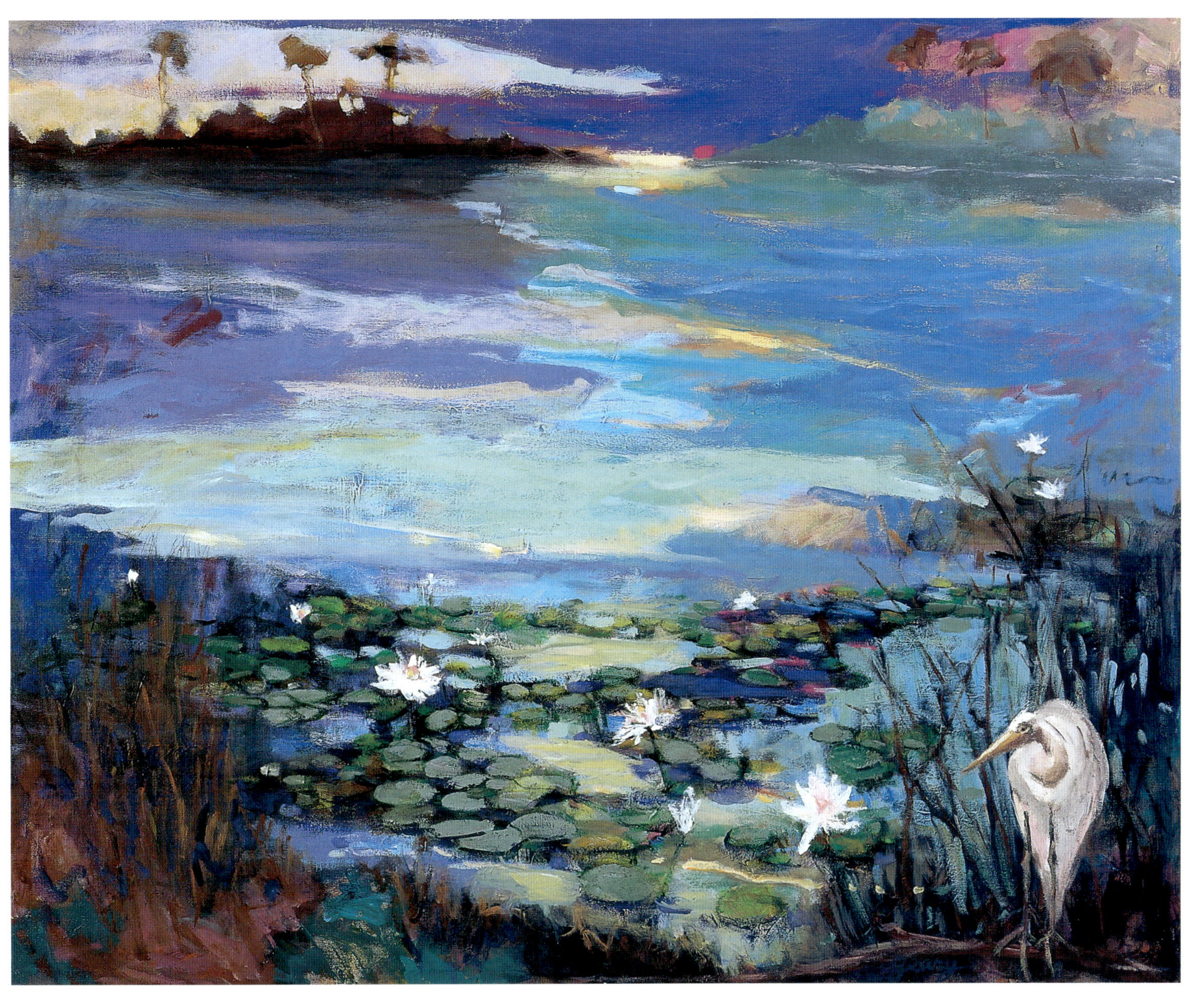

Rosemary Gibson

Spark of Light

1996, Oil on paper, 9¾" x 12¾"

Before the Rain

1996, Oil on paper, 5⅜" x 7⅜"

Born in Naples, Italy, April 24, 1947, the daughter of an American soldier stationed there, Rosemary Gibson spent her childhood in the small, rural towns of Nashville and Sparks, in southern Georgia, attending high school in Adel, Georgia. She moved to Tallahassee, Florida, in 1983. For 20 years, she had a career in fashion merchandising from which she retired in 1992 to devote herself to an art career. Mrs. Gibson does not have a formal art education.

In 1983, inspired by the natural beauty of the hardwood and pine forests, rolling hills and coastal marshes of Northwest Florida, she began to develop her artistic skills seriously, concentrating first on graphite drawings of the landscape. Many of her paintings are inspired by the St. Marks National Wildlife Refuge in Wakulla County, south of Tallahassee, near where the artist lived for 12 years. Her impressionistic works capture the moods of the marsh at different times of the day and seasons of the year. It is what she describes as "regeneration—the constant changes in nature" that inspires her efforts.

Gibson graduated to colored pencils as she developed a need for color in the landscape. In 1987, she began to paint in oils, having found a medium of "brilliant, buttery consistency" that satisfied her sensory needs as an artist. In 1992, Gibson studied with Sandra Wolfe-Nobles as she devoted herself full time to her painting. Later that year, she studied with long-time teacher and painter Joe McFadden at Havana, Florida. In 1994, she began studying with important Florida landscape painter John Stanford, whose moody and colorful impressionism has strongly influenced her overall approach to painting the Florida landscape. Gibson exhibits her work regularly at the Florida Art Center and Gallery, Havana, Florida. Since 1995, she has lived in Bartow, Florida, though she continues to paint the St. Marks area.

Gibson is part of a very prolific group of North Florida painters that has painted views of the St. Marks region and let these stand as a symbol of the real Florida—preserved. St. Marks is a large, protected area of coastal Florida under federal ownership. The St. Marks painters are distinct from the St. Augustine painters like Fritz. Instead of portraying a place to be experienced on vacation, Gibson and the others are capturing the kind of Eden-like sanctuary that Florida residents prize—something right outside their back doors that is an integral part of their everyday experience of Florida.

Spark of Light, 1996, captures a scene near Mounds Pool in the St. Marks Wildlife Refuge, northeast of Lighthouse Point, near Wakulla, Florida, in the panhandle of the state. Gibson selects as her bold, impressionistic focus in this small, oil on paper work a stretch of marshy, golden grassland viewed against a hammock of deep, green palm and palmetto, themselves viewed against a rich, purple background of Florida atmosphere.

When visiting a potential site, Gibson takes numerous photographs of the location, which she brings back to her studio where the painting is created. First, she lightly sketches her selected scene, then sets the charcoal sketch with a brush dipped in turpentine. She then begins to block in areas of the underpainting. For *Spark of Light*, Gibson used cadmium yellow directly from the tube to depict the vibrant, intertwining, bright yellow grasses that dominate the midground of the painting in this bold study of an isolated bit of Florida's beautiful and spacious topography filled with a sense of light and color.

In *Before the Rain*, 1996, Gibson closes in on the scene by directing the viewer's attention along a path that functions as the broad, central axis of the oil painting on paper. Gibson creates a moisture-filled, winter afternoon by her careful handling of color and bold visible brushstroke—as a hazy, purple sky charged with rain promises to refresh the late winter Florida scrub landscape about to come alive with early spring growth.

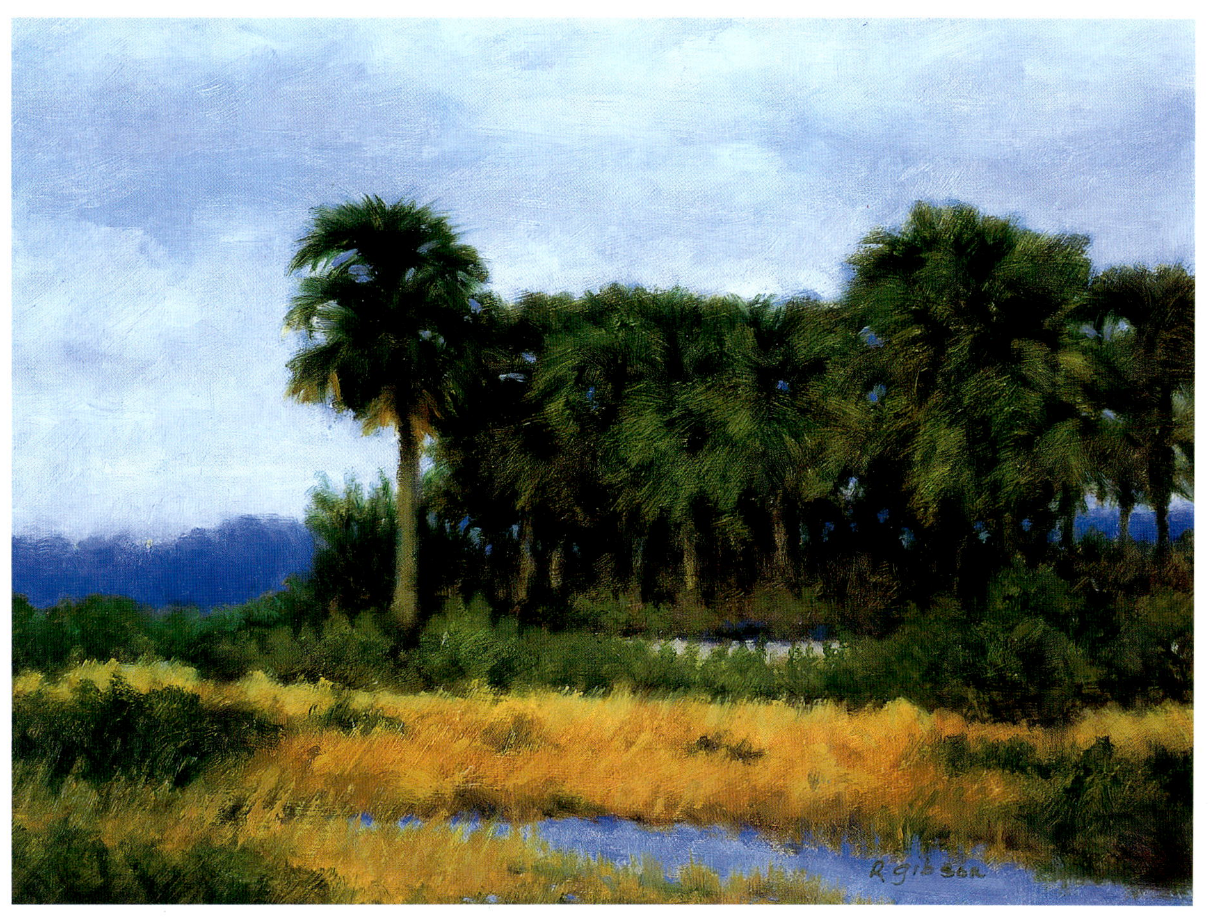
Rgibson

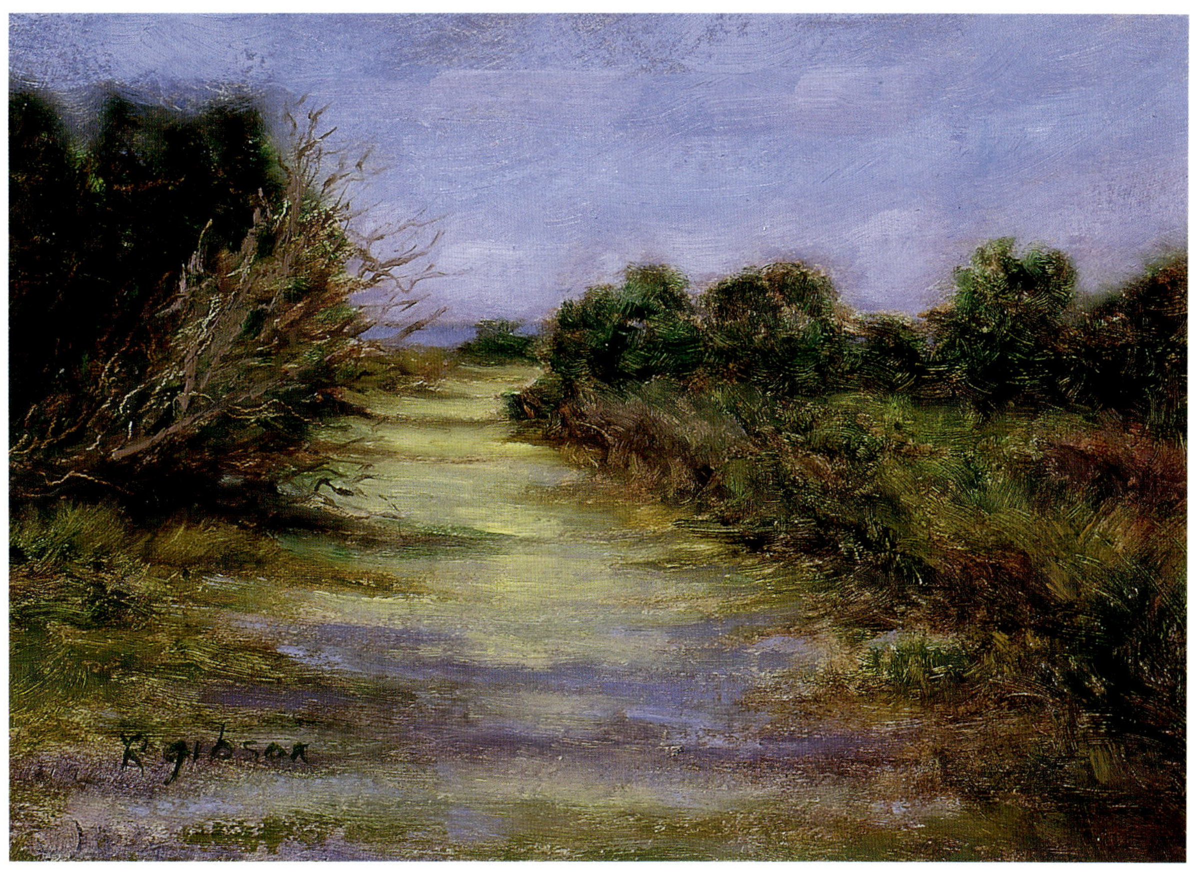
Rgibson

René Guerin

Gainesville Quarry

1991, Oil on canvas, 8" x 16"

René Guerin was born in 1950 in Fort Bragg, California. In 1952, she and her family moved to Vero Beach, Florida, where she received her early education. From 1968 to 1970, Guerin attended Stetson University in DeLand, Florida, on a scholarship. From 1970 to 1972, she attended Florida State University in Tallahassee, where she received a bachelor's of fine arts degree in painting. Guerin continues to work and live in Vero Beach.

Guerin's work has been shown in many solo, juried and group exhibitions in Florida, including the Backus Gallery, Fort Pierce; the Boca Raton Museum of Art, Boca Raton; the Brevard Museum of Arts and Sciences Inc., Melbourne; The Center for The Arts, Vero Beach; the Florida Gulf Coast Art Center, Belleair; the Martin County Council for the Arts; the Sherry French Gallery, Palm Beach; and the Society of Four Arts, Palm Beach; in Georgia at Brenau College, Gainvesville; the Gertrude Herbert Institute, Augusta; the Lyndon House Art Center, Athens; the Macon Museum of Arts and Sciences, Macon; the Madison-Morgan Cultural Center, Madison; Mercer University, Macon; Old Government House, Augusta; the State Botanical Gardens, Atlanta; University of Georgia, Athens; and Wesleyan College, Macon; in Alabama at the University of Mobile; and in North Carolina at Appalachian State University, Boone; and the Mint Museum, Charlotte. Her work is included in the permanent collection of The Center For The Arts, Vero Beach, Florida; the Brevard Art Center and Museum (now Museum of Arts and Sciences), Melbourne, Florida; Morris Communications Inc., Atlanta, Georgia; and The Morris Museum, Augusta, Georgia.

Guerin is a plein aire painter who has worked in many different parts of the United States, as well as in Italy and South America. Her paintings are realistic in the tradition of American painters Charles Burchfield and Edward Hopper. Guerin says her realist landscapes have evolved into intuitive paintings, using composition and color in an emotional way. "I focus on essence rather than detail, and I join aspects of expressive painting and traditional landscape painting." Her paintings generally have a light and rich surface, and are done in a fluid, painterly manner in which edges are not linear but are created by strokes of paint that model and define them. An expressionist in her exaggeration of mood, Guerin does not confine herself to objectively depicting what she sees. Her work has a lyrical quality and it often romanticizes scenes of everyday existence in Florida—sport fisherman on a jetty, farmers loading turkeys on a trunk, cattle grazing, an orange grove, a place where an interstate highway with trucks crosses a rural road.

Gainesville Quarry is an oil on canvas completed in 1991. The painting was begun on an excursion with friends in September 1991. The location is a quarry on the outskirts of Williston, Florida, about 15 miles southwest of Gainesville. Guerin worked on a canvas tacked to a board. Her canvas was prepared with a colored ground. She dilutes a small amount of pigment in turpentine before brushing the solution onto the canvas. She then wipes the canvas, leaving a light stain. The painting captures a view looking southeast on what Guerin remembers as a "very hot morning." In 1991, Guerin was using a pure palette of primaries, earth tones and white.

Guerin's small, jewel-like oil captures a bright woodland scene of hardwood trees and shrubs accentuated by the gray outcroppings of limestone boulders and large, moss-covered oak trees, similar in feel to the earlier work of Charles Burchfield, but more rigorous and dynamic in brushstroke and color key. The palette is loose and painterly as Guerin presents her view of this unique Florida terrain under a billowy and threatening sky.

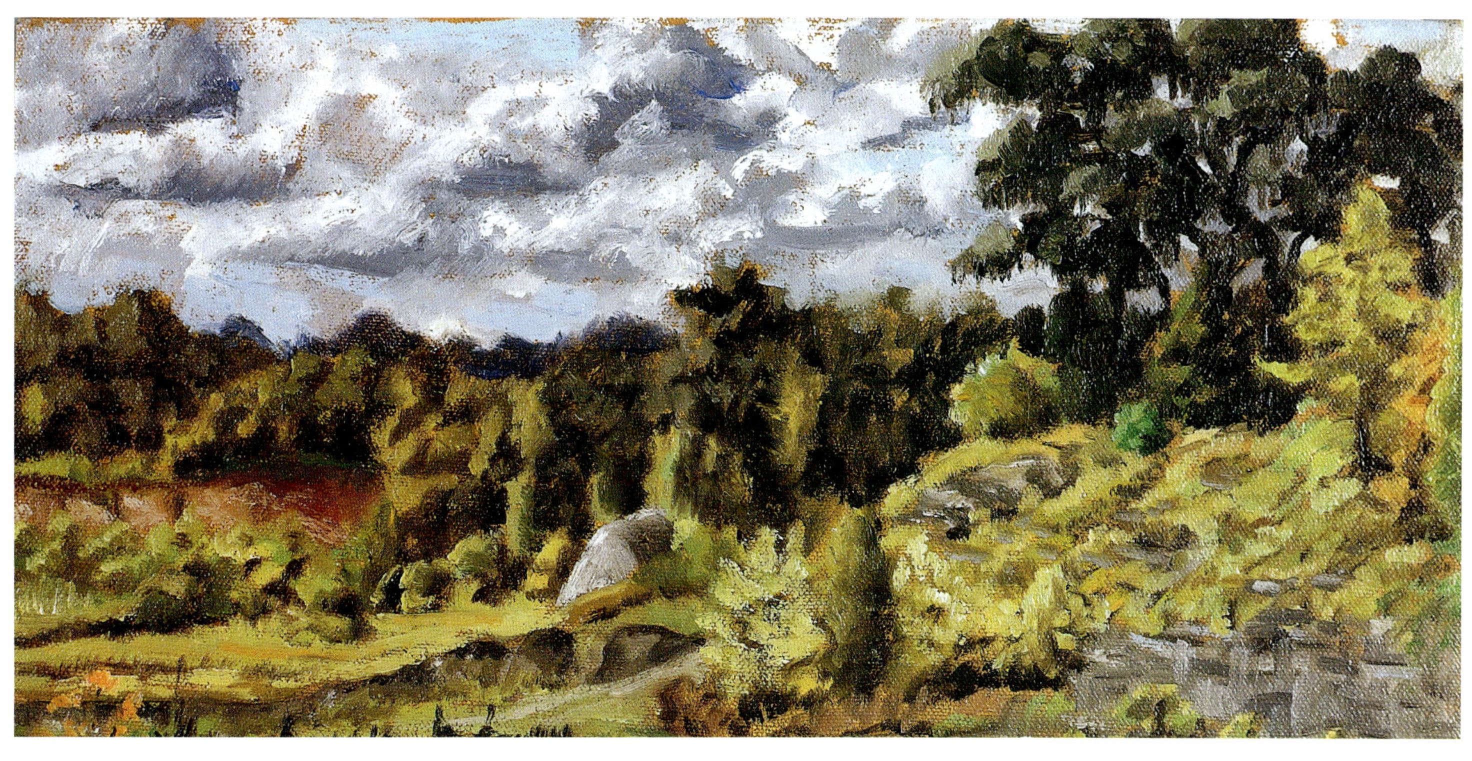

John Gurbacs

Lettuce Lake

1985, Oil on canvas paper, 16" x 20"

John Gurbacs was born in Budapest, Hungary, in 1947. He came to the United States with his family in 1957, after the 1956 Hungarian Revolution. Gurbacs graduated from Miami Edison High School in 1965 and received a bachelor's of fine arts degree from Florida State University in 1970. After a brief period of teaching at the University of South Florida in Tampa, Gurbacs set up a studio in Ybor City where he continues to work. He also teaches in Hillsborough County's Artists in the Schools program.

Gurbacs considers himself to be "an artist who is concerned with our fragile environment." Environmental issues are more explicit in his work than in that of most other Florida landscape painters, even though concern for the protection and conservation of Florida's natural beauty is a motivating force for many of the contemporary landscape painters. Gurbacs uses landscape painting to explore his formal interests in nature—especially the recurrence of similar forms—as well as the relationship between humans and the natural environment. In his most recent paintings, he combines his interest in fractals—geometric forms that are repeated in different realms (e.g., the branches of tree and a bolt of lighting or the shape of a human hand)—with scenes from everyday environments that make a clear statement about his concerns. One painting, for example, contrasts a school of fish with a junkyard of trashed cars. His environmental paintings have evolved over the past two decades from works that explore patterns, both recognizable and abstract, to those that explicitly confront human destruction of natural forms.

Gurbacs exhibits widely and has participated in exhibitions at the Tampa Museum of Art, Tampa, Florida; The Polk Museum of Art, Lakeland, Florida; the Museum of Florida History, Tallahassee, Florida; Scarfone Gallery at the University of Tampa, Florida; Society of the Four Arts, Palm Beach, Florida; Florida State University Arts Gallery, Tallahassee, Florida; Florida Center for Contemporary Art, Miami, Florida; and the Florida Gulf Coast Art Center, Belleair, Florida. His work is included in the permanent collections of the Florida House of Representatives, Tallahassee; the University of Central Florida, Orlando; the Polk Museum of Art, Lakeland; and the Tampa Museum of Art, Tampa. John Gurbacs has also been awarded both a National Endowment for the Arts Fellowship and an Individual Artists Fellowship from the Florida Arts Council.

Lettuce Lake followed a series of studies of water surfaces completed by the artist in the early 1980s. At that time, Gurbacs was preoccupied with capturing close-up, abstract views of the surface of water, including reflections and views that penetrated the water surface allowing for mysterious peeks below the surface. In late 1983, Gurbacs began a series of four water reflection paintings on paper canvas, including *Lettuce Lake* of 1985. These paintings were inspired by reflected colors and forms in the Hillsborough River observed by the artist at Lettuce Lake Park in north Tampa. Like much of Gurbacs' later work, subject matter here is both representational and abstract as the still, reflective surface of the water is distorted by a slight breeze or scrambled into wildly abstract patterns by a strong wing. With mysterious and unusual imagery, Gurbacs' *Lettuce Lake* is a challenging painting that asks the viewer to look down at, and into, the surface of the water as it reflects the bright, white Florida light, black trees overhead and yellow flotsam in a Zen-like reductive view of a special bit of the landscape in Florida.

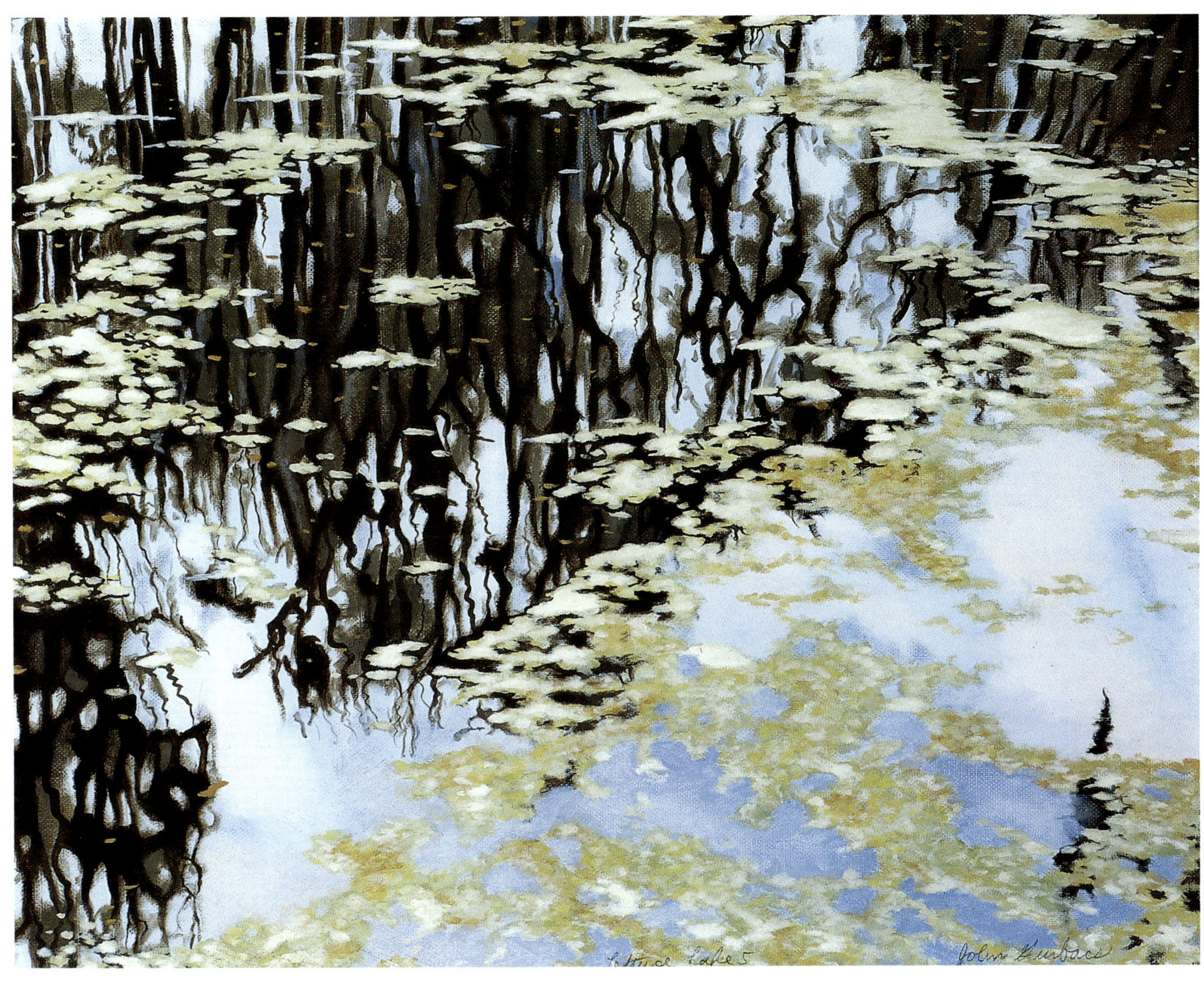
Lettuce Lake 5
John Gurbacs

MICHAEL HARRELL

ODESSA STREET, SEASIDE
1994, WATERCOLOR ON PAPER, 5½" X 10½"

OYSTERING
1992, WATERCOLOR ON PAPER, 18" X 25"

A resident and native of Tallahassee, Florida, born in 1964, Michael Harrell graduated from the University of Georgia in 1988 with a bachelor's of fine arts degree, majoring in graphic design. He began painting at the age of seven and describes himself as a self-taught watercolorist and illustrator.

Harrell considers himself an "American realist in the tradition of Winslow Homer, Andrew Wyeth and Edward Hopper." For years, Harrell was a commercial artist and graphic designer whose clients included American Express. Harrell's fine art has been featured in exhibitions at the National Parks Academy of the Arts, Jackson Hole, Wyoming; the American Artists Professional League at the Salmagundi Club, New York, New York; the Museum of American Illustration, New York, New York; the North American Marine Arts Society, Gloucester, Massachusetts; the Nature Center of Fort Myers, Florida; and the Museum of Science and History of Jacksonville, Jacksonville, Florida.

Harrell is a somewhat eclectic painter in his choice of subjects, which include landscapes from different parts of the United States, architecture, wildlife, boats, and social-realist studies of typical southern coastal scenes. Subject matter in the majority of his work can be found in the coastal areas of Northwest Florida and the low country of Georgia and South Carolina. He is interested in the effects of light on his subjects, as well as in capturing typical coastal scenes.

Odessa Street, Seaside, a bright watercolor on paper from 1994, is presented in a clear and crystalline manner with invisible brushstroke, made more startling through the use of white gouache to highlight certain architectural details, including the pavilion, clearly viewed at the end of the wide promenade of this formal view of one of America's newest seaside cities. This painting is a good example of Harrell's blending of commercial and fine art interests. It was one of a series of 25 views of this planned beach community in Walton County on the Northwest Florida Gulf Coast, commissioned by the developer to promote sales and vacation rentals of the many architecturally interesting houses.

Seaside represents an architectural and urban planning movement in Florida with the focus of designing communities that promote social interaction and are less destructive of the environment in which they are situated. Harrell's *Odessa Street* captures the ambiance of Seaside, as well as the atmosphere of "being at the beach" in Florida, an activity most people associate with this state, but a subject few painters have chosen to depict. Underlying Harrell's painting is the contemporary concern for preserving Florida's natural beauty. In this case, he has documented a new type of Florida community. This is consistent with his desire to paint things he "would like to preserve" for future Floridians.

In *Oystering*, a monochromatic watercolor on paper from 1992, Harrell presents a traditional, transparent watercolor on white paper in the manner of Winslow Homer, who painted similar scenes in both Florida and the Bahamas. Harrell is preoccupied with capturing the quality of winter light on Apalachicola Bay, a large inlet on the panhandle coast of Florida. The view is from the causeway west of Eastpoint. The watercolor captures an oysterman sorting through his haul of oysters against a slate blue sky and deep blue sea. This careful and precise work is one of a series completed by Harrell that salutes this important Florida pastime and industry. Harrell literally captures a disappearing way of life as Florida continues to industrialize her relationship with the sea.

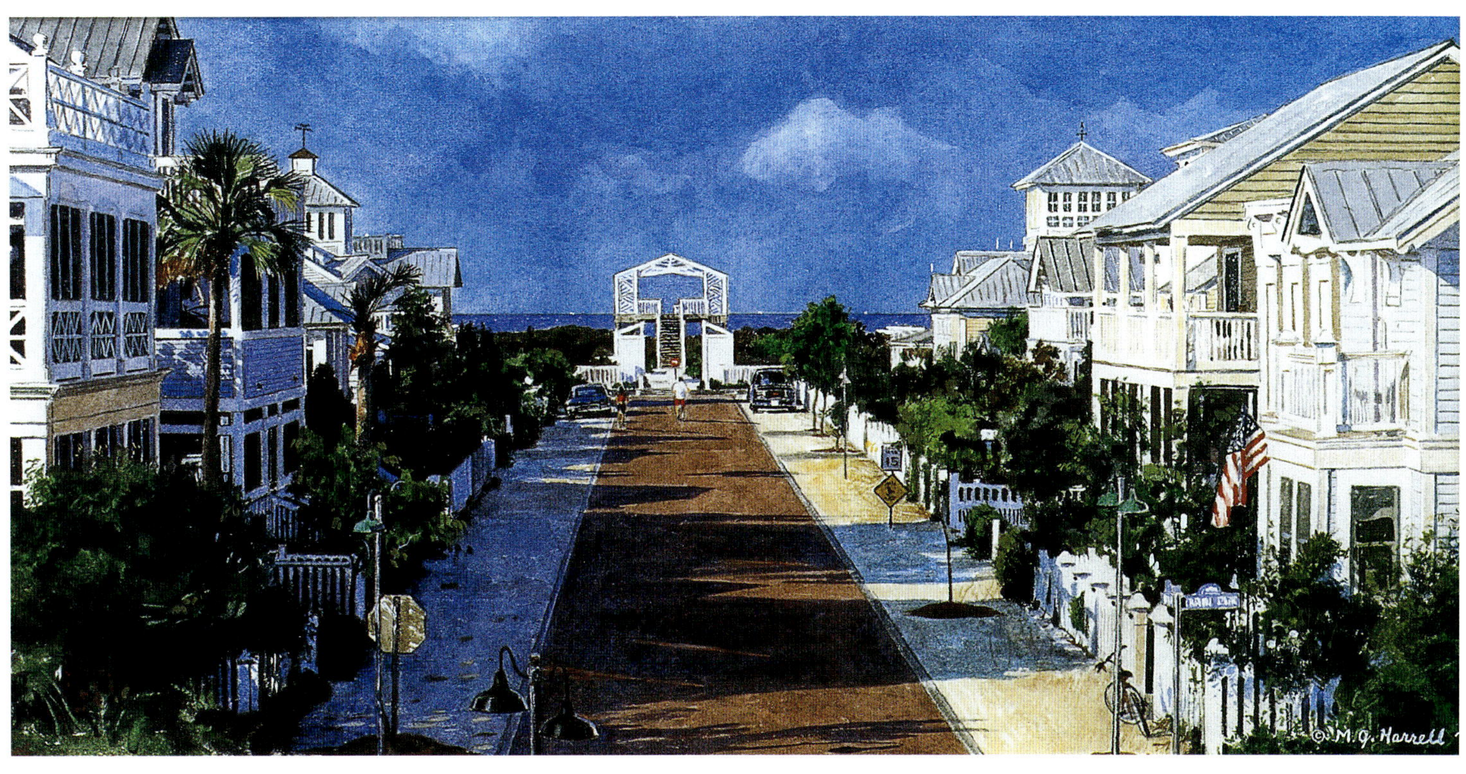
© M.G. Harrell

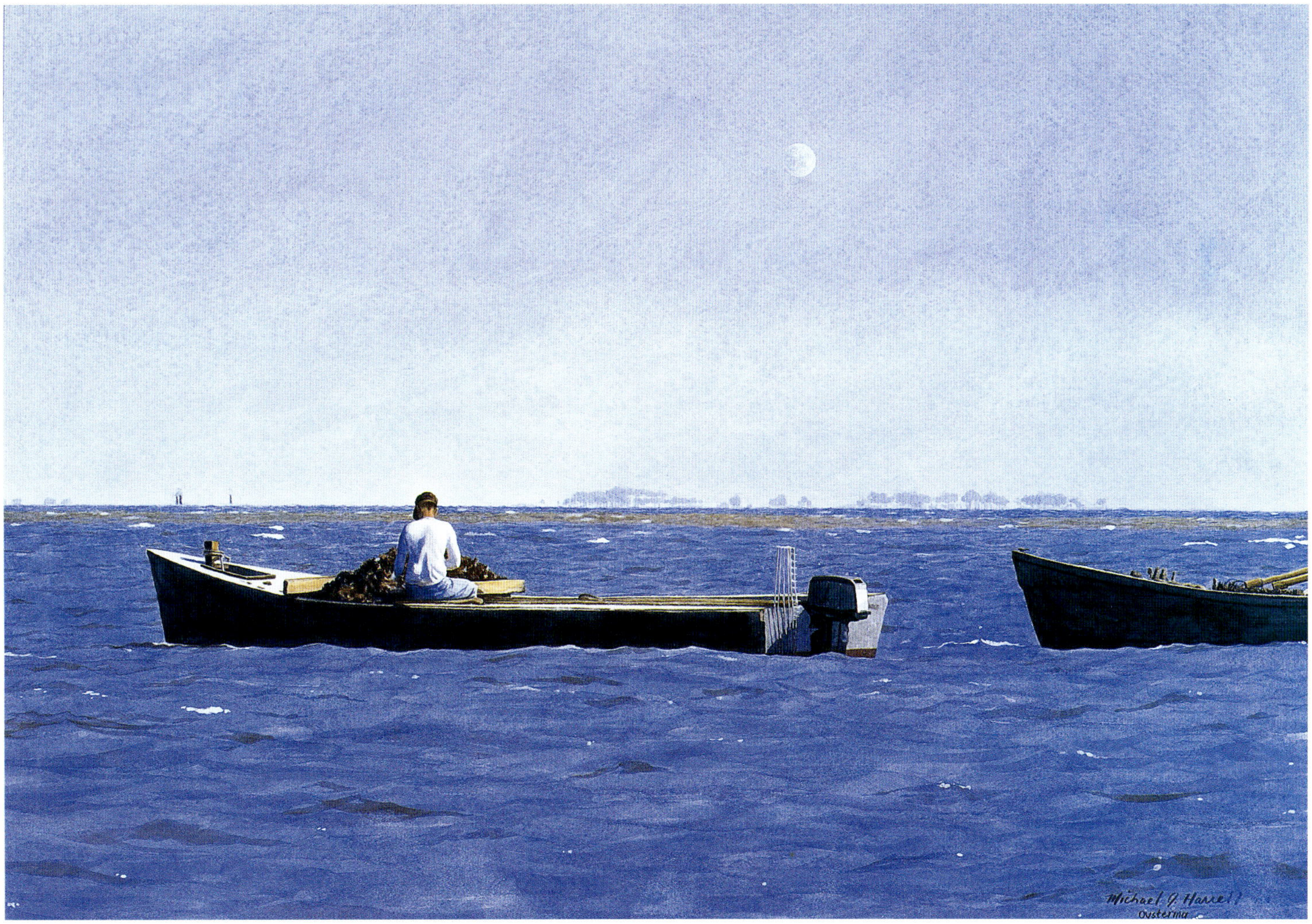

Rachel V. Hartley
1884 - 1959

Untitled
ca. 1930, Oil on canvas, 24" x 36"

Born into a family of artists in New York City on January 4, 1884, Rachel Hartley was the daughter of sculptor Jonathon Scott Hartley and Helen Inness Hartley. Her grandfather was George Inness, one of America's greatest 19th century painters. She was raised in Montclair, New Jersey, and educated in private schools there. At age 17, Miss Hartley entered the Art Students League in New York City. After her studies at the League were over, she worked in a studio next to her father's and devoted herself to portraits. In 1916, she was invited to accompany her brother on the first William Beebe expedition to South America. Hartley was the official artist on the expedition organized by the American Museum of Natural History. The team spent six months at the Tropical Research Station of the New York Zoological Society in British Guiana. During the trip, Hartley perfected her loose representational style and developed an interest in the pure landscape expressed through vivid colors and dramatic use of light.

Rachel Hartley often said that her "artistic career really began on a train bound for Tarpon Springs, Florida, with her grandparents," who maintained a vacation home there. Florida was to play an important role in the life of this suffragette artist throughout her long and prolific career. Hartley maintained residences in New York City and Southampton, Long Island. Typically, she spent summers partly in Southampton and partly in Provincetown, Gloucester, or elsewhere in New England. She also spent part of the year painting in Florida and other southern states, especially Virginia and the Carolinas. She exhibited her works principally in the Northeast in Boston and New York, including exhibitions at the Ainslie and MacBeth Galleries. Her paintings are included in many North and South American collections, including the National Gallery in Georgetown, British Guiana.

The present painting is an untitled work of ca. 1930. It is based on a location somewhere between Ormond Beach and St. Augustine on the northeast coast of Florida. In the oil on canvas, Hartley selects a large oak tree as the subject of her landscape. In the foreground, loose brushstrokes define a sparse groundcover accentuated by strong, purple shadows cast by the majestic oak. The bright yellow midground reflects the bright Florida sun partially viewed through the Spanish moss-covered limbs of the tree. Tall, dark pines help define the background, which gives way to a distant body of water framed by a shoreline rendered in atmospheric perspective. The light pink sky is accentuated by golden light in this vibrant, energetic, sun-charged painting of the Florida landscape.

Trees played an important role in Hartley's life. She often commented that her early childhood was literally spent climbing trees. Many of her South American paintings featured the exotic and unusual trees of the tropical jungle. Rachel Hartley equated the tree with immortality in many known and titled works from the period after 1923, the date of her return from a second trip to South America. It is hard to discern whether Hartley implies a prelapsarian Eden, before the Fall, or a postlapsarian Eden bereft of humankind, or both. What is obvious, however, is her use of a dramatic Florida setting with the sun rising in the east in which to place her tree—perhaps a reference to the knowledge of good and evil as Florida begins to lose her isolation and primitive beauty after World War I. This painting came from Hartley's "Barnyard" studio in Southampton, originally owned by her grandfather. At the time of her death, there was a large collection of her works—more than 150 oils, gouaches, and works on paper—in the studio. This work was among them. While the largest number of oils were still lifes, the collection also included paintings done during her 1916 and 1923 voyages to South America with the Beebe expeditions, and a number of works done in Florida and other southern states.

This painting is an interesting one for Florida. Its bravura technique and subject reflect the influence of the independent movement in American art spearheaded by Robert Henri and John Sloan. The transition from 19th century academicism to early 20th century realism is not well represented in known Florida landscapes. Hartley was certainly not the only northeast artist regularly coming to Florida in the early decades of the 20th century. Her painting suggests there is still much to be discovered or unearthed from private collections about the influence of developing styles in American art on the landscape tradition in Florida.

Hartley was a life member of the Art Students League, a member of the Pen and Brush Club, the National Arts Club and the American Association of Painters. She died in 1959.

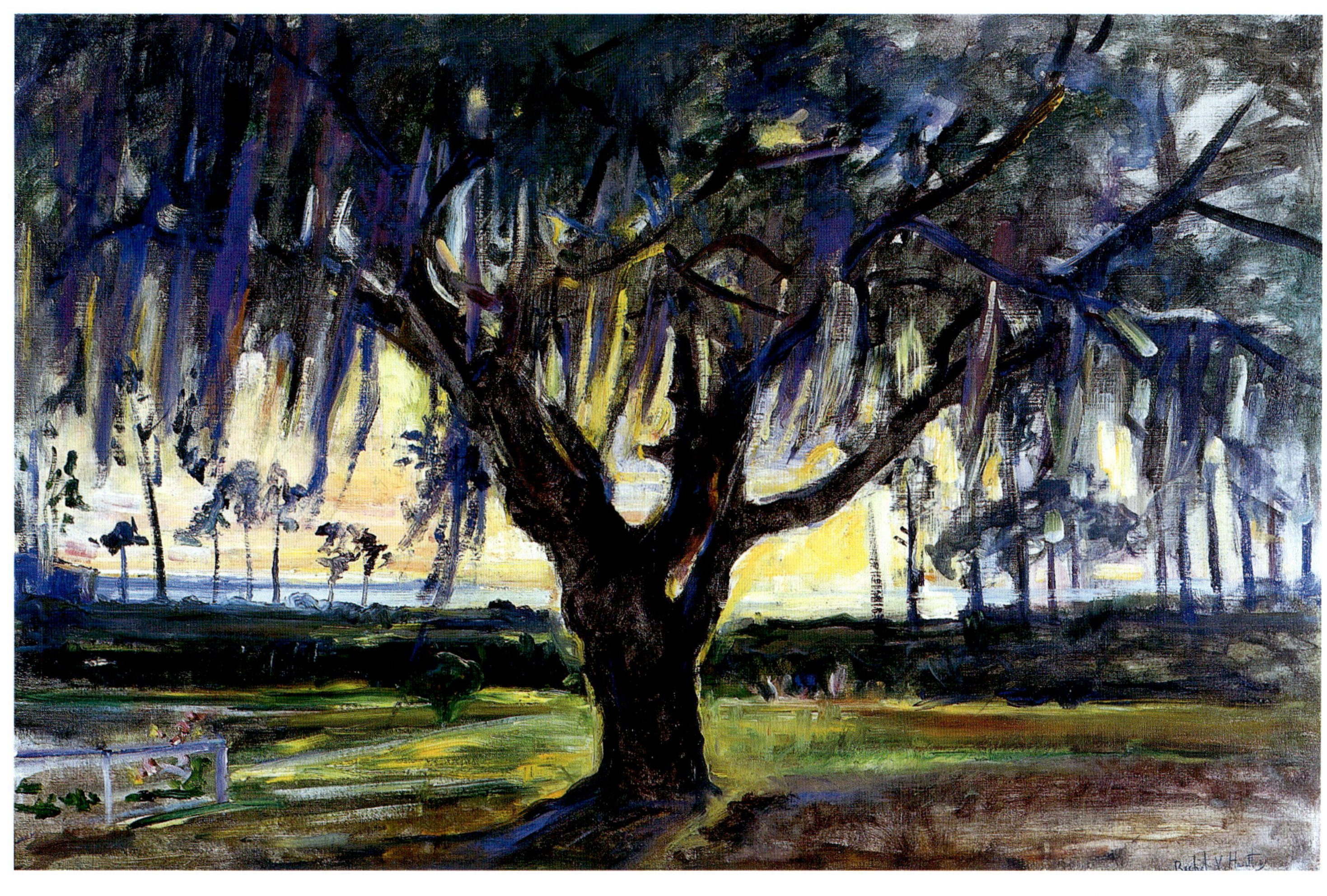

John David Hawver

Low Tide and Green Grass Forever

1995, Pastel, gesso and water on paper, 24⅞" x 38"

Born July 17, 1949, in Binghamton, New York, John David Hawver moved to Miramar, Florida, at the age of 10. He graduated from Miami-Dade Community College and the University of Florida. In 1973, he received a master's of fine arts degree from the University of Miami. For years he worked as a commercial artist and illustrator while also teaching at the University of Miami, Miami-Dade Community College, and the New World School of the Arts, Miami, Florida. He now paints full time, maintaining studios in Hollywood, Florida, and in Matecumbe Key, Florida, near Key West.

Hawver has exhibited widely in Florida and the South with more than 30 shows, including the Cummer Gallery of Art and Gardens, Jacksonville, Florida; the Museum of Art, Fort Lauderdale, Florida; the Ormond Beach Memorial Art Museum, Ormond Beach, Florida; Salem College Art Museum, Winston-Salem, North Carolina; the Art and Culture Center, Hollywood, Florida; Miami-Dade Community College, Miami, Florida; and the Ritter Gallery of Florida Atlantic University, Boca Raton, Florida. His work is included in the permanent collections of the Boca Raton Museum of Art, Boca Raton, Florida; the University of Miami, Miami, Florida; the University of Florida, Gainesville, Florida; Tropicana Corporation, Bradenton, Florida; Southern Progress Corporation, Birmingham, Alabama; The Society of the Four Arts, Palm Beach, Florida; RCA Records, Nashville, Tennessee; and the Art in Public Places programs in Dade and Broward counties, Florida.

Hawver's work is inspired by the energy and excitement of the natural environment of Florida. He began his career as a figurative and portrait painter, but quickly moved to the animated Florida landscape as his primary subject. Hawver does more than capture a literal view of the landscapes he creates in mixed media paintings on paper. Hawver's landscape world is a teeming, kinetic place of pure atomic energy, free from man-made objects. This is his way of "addressing modern life, urban sprawl, and the depletion of natural places. I document the splendor of what is left in Florida." Hawver feels that his work is also about the act of painting—the act of making marks, brushstrokes and color—not just what they represent. He is interested in creating surface tension in his work, undercut by a sense of space and atmosphere. In many ways, Hawver is both a landscape and color-field artist painting an abstract surface with personal feeling and emotion. He feels that his work could not have evolved if not for the unique light and color of South Florida, "where sky, land and water meet." Hawver often states that in his painting "clouds are the performers, light is the theme, and water is the stage."

Low Tide and Green Grass Forever, 1995, captures a view from U.S. Highway 1, at marker 74, on lower Matecumbe Key, north of Key West, Florida. The painting on paper catches rising mid-morning light and low tide that exposes and celebrates a mass of sinuous sea grasses viewed against a shimmering, blue ocean. To the right, a stretch of beach arcs toward the background creating depth and perspective to this highly charged scene.

Overhead, a bright blue, cloud-filled sky further animates this scintillating and living scene where drawn pastel is lightly washed with water. After drying, Hawver then draws over the wash. Often he adds gesso for highlights creating a many-layered combination of drawing and painting in his personal vision of the scene that celebrates living nature in Florida.

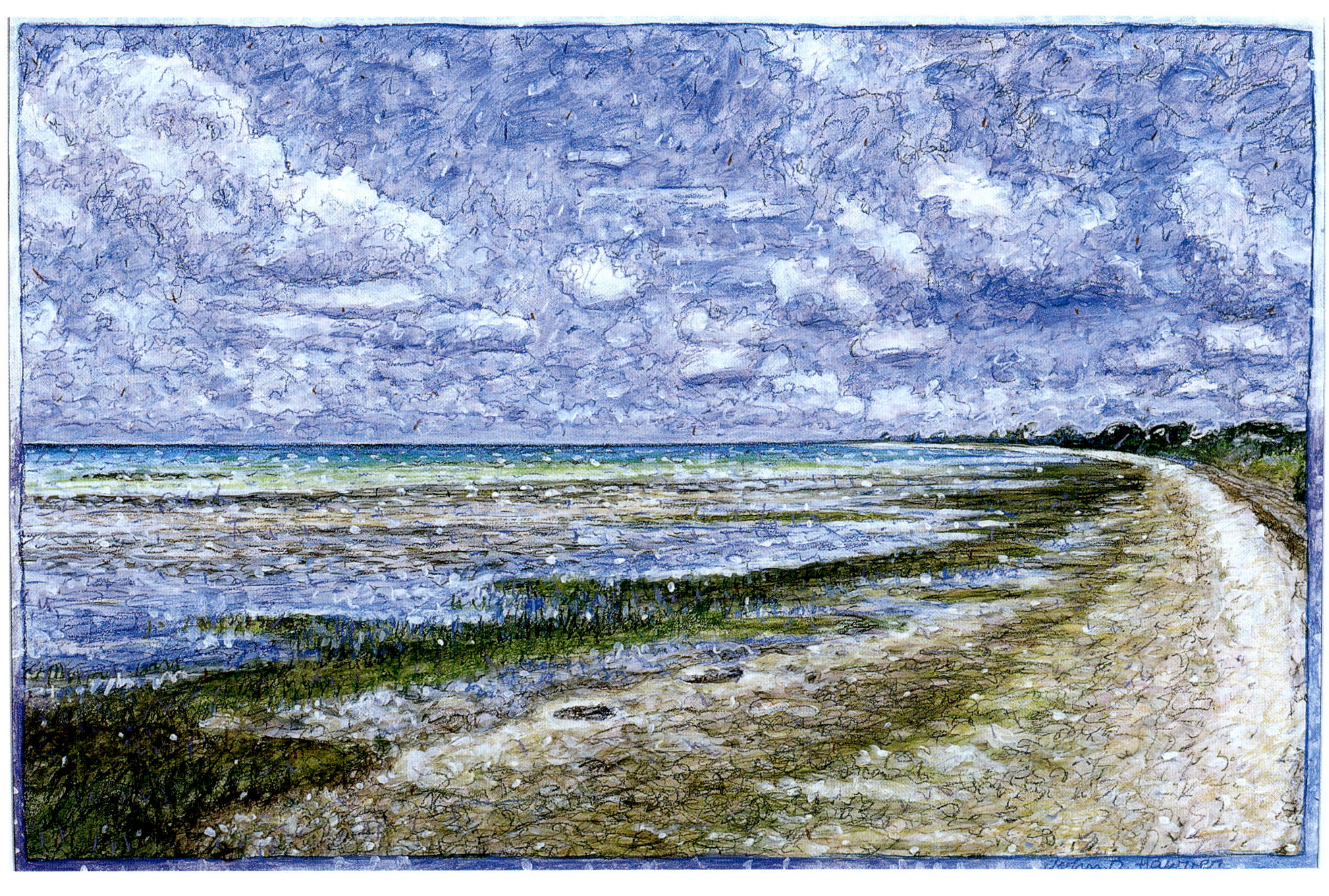

PETE NOAH HINSON

MILLER'S LANDING ROAD
1992, WATERCOLOR ON PAPER, 25" X 40"

OCHLOCKONEE RIVER
1993, WATERCOLOR ON PAPER, 14¼" X 21¼"

Pete Noah Hinson was born in Quincy, Florida, in 1957. He was one of 12 children of Anna and the Reverend Jimmy L. Hinson Sr., a Holiness minister and rural farmer. As a child, he accompanied his parents in the tobacco and peanut fields of North Florida where he learned to "love and respect the Earth reflected in its physical beauty." Hinson graduated from Shanks High School in Quincy and went on to the Cleveland Institute of Art and Case Western Reserve University Medical School where he received a degree in medical illustration while minoring in printmaking in 1980. After college, Hinson returned to North Florida. From 1980 to 1985, he was the art director for WCTV in Tallahassee, Florida. Since then, he has been self employed as a medical illustrator and artist. Hinson has been an award winner throughout the South since grade school. His work has been widely exhibited in North Florida and is included in corporate and private collections. In junior high school and high school, Hinson was part of a school art team made up of talented African-American students. The team was the idea of their junior high school art teacher who recognized the talent of Pete Hinson, Dean Mitchell and others. He formed the group to encourage the young men in developing their art skills.

In his opaque watercolor, *Miller's Landing Road*, 1992, Hinson describes a "canopy road" scene from the Tallahassee area. Here, dappled sunlight barely penetrates the heavy tree cover as it puddles in the rich, reddish-brown earth of the dirt road that divides the avenue of oaks planted by North Florida philanthropist John H. Phipps. In creating his tribute to this shady and beautiful location, Hinson uses standard watercolor on paper. He layers his transparent washes until a targeted richness of tone is achieved. His whites are actually the watercolor paper showing through the rich build up of adjacent color. Finally, Hinson glazes certain areas of his watercolor to "stress the beauty of a particular shape or color." He often incorporates drawing into the watercolor achieving both a sureness of line and a structure for the rich areas of layered watercolor in his painterly compositions.

In his *Ochlockonee River*, 1993, Hinson relaxes his grasp somewhat, producing an airy and luminist-inspired watercolor of this tranquil river in Northwest Florida. Here Hinson minimizes drawing. Instead, shoreline areas are suggested by a heavy wash of dark watercolor that defines the shoreline as it wraps the work dividing it between water and sky. A large mass of purple clouds floats in an orange sky. Their reflection fills the foreground in this loose and painterly celebration of sunset and its transforming magical quality on the isolated river and adjacent landscape.

Pete Hinson has a unique perspective on rural North Florida. No other artist (other than Dean Mitchell, who now resides in Kansas City) has depicted rural, inland North Florida scenes and people. Hinson's subjects include not only the natural landscape but, perhaps more importantly, cultural landscapes (cotton and peanut fields, for example), rural architecture and cultivated and wild flowering trees and bushes. He is also very aware of the special beauty of North Florida and is concerned to capture it before it is lost. Miller's Landing Road, for example, is now paved.

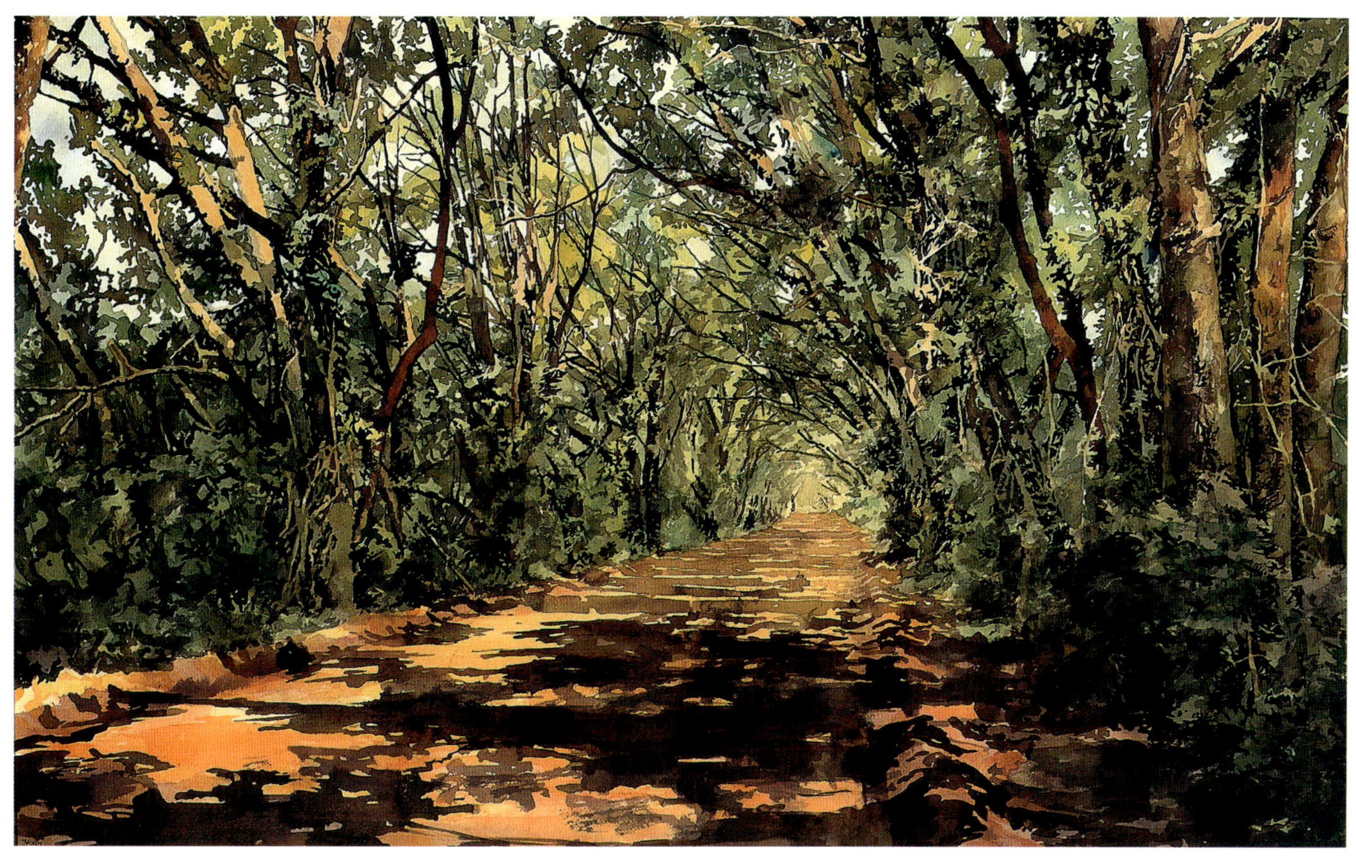

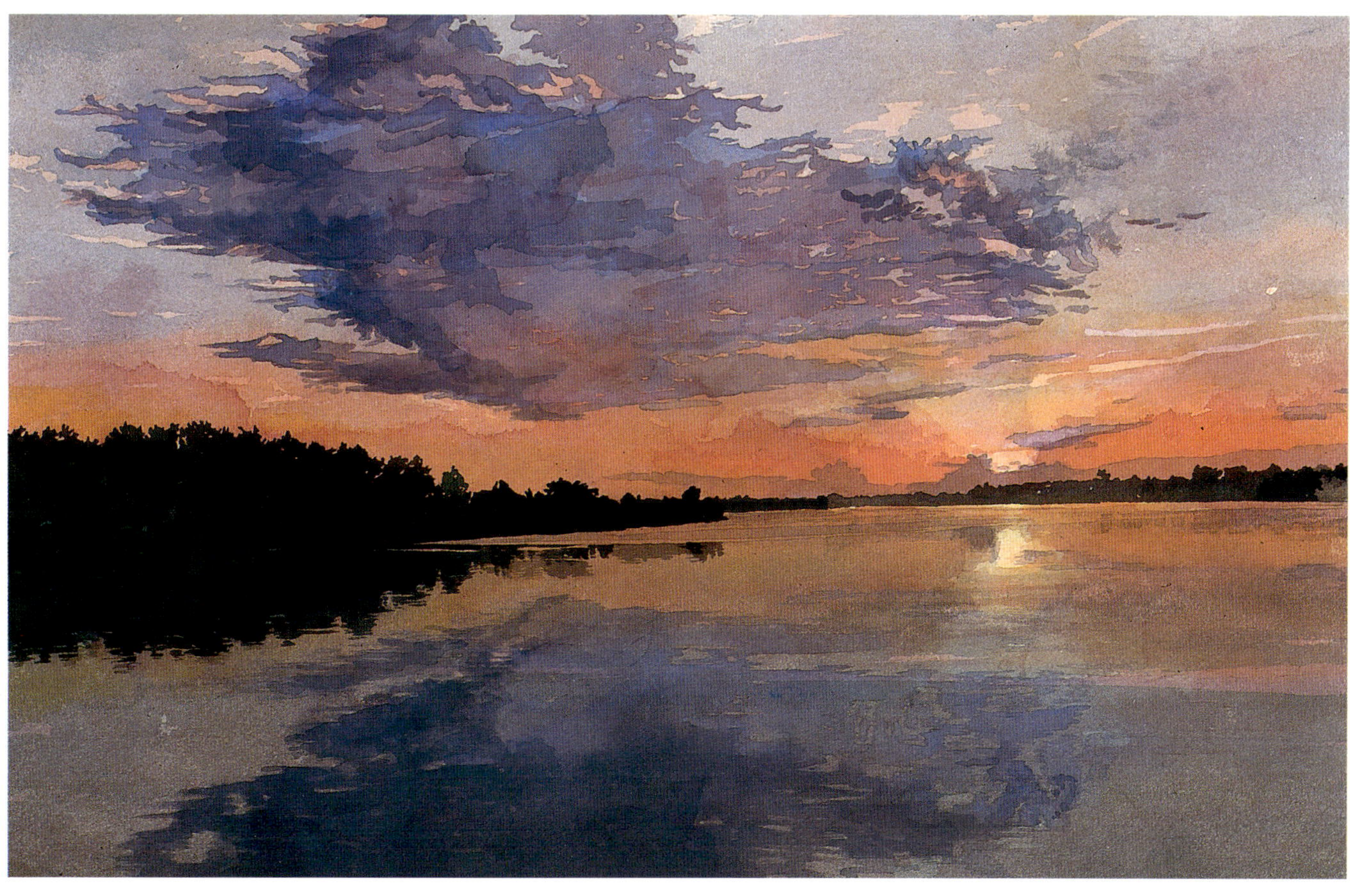

MARIA HOCH

GULF ISLANDS NATIONAL SEASHORE

1996, WATERCOLOR AND PASTEL ON PAPER, 20" X 30"

Born in Melbourne, Florida in 1953, Maria Hoch was one of six children in a family that moved frequently around the United States. After finishing high school, she attended both Auburn University and the University of Alabama in Huntsville. In 1981, she returned to Florida with her two teenage children. The beach was her principal destination because of its affordability and special ambience. After a short time, the "need to go to the beach" convinced her to settle on the coast at Pensacola, Florida, in the panhandle.

Since 1976, Hoch has exhibited her work in invitational and commercial one-person and group shows in the Pensacola area and elsewhere in the Southeast. In the 1970s, she was a private art teacher. In 1994, she was an artist in residence for Escambia County's middle and high school system. In 1995, she taught art at an area Montessori Middle School. Since 1996, she has painted full time producing both commissioned work for clients and work for several galleries in North Florida. Most of her work is in private collections.

Most of Hoch's landscape work begins with pastel on paper. She then adds water softening the pastel into a wash. Recently, she has incorporated watercolor into her mixed media paintings of the spacious and exhilarating beaches of Florida. Hoch works downward on the page establishing a dark, deep sky in contrast to the white of her cloud formations. "There is such an intense delight when I first establish that deep blue outline of the divide between sky and clouds, and then load a brush with water to spread outward from it describing the rest of the sky on paper."

Many of her paintings are inhabited spaces, especially people at the beach. The artist is intrigued by the contrast between the sights and sounds of groups of people on the beach with their paraphernalia and the natural colors and sounds of the seashore. Pure landscapes, like the present example, are less usual for her. Hoch believes deeply in the restorative qualities of the Florida landscape. While not involved in any political or social organizations concerned with the Florida environment, Hoch is "thankful for the preservation of the National Seashore. It is such a gift whose creative influence has increased on me over the years."

Hoch's mixed media *Gulf Islands National Seashore* approximates a scene near Santa Rosa Island, south of Pensacola. Hoch's works are actually composites of reality and fantasy, mixing images and locations in a romantic landscape that recreates a unique mental image based on reality but slightly different. And, while the land mass seen in the distance is probably the Naval Air Station viewed from the area of Ft. Pickens, a historic Civil War masonry fort on Pensacola Bay, Hoch added the thin line of green land weeks after she completed the billowy skyscape and sea because "the painting just needed it." Many of the clouds included in this piece are based on cloud formations captured in Polaroids in Hoch's backyard and are transformed here into thunderheads in the bright, blue sky of a protected piece of Florida's unique landscape. Hoch has tried to convey the realities of place that are most important to her and strike her as the transcendent qualities of the seashore; a sense of timelessness, the endurance of the sea, sky and the land masses, a stage setting for Civil War forts and modern beachgoers escaping from urban stress, and outlasting them all.

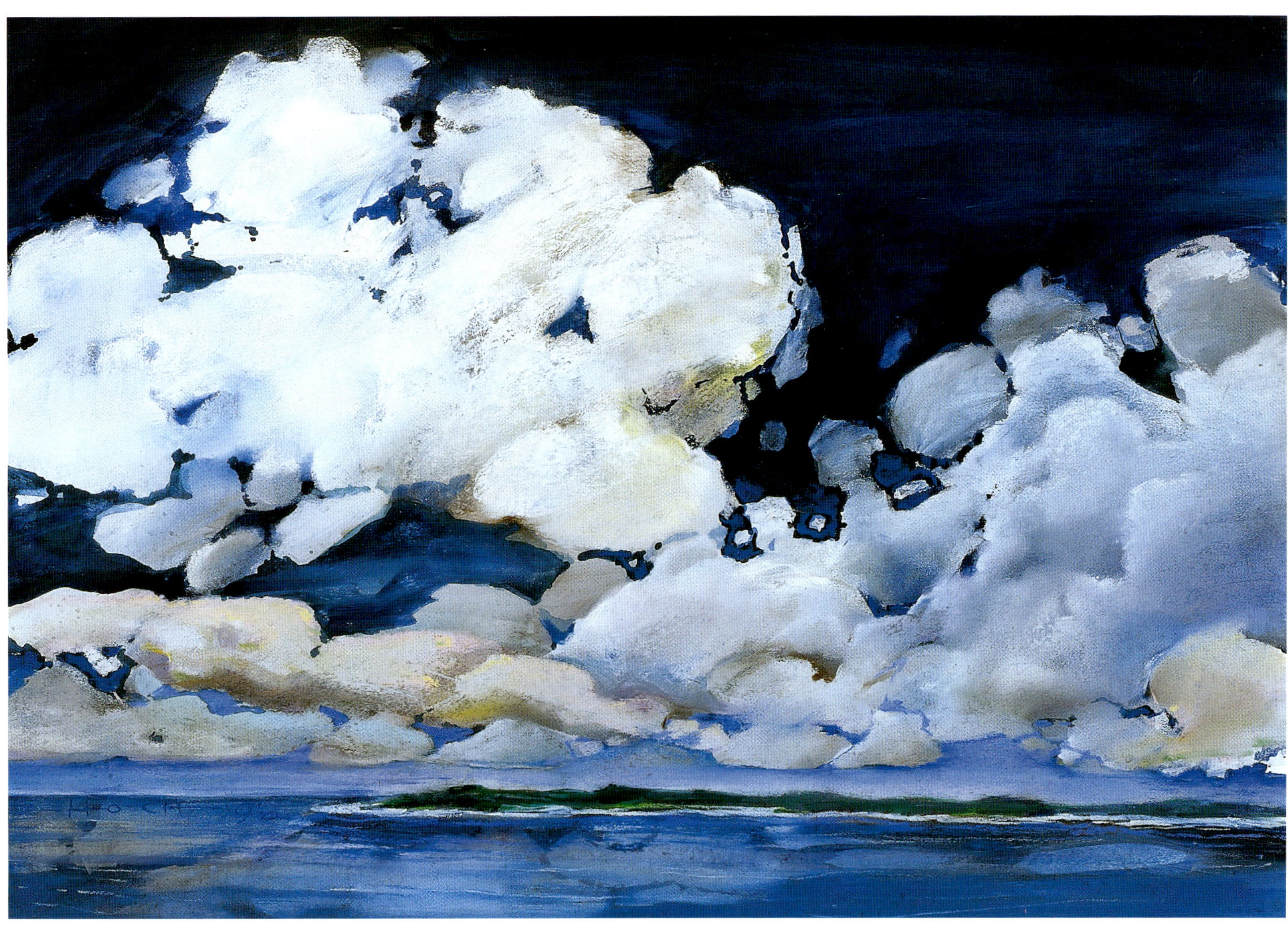

Larry Horn

Blackwater Bay From Escribano Point

1996, Pastel on paper, 7¼" x 10¼"

Pastel artist Larry Horn was born in 1939, in Mobile, Alabama, on the Gulf Coast, where he received his early education. Horn studied at the Ringling School of Art in Sarasota, Florida. He also studied with Albert Handel and Robert Frank. Horn has exhibited widely in commercial galleries and has been included in exhibitions at the Art Museum at Fort Walton Beach, Florida. He is an affiliate of both the Pastel Society of North Florida and the Southeastern Pastel Society. Since 1992, Horn has specialized in capturing the special nature of isolated spots in Santa Rosa and Escambia counties, Florida, the westernmost parts of the Florida panhandle. He now resides in Pensacola where he maintains a studio. In 1996, he completed a series of pastels after spending 15 months traveling through the bays, bayous and landscapes of Northwest Florida.

Horn works on sanded paper because it can accept more pigment than other surfaces. He usually works from dark to light, background to foreground, hard pastel to soft pastel as he creates his equivalent visions of the Florida landscape. Horn works in a studio where slides, sketches, prints and notes act as stimulants to his creative process. He often describes himself as more technical than intuitive as he explores both the surface of the world he creates, as well as its deeper meanings, in pastels of sensitive and colorful strength that both describe and analyze the rural landscape in Northwest Florida.

Blackwater Bay from Escribano Point, 1996, captures a typical stretch of land and water along the east side of Blackwater Bay, a body of water formed where the Blackwater River and the Yellow River enter Pensacola Bay. The scene is some eight miles from downtown Pensacola. The artist is looking northeast with the calm and reflective surface of Blackwater Bay to the viewer's left. Hidden by the trees in the center is the mouth of the Yellow River.

Horn chooses an early afternoon on a mild, spring day. The treescape is abundant with oak and pine. To the right, the bright yellow and green undergrowth results from freshwater run off and the seeds it carries that germinate at the edge of the brackish bay water. Horn is a realist and is concerned with capturing not only the specifics of the landscape but also the reflection of sunlight and clouds in the tranquil blue waters of the bay. "I enjoy recording these images that are prompted by natural beauty while it's still here. The beauty of nature requires space. People require space. People tend to displace and destroy the beauty that attracts them. Nature is defenseless. I want to experience the serenity of what natural beauty remains and record some of it." The qualities of Florida that Horn describes—mild weather, natural beauty, casual serenity and balance—are the same attributes in very similar words that struck Ralph Waldo Emerson a century and a half earlier in his descriptions of this part of Florida. Emerson praised the casualness of the place; Horn regrets its passing.

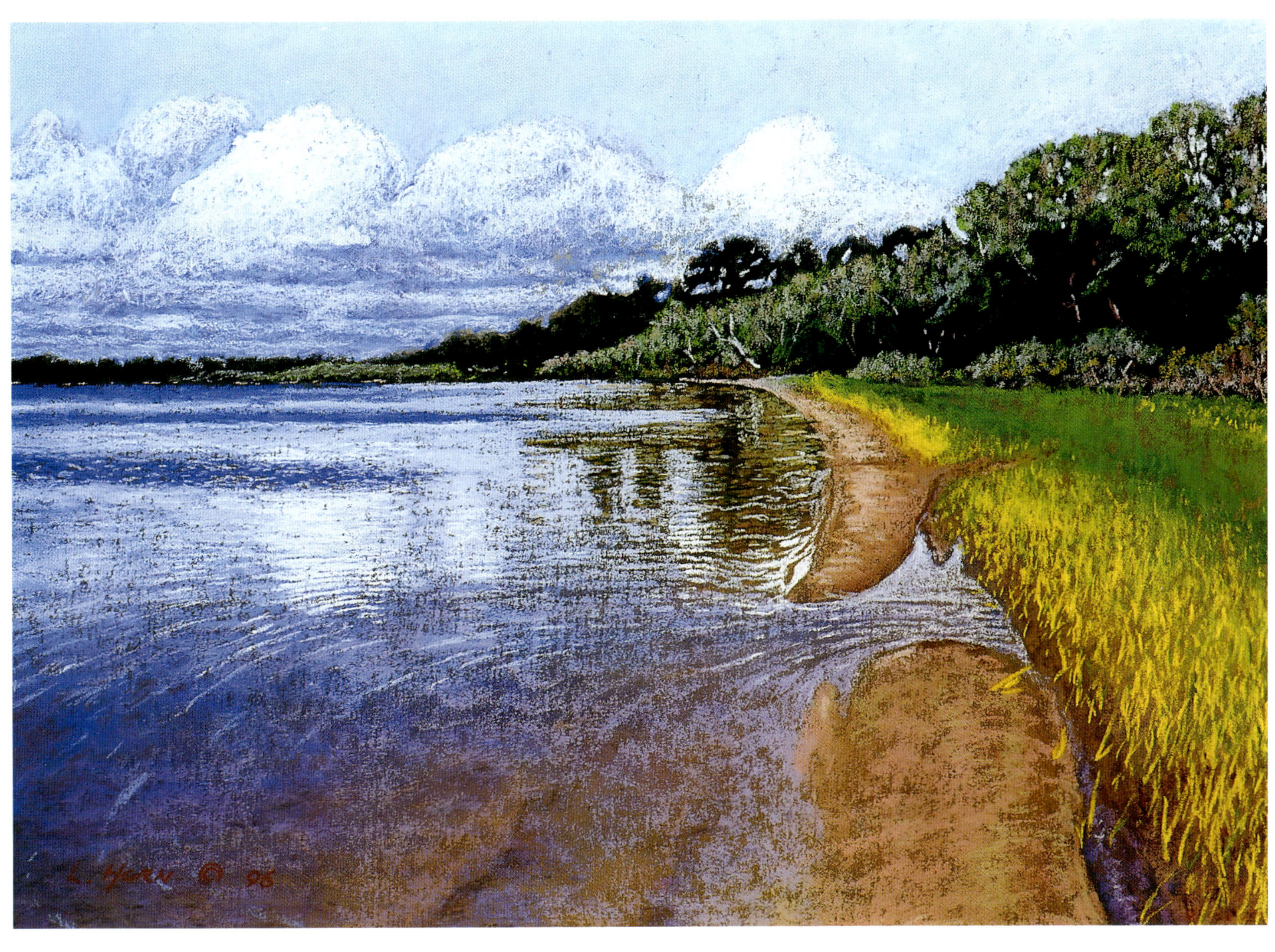
L. HORN © 96

Artemis Skevakis Jegart Housewright

The Field (Evening Comes to Tennessee Street)

1957, Polymer, tempera, collage and oil on wood panel, 34" x 48"

Artemis Housewright was born in Tampa, Florida, in 1927, the daughter of a Greek father and an English mother. She was raised in St. Petersburg, Florida, where her father served as chief engineer at Bay Pines Hospital.

As a child, Housewright attended classes sponsored by the Works Progress Administration while attending public schools in St. Petersburg. She earned a bachelor's of arts degree at Florida State University, Tallahassee, and worked briefly (1949-1951) in Atlanta, Georgia, as a graphic artist. After a tour of Europe in 1951, she returned to Florida State where she received a master's of arts degree in painting in 1953. During this period, she was an art student of both Edmund Lewandowski and the European expatriate painter Karl Zerbe, a major force in the modernist movement in the South after the second world war. From Lewandowski, she learned his appreciation of interesting architecture. Working with Zerbe, she developed her distinctive technique in painting using small palette knives that she fashioned from broken razor blades. They enabled her to apply oil paint in precise ways. In 1956, an oil, *Saturday Afternoon on Adams Street* (Tallahassee, Florida), won the Mead Paper Company Painting of the Year Award. In 1957, she won her first prize in the National Oil Painting Competition held in Jackson, Mississippi.

Since that beginning, Housewright has exhibited widely, including shows at The Butler Institute of American Art, Youngstown, Ohio; The University of South Florida, Tampa, Florida; The John and Mable Ringling Museum of Art, Sarasota, Florida; The Society of the Four Arts, Palm Beach, Florida; The New Orleans Museum of Art, New Orleans, Louisiana; The Columbia Museum of Art, Columbia, South Carolina; The Mississippi Art Association, Jackson, Mississippi; The Jacksonville Museum of Contemporary Art, Jacksonville, Florida; The Birmingham Museum of Art, Birmingham, Alabama; The LeMoyne Art Center, Tallahassee, Florida; and the Cosmos Club, Washington, D.C. She has received hundreds of commissions and her work in both oil painting and shell mosaic can be enjoyed throughout the United States, including at the University of Maryland, Baltimore, Maryland; Louisiana State University, Baton Rouge, Louisiana; Florida State University, Tallahassee, Florida; Sarasota Art Association, Sarasota, Florida; the National Museum, Havana, Cuba; Old Westbury Gardens, Long Island, New York; and the City of Tallahassee, Florida, Municipal Airport. She continues to be listed in numerous publications on American art and artists, and maintains a studio in Frederick, Maryland.

The Field (or *Evening Comes to Tennessee Street*), 1957, captures a scene located on Tennessee Street near High Road in Tallahassee, Florida. *The Field* was drawn from a typical scene, with a shack or two added to the hot, red clay field for the sake of composition. The field hands were coming home in the late afternoon." The mixed media work of polymer, tempera, collage and oil on wood panel is a large, modernist work where Housewright has collapsed perspective and stacked her images. Broad, abstracted areas of color convey the atmosphere of rural North Florida—the dazzling white heat of midday, orange-red riotous sunsets, silver-grey cypress siding, lush green growth, the cool shade of oak trees, and a quiet desperation in the lives of poor, rural, black families. A group of black men is returning home at the end of the day, trudging slowly. Tired women are waiting on the porches of each shack. And, while the viewer is invited to enjoy the rich colors of the different times of day, this is a portrayal of the rural South; part of the "Other Florida" described by author Gloria Jahoda in 1968: "Housewright has made an Other Florida of her own with beauty entrapped in the simple, compassion eloquent in the telling detail, history vivid in the evidence of human lives daily lived...."

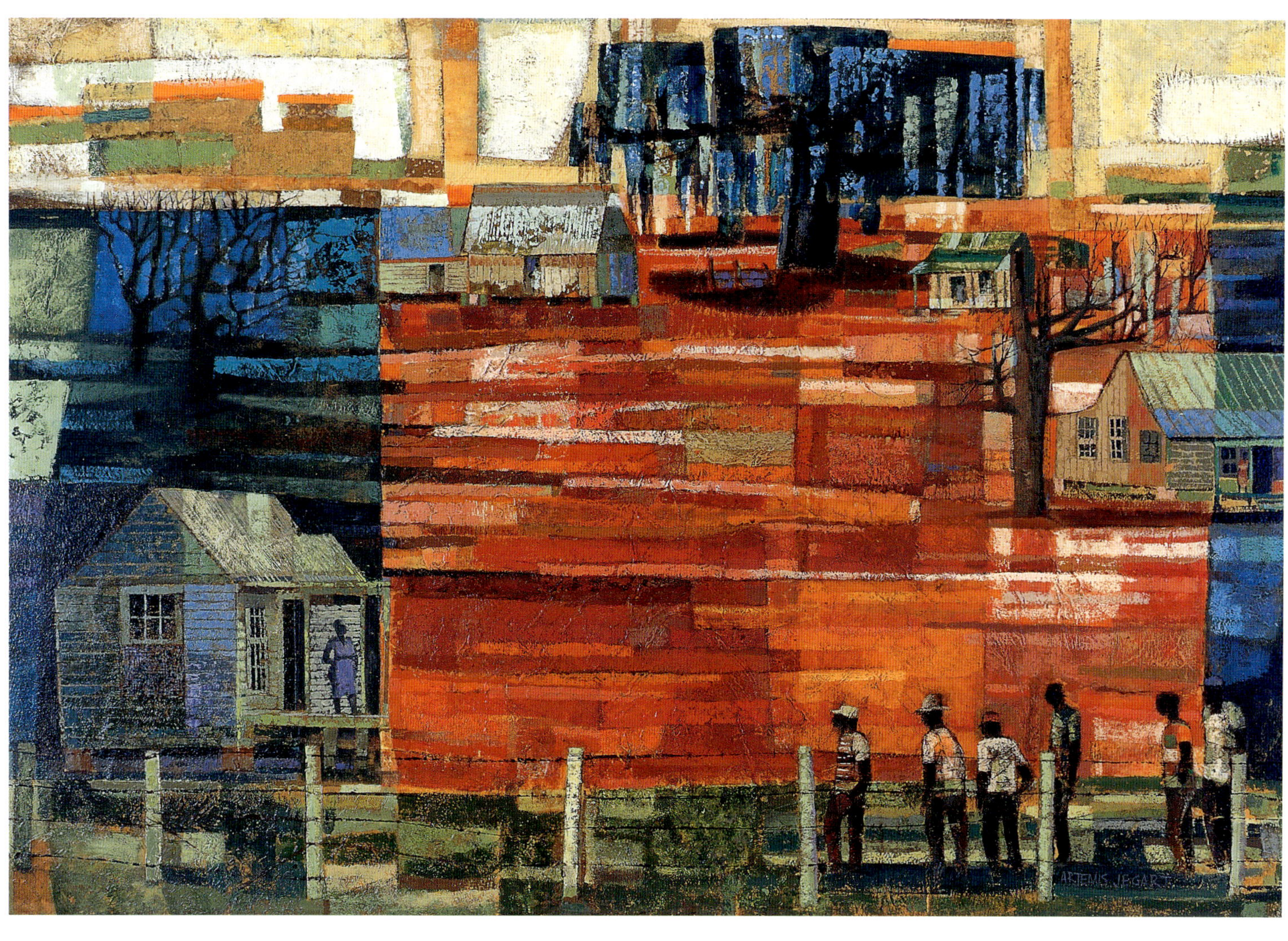
ARTEMIS JEGART

WILLIAM JAMES

ROYAL POINCIANA TREES
1990, PASTEL ON PAPER, 27¼" X 29³⁄₁₆"

CHURCH IN THE GABLES
1995, PASTEL ON PAPER, 25½" X 19⅜"

Illustrator-artist William James was born October 7, 1943, and raised in Forty-Four, Pennsylvania, a small town near Wilkes-Barre. He received a bachelor's of fine arts degree from Syracuse University in 1965. After college, he spent a year in Washington, D.C., but moved to Miami, Florida, partly for the weather and partly because he felt it was a fast-growing area where he would have more opportunities to become established as an illustrator.

James is a commercial illustrator and fine artist who works in pastels and watercolor. His favorite subject is people, but he also paints landscapes and architecture. His paintings depend heavily on drawing, reflecting the skills he has developed as an illustrator. He is a member of the Society of Illustrators, the Pastel Society of America (PSA), the American Watercolor Society (AWS), the National Watercolor Society, and the Knickerbocker Artists U.S.A. He exhibits widely and has received numerous awards, including the M. Grumbacher Award (PSA), the Elsie Ject-Key Memorial Award (AWS), the Salmagundi Club Award and the Andrew Giffuni Award (both PSA), the Award of Exceptional Merit from the Degas Pastel Society, Best in Show awards from the Louisiana Watercolor Society, Mississippi Watercolor Society, Watercolor Society of Alabama, and the Georgia Watercolor Society. James has been featured in *Communication Arts Magazine*, 1982; *Step-by-Step Magazine*, 1995; *American Artist*, 1984, 1989 and 1996; and *The Artist's Magazine*, 1988 and 1995.

James works in his studio at home. He generally starts with photographs of a subject that interests him. These are a point of reference for composing a final image. He first makes a rough sketch in colors that are complementary to the actual subject. He then refines his image with strokes of related colors. James describes his style as impressionist, influenced strongly by Mary Cassatt and using a loose, color-separated technique similar to her color strokes, which are not blended but are applied side by side. From a distance, the colors blend and produce a realistic image, as well as "the effect of vibration and movement." James also paints with bright colors and many complements, heightening or exaggerating actual colors to further enhance the sense of excitement or movement in each painting.

James' *Royal Poinciana Trees* is a 1990 pastel on Canson Mi-Tientes paper, which is dark colored and makes the colors stand out. It is one of his first Miami landscape paintings and depicts royal poinciana trees near his home. He was intrigued by the design they made, along with the schefflera trees behind them. He has set the trees against a substantial sky painted in a warm, ultramarine color "to go along with the bright red flowers. I added some clouds and painted them to repeat the rolling effect the group of trees made." He omitted adjacent houses, telephone poles, and street signs to uncover a simpler and more beautiful scene in a modern statement of the Florida idyll.

Church in the Gables is a pastel completed in 1995 and featured as a cover for the April 1997 issue of *American Artist* magazine. Again, James used his impressionist technique in capturing this landmark located directly across the street from the famous Biltmore Hotel in Coral Gables, Florida. James' aim was to illustrate "a beautifully designed building on a warm, sunny day." James photographed his subject from many angles. Back in his studio, he selected a vertical format for the work to accentuate both the steeple and the palms located in front of the church. He painted the sky a heightened blue to contrast with the yellows, pinks, oranges and whites of the building. James added clouds and created dramatic shadows on the building to simulate a bold chiaroscuro on this familiar landmark and typical architectural style of the urban landscape of South Florida.

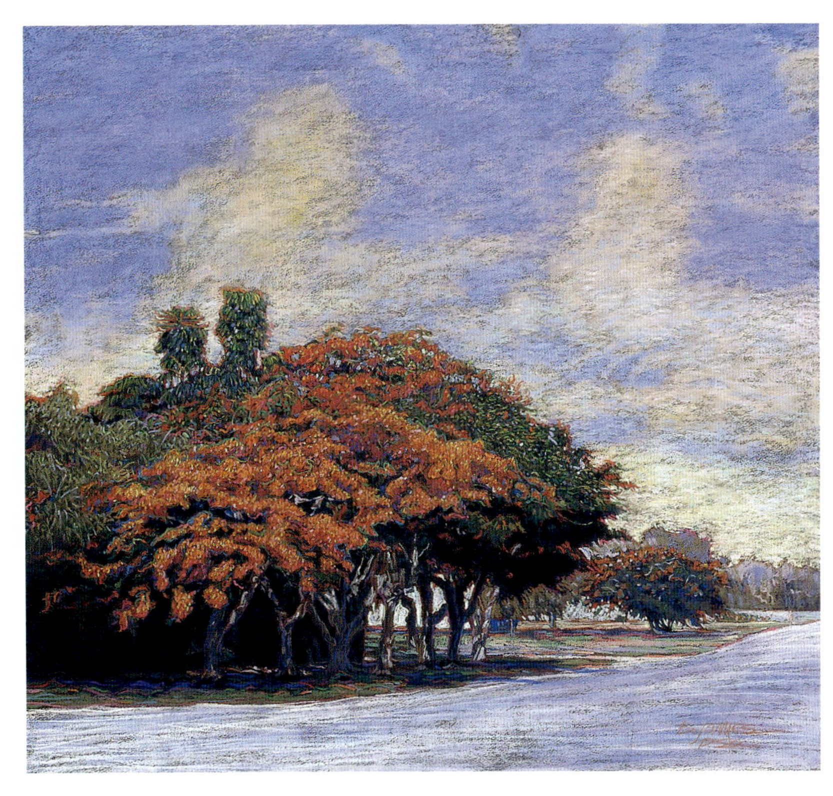

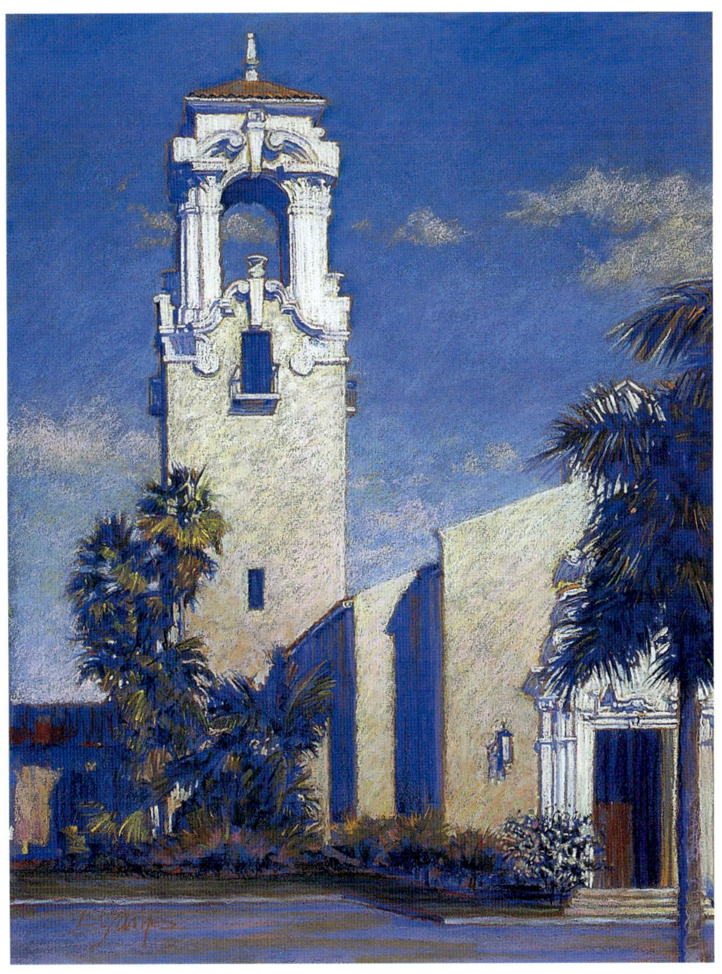

F.W. KENNISTON

DUNE COUNTRY #9

1995, OIL ON WOOD PANEL, 17¼" X 20⅜"

F.W. (Ken) Kenniston was born in Bourne, Massachusetts, on Cape Cod, in 1919. He received his early education in Cambridge, Massachusetts, where he graduated from high school. He attended the Massachusetts School of the Arts for two years; 1938-1940. Kenniston also studied at the Chicago Art Institute. From 1954 to 1964, Kenniston was a full-time graphic designer in Chicago, Illinois, serving as art director at the Leo Burnett Advertising Agency from 1964 to 1970.

Kenniston came to Florida in 1971 to teach art at Florida State University, Tallahassee. He was an associate professor from 1971 to 1988, and served as chairman of studio art from 1978 to 1980. While teaching and painting, he also served as consulting art director for Nedham Worldwide Advertising from 1981 to 1986. In 1988, Kenniston retired from Florida State University to devote his full attention to painting and writing from his studio in Apalachicola.

Kenniston has participated in more than 40 exhibitions, including The Art Institute, Chicago, Illinois; The Florida State University Gallery, Tallahassee, Florida; The El Paso Museum of Art, El Paso, Texas; The Lemoyne Center for the Arts, Tallahassee, Florida; and The Arts Club of Chicago, Illinois. His work is included in many public, corporate and private collections, including City National Bank, Baton Rouge, Louisiana; Florida State University and The City of Tallahassee, Florida; and Diagonal Data Corporation, Lakeland, Florida.

Kenniston shifted his interest to the Florida landscape about 10 years ago. "The rivers, pine forests and coastal dunes of the North Florida panhandle have been the inspiration for my landscape interpretations. My images are as much a result of invention as direct observation."

Dune Country #9 is an oil on wood panel completed in 1995. "In this work, I have tried to capture the color, characteristic light and ambience of a certain kind of geographical area rather than document a specific location. This painting is the final result of many revisions and reworkings. It is based on the remembered experience of many such places." Kenniston's *Dune Country #9* presents the viewer with a light and spacious imaginary Florida landscape of dune, sky, palm and ocean dominated by a single palm and a dense thicket in the midground rendered in a deep green and purple. The foreground of greens and yellows suggests a beachy ground cover. The background is dominated by a large dune of pink and mauve against a bright, blue-green sea in this abstract and cerebral recollection of a Florida beach landscape.

"My intention is to try to memorialize the still relatively unspoiled quality of the rivers, wetlands, forests and coastal dunes of this quiet, enchanted region. [My] paintings are meant to be neither documentary nor narrowly descriptive, but are an attempt to visually evoke that kind of poetic memory that is the stuff of myth." Even though *Dune Country #9* is a composite of images, it captures the character of the high dunes along the Northwest Florida Gulf Coast, especially in the western panhandle. The dunes are extensive and almost desert-like at the height of a hot summer day when the colors are baked out. The colors of sand and vegetation change dramatically depending upon the light and time of day.

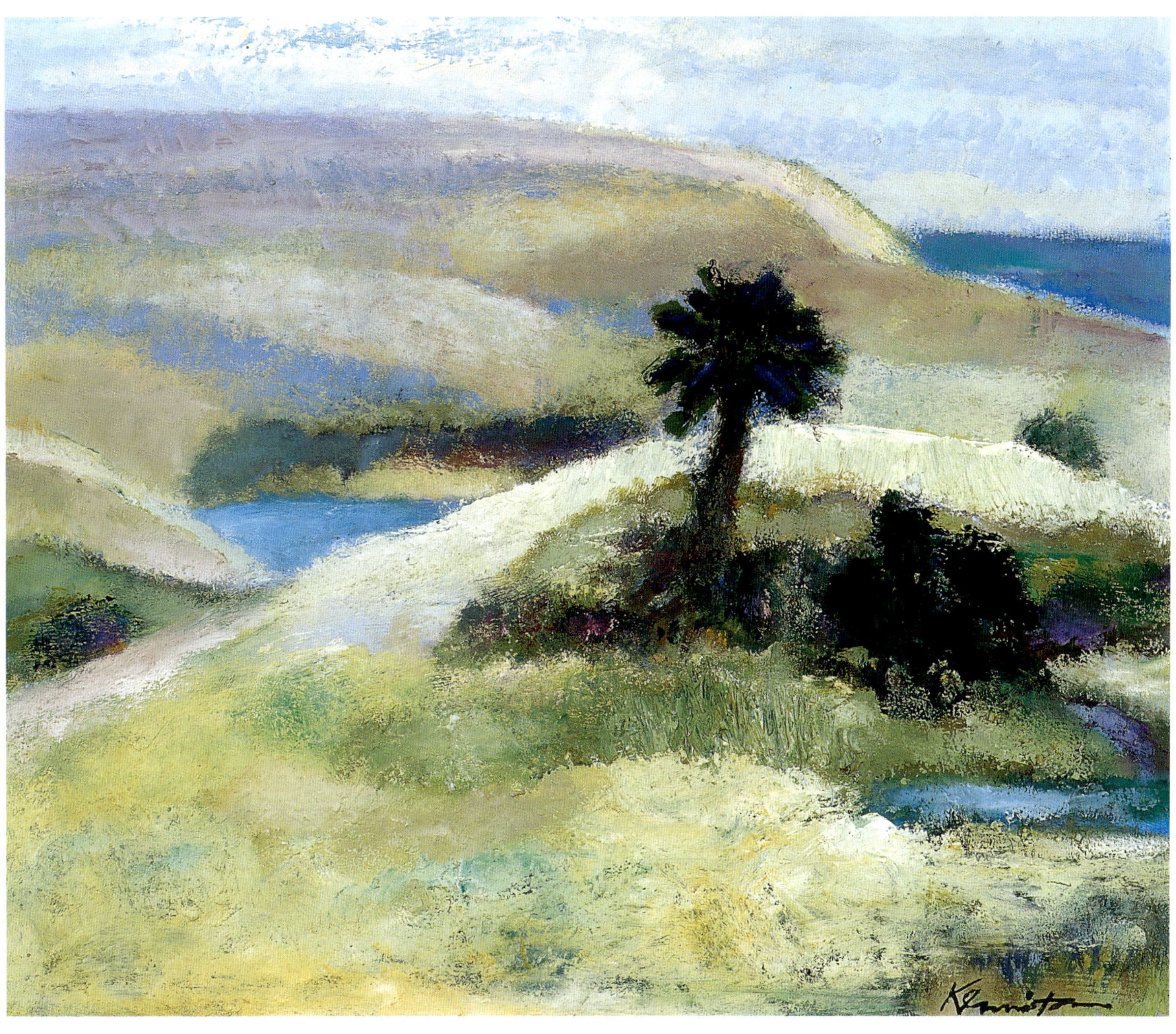

Susan Klein

My Siesta Key Five

1994, Acrylic on canvas, 17½" x 22½"

Susan Klein was born in Dayton, Ohio, October 30, 1944, and attended elementary and secondary schools there. She later attended Ohio State University in Columbus, first majoring in elementary education. After her junior year, she shifted interests and attended Youngstown State University, Youngstown, Ohio, where she received a bachelor's of arts degree in studio arts with a minor in English literature. In 1977, she received a master's of fine arts degree from Kent State University, Kent, Ohio, with a major studio emphasis in painting and a minor in sculpture. In 1979, Klein owned and operated a commercial gallery in Youngstown, while teaching at both Youngstown State University and The University of Akron. In 1985, she directed the Trumbull Art Guild in Warner, Ohio. Since 1990, she has pursued her career as a full-time professional artist. She moved to Florida in 1990.

Klein has exhibited widely, including shows at the St. Petersburg Center for The Arts, St. Petersburg, Florida; The Self Family Arts Center, Hilton Head, South Carolina; The Barrier Island Group for the Arts, Sanibel, Florida; Youngstown State University; Youngstown, Ohio; the Davis Gallery of the University of Akron, Akron, Ohio; and the Dayton Art Institute, Dayton, Ohio. Her works are included in public and private collections, including The Hoyt Institute of Fine Art, New Castle, Pennsylvania; Youngstown State University, Youngstown, Ohio; and Kent State University, Kent, Ohio.

Klein's images are drawn from the Florida landscape. Her style is grounded in Pop Art and the expressive use of color and line by French post-impressionist painters like Gauguin, the Nabis and the Fauves. Like the Fauves, Klein translates her feelings about the Florida landscape into colors. Her shapes are naturalistic but simplified, like the imagery of Pop Art.

Klein is very philosophical about her commitment to landscape painting. "Nothing makes me feel so alive, so safe, so at peace with myself as when I'm surrounded by, and immersed in nature. From the solitude of the landscape I am able to express those most positive feelings toward life that can easily be doubted in other circumstances." For Klein, the landscape as art is a variation of reality in the Fauvist tradition where color is chosen for meaning and for its impact on the senses. Klein believes that "composition is the skeleton; color is the muscle."

Painting for Klein is also a political exercise. "What I am doing is very political. We are in a struggle to safeguard the health of our environment. My landscapes are a cry for awareness of the preciousness of the environment."

For Klein, each painting is "special and specific" to a given place and time. Klein first captures her reaction to special places in drawings and sketches done on site. Later in the studio, she works from this shorthand where the sketch conveys the necessary creative memories through the energy of the drawn line, which captures, for Klein, sentient memories of her subject, including breezes and the smell of trees, sky, water and grass.

My Siesta Key Five, 1994, is an acrylic painting with metallic pigments on canvas. The group of five cabbage palms was selected from a landscape at Siesta Key Beach, on Florida's Gulf Coast near Sarasota. In reality, they are located next to volleyball courts, a lifeguard building and a parking lot. A picnic table and trash container are within the circular space they describe. The artist, in her vision, however, has isolated the palms from the surrounding beach clutter. In the energy of the atmosphere, and the rhythm of the sea and the light, the distinctive shapes of the palms represent a space for "joyful and peaceful contemplation." Klein believes in nature's self-healing powers. This picture also demonstrates the ability of Klein's technique to capture energy in nature. Her metallic pigments give this painting an electricity that conveys excitement while the elegant blue and green palms, dark blue sea, and blue and violet sky convey the serenity and majesty of nature in this peaceful, modernist Florida landscape.

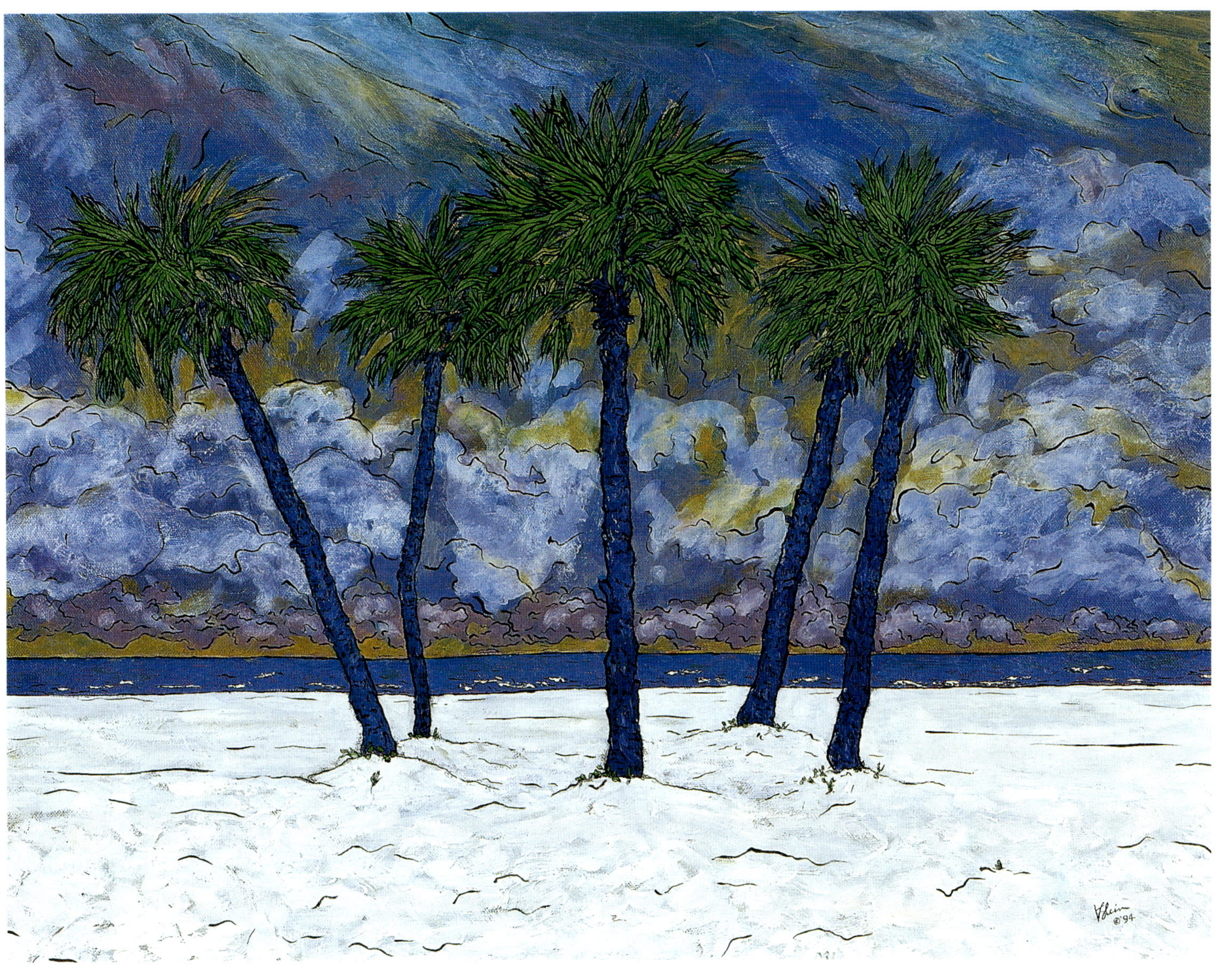

Mitchell Lee Kolbe

Cat-Head Pine
1993, Oil on canvas, 23½" x 17"

Homosassa Springs
1995, Oil on canvas, 24" x 20"

Born in Charlotte, North Carolina on March 12, 1955, Mitchell Lee Kolbe attended schools in the Charlotte-Mecklenburg area. In 1973, he moved to New York City to study with Robert Schultz, Jack Faraggaso, and John H. Sanden at the Art Students League as a scholarship award student. He also studied privately with Lou Dedonato at the Salmagundi Club. In 1977, Kolbe studied photography at Queens College in Charlotte, and enjoyed his first one-person exhibition of paintings at the Robinet Art Gallery there. It was also in 1977 that he first visited and exhibited in Florida, at Tarpon Springs.

Mitch Kolbe is a free spirit. His art background and work experience are as varied as any contemporary Florida artist. Since New York, he has lived in Charlotte, North Carolina, Atlanta, Georgia, and Tarpon Springs, Florida. He has worked as a commercial artist, muralist and sculptor, while pursuing his fine art painting. In Atlanta, he worked on the restoration of The Atlanta Cyclorama. At Kennedy Space Center, Titusville, Florida, he completed a series of realistic murals describing natural Florida. He produced 92 life-size sculpted heads of children from around the world for the 1996 Centennial Olympic Games, also in Atlanta.

In 1983, Kolbe moved to Tarpon Springs, Florida, where he established a studio in 1985 dedicating himself to oil paintings. His studio was once the studio of American landscape painter George Inness Jr. Kolbe's fine art paintings consist principally of landscapes representing the central west coast region of Florida, including scenes of Tarpon Springs. He is a realist, somewhat conservative, and his works are scenic and romantic with a classical feel and rich colors that are immediately appealing. There are few passages that are difficult for the viewer to understand. Even though Kolbe is distressed by the adverse effects of growth in Florida, the world in his paintings is Edenic. Perhaps as much as any contemporary Florida artist, Kolbe is able to convey a sense of the ideal place we are in danger of losing. Kolbe's strongest ties are to the premodernist painters who began portraying Florida more than a century ago. This approach is still one of the most powerful in conveying the distinctive qualities of the landscape.

Typically, Kolbe begins his paintings on location. He starts each oil painting with a board or canvas he tints red in order to capture Florida's subtropical atmosphere. Then, he quickly sketches in shapes using turpentine and umber pigment. Next, he amasses large areas of color to establish his light, middle, and dark tones. His technique is additive, starting with thin paint and building thicker textures as he moves toward completion.

On the first day, Kolbe likes to concentrate on his drawing and the values of light and dark. He then adds color and detail, correcting his drawing as he works for the next three to four days. He then moves back to his studio where he adds or deletes detail, decides on color changes, and often glazes his finished image to produce special highlights and emphases.

Kolbe's *Cat-Head Pine*, 1993, image captures a large Florida pine on Seminole Drive in Tarpon Springs. Kolbe was "first taken with the beauty of the late afternoon sunlight trapped in the massive boughs of this old giant." He completed the painting in early May at twilight, around 6 p.m. on consecutive days. The term "cat-head" refers to the shape of the scars left on these trees from turpentine harvesters who carve into the trees to induce sap flow. Kolbe's richly textured, realistic oil on canvas carefully recreates the golden light of the late afternoon as it illuminates the surrounding palms and the warm browns of the bark of this majestic survivor of Florida's agricultural past. Kolbe is a master technician whose near-invisible brushstroke celebrates this palm and pine hammock as something representative of a rapidly disappearing Florida. "I'm painting contemporary Florida as fast as I can in hopes that others will also take note of its natural limitations."

In his *Homosassa Springs*, 1995, Kolbe moves to a lighter and less-dense format as he describes the lush and tropical freshwater spring and its crystal clear, blue and green waters. Kolbe selects a cool, January midafternoon as he paints the "fish bowl" area of this unique spring located about 45 minutes north of Tarpon Springs in Citrus County. Here, carefully drawn and accurately rendered lush palm and palmetto frame the white-sand-bottomed, freshwater spring as it bubbles out into this fountain of youth created by the limestone topography of Central and North Florida. Florida is a wet state with many rivers, lakes, springs and sinkholes breaking the surface of the land, thus determining the character of the topography and vegetation. In this picture, Kolbe captures a quintessential Florida place. "The first time I saw Homosassa Springs, I couldn't believe my eyes. After swimming there, I'm convinced that the story of the fountain of youth is true; it's almost a religious experience."

Mitchell Lee Kolbe is concerned about growth and its negative effect on the Florida landscape. "In the latter half of the 20th century, it is increasingly difficult for any landscape painter to find truly unspoiled wilderness and this is especially true of Florida. I see myself as sort of a visual timekeeper trying to live and accent, rather than destroy, the reason each and every one of us chose to come here in the first place."

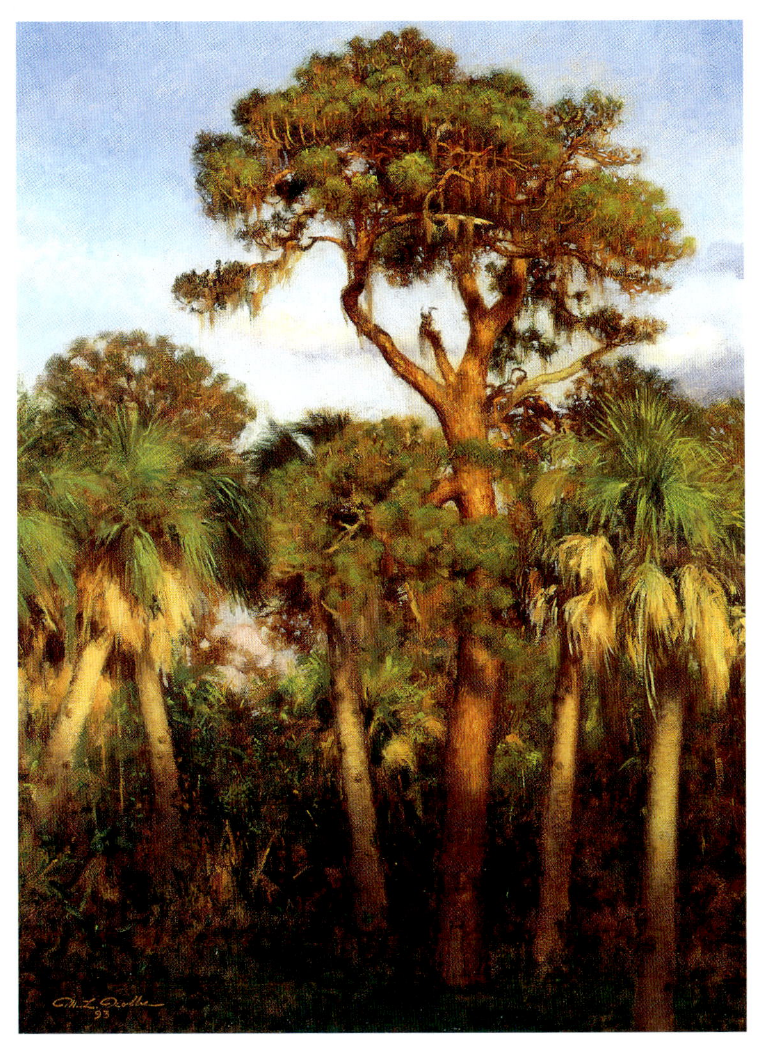

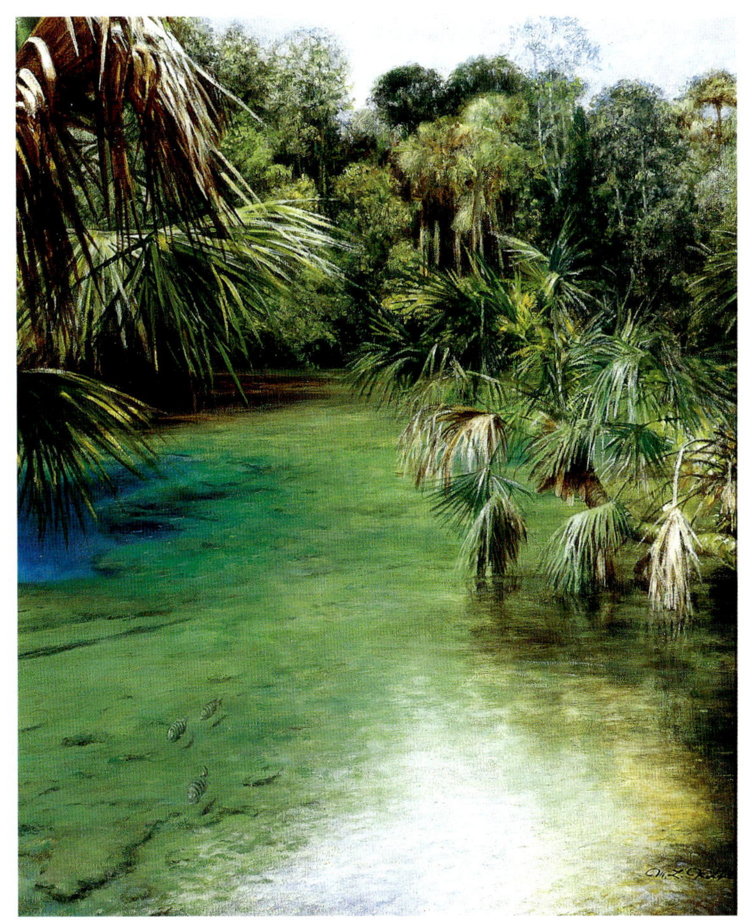

Robert Larsen

Myakka Lake

1995, Oil on wood panel, 8" x 12"

Robert Larsen was born in Aurora, Illinois, in 1923. His early years were spent in the Midwest where he first developed an awareness of art and its influence on life. Larsen's early education was completed in Illinois.

In 1946, Larsen attended the Kansas City Institute of Art and Design, Kansas City, Missouri. In 1947, he attended the Detroit School of the Society of Arts and Crafts, Detroit, Michigan. In 1950, he moved to Florida, attending the Ringling School of Art and Design in Sarasota, where he has enjoyed an extensive career as an influential teacher and painter of regional significance for nearly 50 years. Between 1966 and 1990, he taught figure painting and figure drawing at the Ringling School.

Larsen has exhibited throughout the Southern United States including exhibitions at The Corbino Gallery and the Sarasota Art Association, Sarasota, Florida; The Gallery at Edison Community College, Fort Myers, Florida; The Polk Museum of Art, Lakeland, Florida; The Columbus Museum, Columbus, Georgia; The Columbia Museum of Art, Columbia, South Carolina; and The Tampa Art Institute, Tampa, Florida. He also exhibited at several well-known, but now-closed private galleries in Florida, including the Hilton Leech Gallery, Hodgell-Hartman Gallery, and the Joan Hodgell Gallery, all formerly of Sarasota. His work is included in the collections of The High Museum, Atlanta, Georgia; and The Polk Museum of Art, Lakeland, Florida. His works include still life, figures, and landscapes in a modernist style with a cubist influence. After art school, in addition to painting, Larsen was a wood sculptor and also worked in concrete and plaster. He also built props for Ringling Brothers and Barnum and Bailey Circus. There is no doubt that his work in three-dimensional forms affected his painting.

Larsen's first experience with painting the Florida landscape began in 1951 when Siesta Key near Sarasota was still undeveloped. "It was wild and beautiful...almost breathtaking then." He has continued to paint the landscape that helps express his personal feelings for the poetry of tropical light and its transforming affect on nature. His personal obsession with the landscape has been called "a perceptive commentary on the prevailing concerns for the future of our native land."

Larsen's landscapes have a hazy or misty quality, which he sees as characteristic of Florida where rising moisture in the air softens the light. His colors are also soft, often jewel-like pastels, which are intensified by contrast with adjacent colors. Even though the light is soft, the forms in his landscapes are sculptural and stable, structured as a series of cubist, refractive planes in a classically balanced composition. His subjects are often ordinary places, but through his use of color, he elevates the ordinary into a very intense experience of reality.

Larsen usually begins a painting by creating a series of watercolor sketches on site. He calls these "color and shape notes." He then reassembles these bits of information in the studio as he begins to abstract his vision by adding more opaque colors and geometric forms as he literally reinvents a Florida landscape. Larsen usually uses umber to first sketch in his subject. He then builds images with layer upon layer of underpainting. His use of linseed oil allows him to carefully control his oil often opting for a rich, flat matte texture to the surface of his painting. And, while Larsen insists that he is not a symbolist or a metaphorical painter, his landscapes can be enjoyed as misty existential illusions of a universal Florida, fast disappearing into the anxious modern world, but captured in its pristine form in his carefully constructed and elegantly painted canvases of the Florida wilderness.

Larsen's *Myakka Lake* of 1995 is the end result of "a pencil sketch and my memory." Larsen remembers that his explorations of the lake located on the Myakka River in Myakka River State Park, east and inland from Sarasota, were in springtime and around noon. "The colors and shallowness of the lake tell me that."

And, while he hesitates to assign any specific meaning to the painting, he does admit to painting the area "because it's one of the few beautiful areas in Florida that hasn't been messed up by developers. Today, it's much like it was a hundred years ago."

In the top half of the picture, a pale blue-pink, hazy sky holds bands of soft clouds. Below is a strongly structured landscape with planes of green trees and green and pink bushes, in sculptured isolation. In the foreground there are strongly demarcated islands of golden grasses alternating with bands of shallow water. The whole effect is romantic and idealistic, capturing a transitory moment and heightening our response to a typical Southwest Florida marsh.

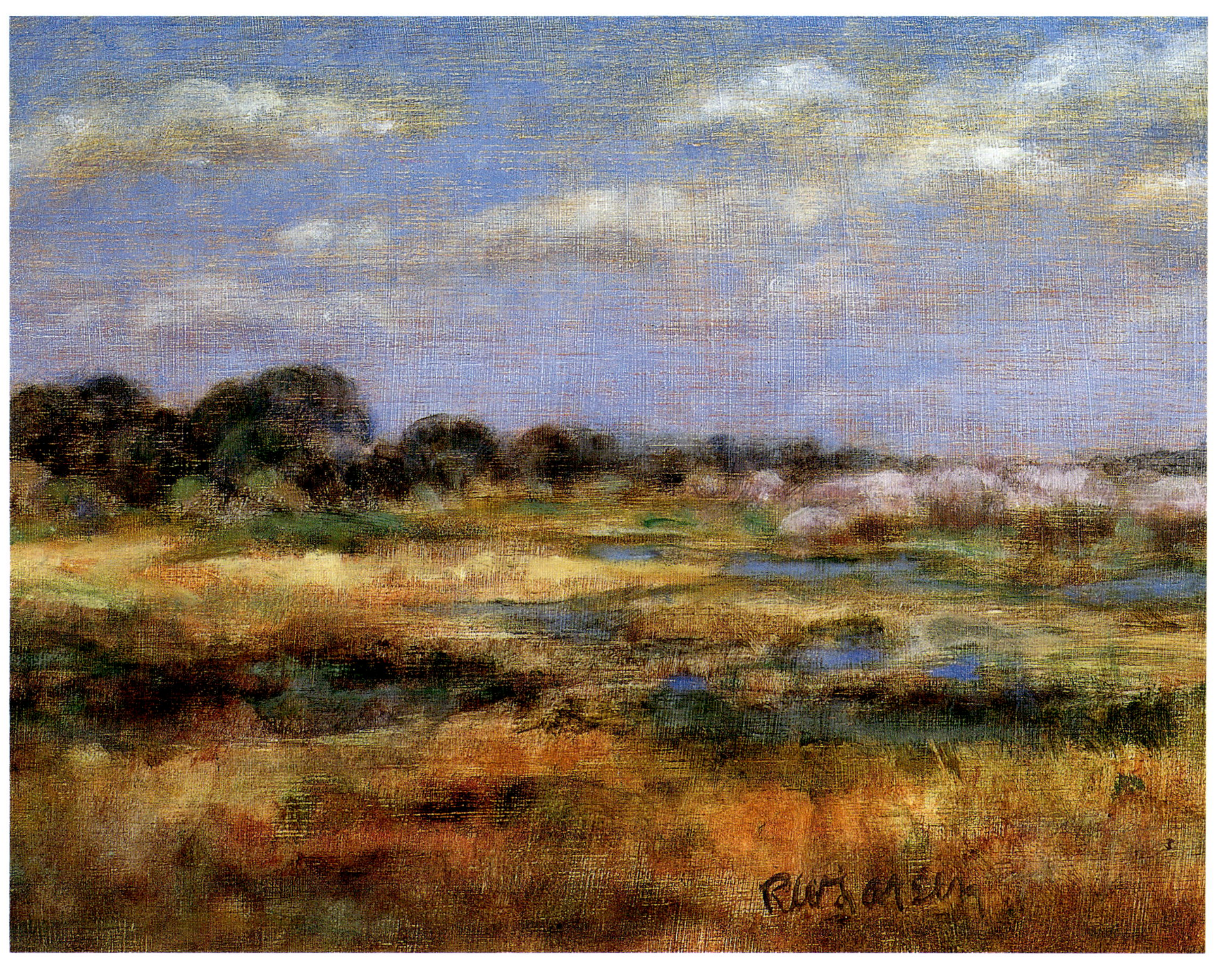

Hilton Leech
1906 - 1969

Untitled
Ca.1950, Casein and colored inks on paper, 22¼" x 30"

Hilton Leech was born in Bridgeport, Connecticut, in 1906, where he completed his formal education through his sophomore year in high school. At that time, he left Bridgeport to literally live in the woods where he existed by hunting, trapping and helping area farmers with chores. Leech was interested in becoming a naturalist writer and artist like John James Audubon, which is why he left rural Connecticut to study at the Grand Central Art School in New York City. There he studied with George Pearce Ennis and Arshile Gorky. At night, Leech studied at the Art Students League where he realized that painting, not writing, had to be his career in life. In 1931, during the depths of the Depression, Hilton Leech came to Sarasota, Florida, to help George Pearce Ennis organize the brand new Ringling School of Art, where Leech also taught. During the summers, Leech taught at his own art school in Amagansett, Long Island, New York. In 1942, World War II forced Leech to leave the Ringling, close his school and move to upstate New York, where he and his wife Dorothy worked as artists in the airplane industry until the end of the war. Then, the Leeches moved back to Sarasota where they opened a new Amagansett Art School on Hillview Avenue. In 1959, the school moved to new quarters as the Hilton Leech Studio on Riverview Avenue in Sarasota. Described often as a Renaissance man, Leech organized in 1962, with scientist Dr. Roger Early, an influential group known as the Friends of the Arts and Sciences, which met weekly to discuss important topics of the day, including the ecology movement in Florida, global warming, and the space industry and its effect on the humanities in the state. He was an active member of the Florida Artists Group and the Sarasota Art Association, and influenced many artists to settle or spend time in Sarasota.

Hilton Leech was a prolific and highly experimental artist who explored multiple styles of art and invented various techniques, as well. However, it was his mixed media watercolors that earned Leech national recognition. His work has been featured in exhibitions at the Metropolitan Museum of Art, New York, New York; The Dallas Museum of Art, Dallas, Texas; The University Gallery Museum, Gainesville, Florida; The Norton Museum of Art, West Palm Beach, Florida; and the Gallery of Hamilton, Ontario, Canada. Leech won many significant awards during his long career, including an American Watercolor Society Purchase Prize, the Knickerbocker Artists Medal of Honor, the Allied Artists Watercolor Award, the Morse Medal at the National Academy of Design, and the Gold Medal of Honor from the Allied Artists of America.

Leech usually worked from memory in his studio. "I usually draw in the composition with a soft pencil, using a good, black line where I know I want strong, dark areas. My first washes establish the values of the big patterns and are generally applied with transparent watercolor...it never worries me if the pencil lines show through...they should become an integral part of the final result. I don't hesitate to use (Higgins) waterproof india ink to help strengthen structural lines and take advantage of the textures that result as the ink reacts to the wet wash of watercolor." Leech often added casein, spreading it richly with a palette knife. He often glazed areas with colored inks to help increase the richness and quality of the paint and the textures created by this mixture of media and materials. Leech preferred working on a heavy, 300-pound, rough watercolor board or watercolor paper, sometimes saturating the ground with Cado inks that bleed interestingly as they react to water. Leech also used plastic spray paint, adding it to his unique mixtures of casein, watercolor, and Cado inks. Leech died in Sarasota, Florida, in 1969. As an artist, teacher and community leader, he was an important force in the development of serious contemporary art in Florida during his long and influential career.

Leech's untitled mixed media work, ca. 1950, combines casein, watercolor, colored inks and pencil on heavy watercolor paper. It accurately captures the sophisticated, minimal and orientalist approach he championed before 1953, when his work became more affected and influenced by Cubism. In this mixed-media study of American wood storks and plovers, Leech places the shorebirds amid calligraphic grasses on a soft, Florida beach. Overhead, a pale blue sky frames this abstract and modernist interpretation of the shore and the Florida birds that inhabit it.

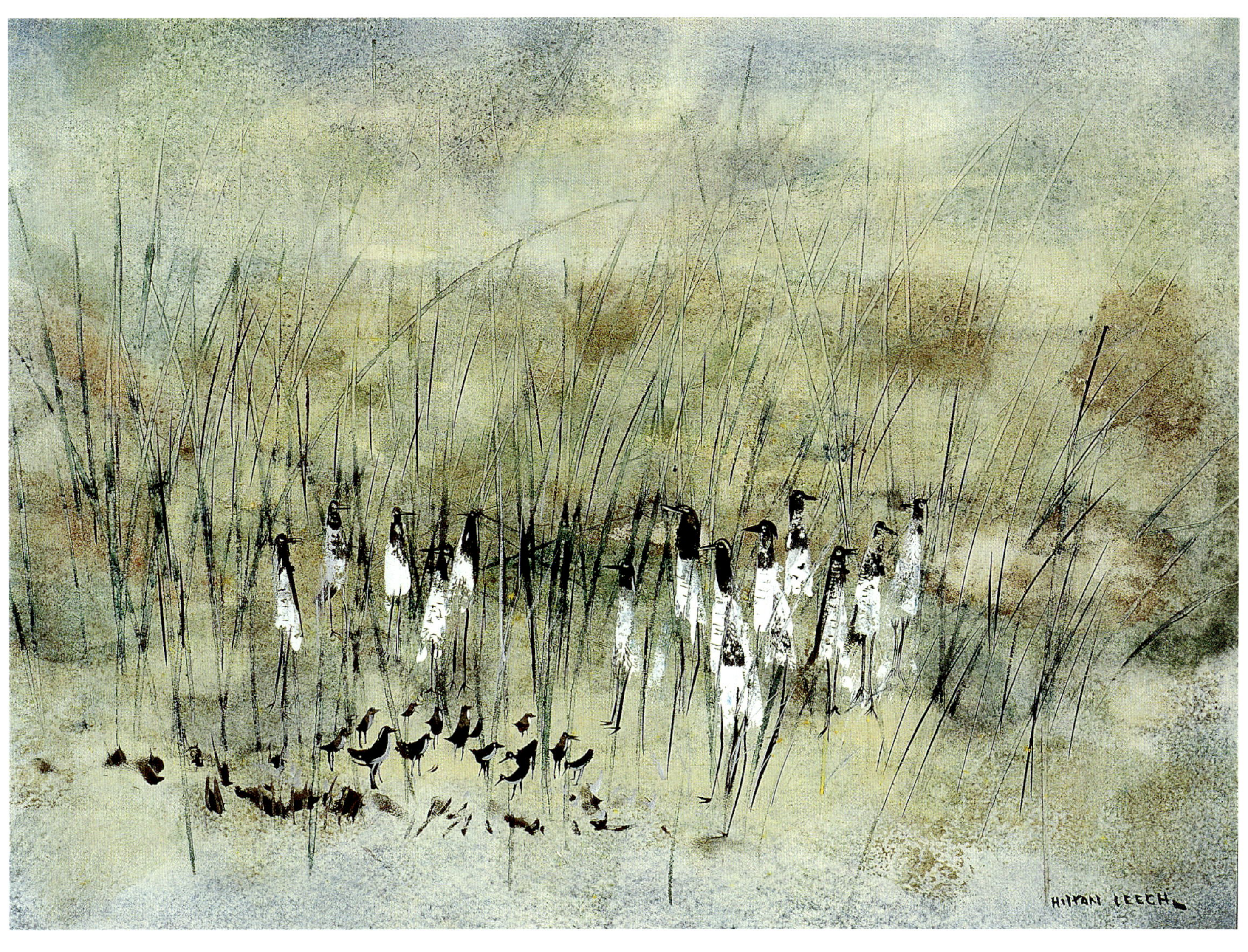
HILTON LEECH

TOD LINDENMUTH
1885 - 1976

FLORIDIA
CA.1950, OIL ON CANVAS BOARD, 16" X 20"

Born in Allentown, Pennsylvania in 1885, Raphael Leroy Lindenmuth was one of four children born to artist-photographer Arlington Nelson Lindenmuth. After a childhood that suggested a career in art, Tod Lindenmuth moved to New York City where he studied at the Chase School of Art with Robert Henri, the driving force of the Ashcan School of artists who chose loose brushstroke to describe urban life—the subject of their art.

As a teenager, Lindenmuth started to spend his summers in and around Provincetown, Massachusetts, on Cape Cod, a major art center in New England. In 1913, Lindenmuth traveled to France where he studied painting in Brittany with George Elmer Browne until the outbreak of World War I. He returned to Provincetown where he studied with E. Ambrose Webster, a disciple of Henri Matisse. Lindenmuth became preoccupied with printmaking at this time and joined the Provincetown Printmakers where he developed a variation of the Oriental blockprinting method. Lindenmuth's early painting style was impressionistic. As he became interested in printmaking, his style evolved to larger blocks of color and design.

In 1925, Lindenmuth married the artist Elizabeth Boardman Warren, an accomplished engraver and etcher who had studied with W.H.W. Bicknell and Charles Simpson R.A. in London. In 1932, the Lindenmuths spent their first winter in Miami, Florida. The next year they wintered in St. Augustine, which became their annual winter home. Summers were spent in Provincetown until 1940, when they moved their summer headquarters to Rockport, Massachusetts. In St. Augustine, they established a gallery on Aviles Street. They were active in the founding of the St. Augustine Art Association and were often visited by friends from Rockport, including Anthony Thieme, Emile Gruppe and other artists. According to Mr. Lindenmuth's daughter, Ann Fisk, the St. Augustine artists of this time did not have much to do with artists in other colonies in Florida. In the late 1960s, the Lindenmuths moved to a retirement home in Jacksonville where they continued to create art. Tod Lindenmuth painted until four days before his death in November 1976.

Tod Lindenmuth exhibited widely. Oil paintings are included in the collections of the Pennsylvania Academy of Fine Arts, Philadelphia, Pennsylvania; Palmer Museum of Art, Pennsylvania State University, Allentown, Pennsylvania; Allentown Art Museum, Allentown, Pennsylvania; The Newark Museum, Newark, New Jersey; and the Toledo Museum of Art, Toledo, Ohio. Block prints are in the Museum of Fine Arts, Houston, Texas; Museum of Fine Arts, Springfield, Massachusetts; the Los Angeles County Museum of Art, Los Angeles, California; and the Bibliotheque Nationale, Paris, France. He was a Life Fellow of The Metropolitan Museum of Art, New York, New York; and a member of the Salmagundi Club, the Provincetown Art Association, and the Rockport Art Association.

Lindenmuth was a prolific artist who believed in a schedule. After rising each morning, he would sketch and paint. He then lunched, which was followed by a nap. After his nap, he sketched and painted until dinner time. Never owning an automobile, the Lindenmuths walked everywhere. Both felt these walks allowed them time to think and to consider potential subjects for his paintings and block prints, and her etchings.

The monochromatic oil on canvas *Floridia* probably dates from the early 1950s when Lindenmuth was exploring the soft and impressionistic brushstroke championed by a second generation of American impressionist and tonalist painters. Moss-covered oaks and tall, mature palms frame a tranquil body of water in a tonalist nocturne reminiscent of both Whistler and Inness, two 19th century American masters of illusionistic suggestibility. Here, atmosphere, not form, conveys the message of a cool, blue Florida night, lit by a bright, white moon, rendered in a loose and painterly style by an influential Florida landscape painter.

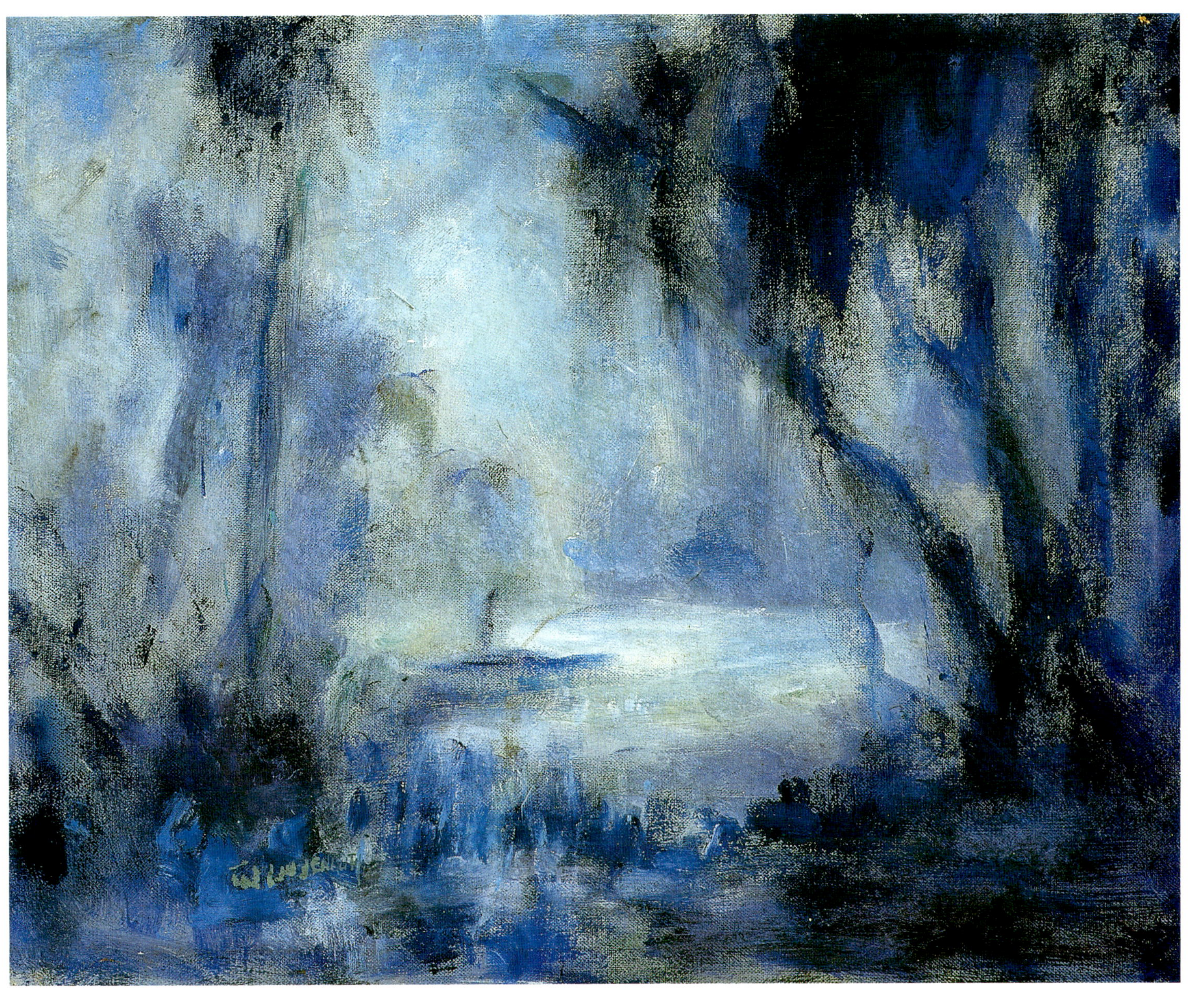

Molly Mabe

The Voice

1997, Pastel, gouache and charcoal on paper, 29¼" x 21½"

Molly Mabe was born in Rochester, New York, in 1942. She moved to Florida with her parents in 1945, and lived in Jacksonville where she received her early education. After high school, she attended Simmons College in Boston, Massachusetts, where she received a bachelor's of science degree in 1964. During this period, she maintained a studio at the Museum School of the Museum of Fine Arts, Boston, and had the opportunity there to immerse herself in one of the country's leading collections of Asian art. In 1970, Mabe finished a master's of fine arts degree at the University of North Carolina, Greensboro, North Carolina. She is currently enrolled in the humanities doctoral program at Florida State University, Tallahassee. She continues to paint from her studio and home in Tallahassee.

Mabe has enjoyed more than 15 exhibitions since 1994, including The Florida Gulf Coast Art Center, Belleair, Florida; The Capitol, Tallahassee, Florida; The LeMoyne Art Foundation, Tallahassee, Florida; The Ormond Beach Memorial Art Museum, Ormond Beach, Florida; Santa Fe Gallery, Gainesville, Florida; and the Fernbank Museum of Natural History, Atlanta, Georgia. Mabe's work is included in a number of private and public collections, such as The City of Tallahassee, Florida; Guilford College, Greensboro, North Carolina; The Museum of Florida History, Tallahassee, Florida; The University of North Carolina, Greensboro, North Carolina; Capital City Bank Group, Tallahassee, Florida; Asset Preservation, Atlanta, Georgia; and the Culpepper Corporation, Tallahassee, Florida.

Mabe has received commissions from The State of Florida, Art in Public Places Program for Nassau County, Florida; The St. Teresa Episcopal Church Sanctuary, Crawfordville, Florida; The Thomas Jefferson Memorial Foundation, Monticello, Charlottesville, Virginia; and The Florida League of Cities, Tallahassee, Florida.

Her predilection for commonplace landscapes and her interest in the super-sensible or metaphysical qualities of the experience of everyday things is strongly influenced by her studies in Asian art. Her style is also "related to the later period of the 19th century landscape tradition when panoramic compositions gave way to more circumscribed depictions, and the natural effects of light were the main subject...the inspiration for much of the work happens to be local, but there is a universal import to what she paints. In her concentration on essentials, and in her deliberate lack of embellishment, she takes a very unromantic stance...Molly Mabe's art would retain its elegant keenness and offer its timeless metaphysical lessons anywhere in the world," wrote William Zimmer, a contributing critic to the *New York Times*, in 1996.

In *The Voice*, a 1997 mixed media composition in pastel, gouache and charcoal on paper, the artist presents an accurately drawn palm head in unusual shades of black, tan, yellow and orange. The entwined husks and fronds are rendered in a bold chiaroscuro that gives depth and richness to the subject. Most interesting is the contrast between the linear and painterly qualities of the work, where the drawing of the fronds breaks down into a kind of action painting.

The combination of the unnatural colors, the use of gestural technique, and the edge where the painting "dances between realistic details and abstraction" enable the artist to convey something more than merely the local experience of a Florida palm. Mabe is interested in the transcendent aspects of the experience of nature that lie behind the visual experience of objects' natural edges. She sees the palm as a symbol of the eternal rise and fall of life: "The palm is the promise of life that moves forward, yet is continuously cycling through life and death. As each year falls away, the palm is marked along the trunk by the boots of older fronds only to be overwhelmed by renewal in a burst of fruit and fronds pushing outward."

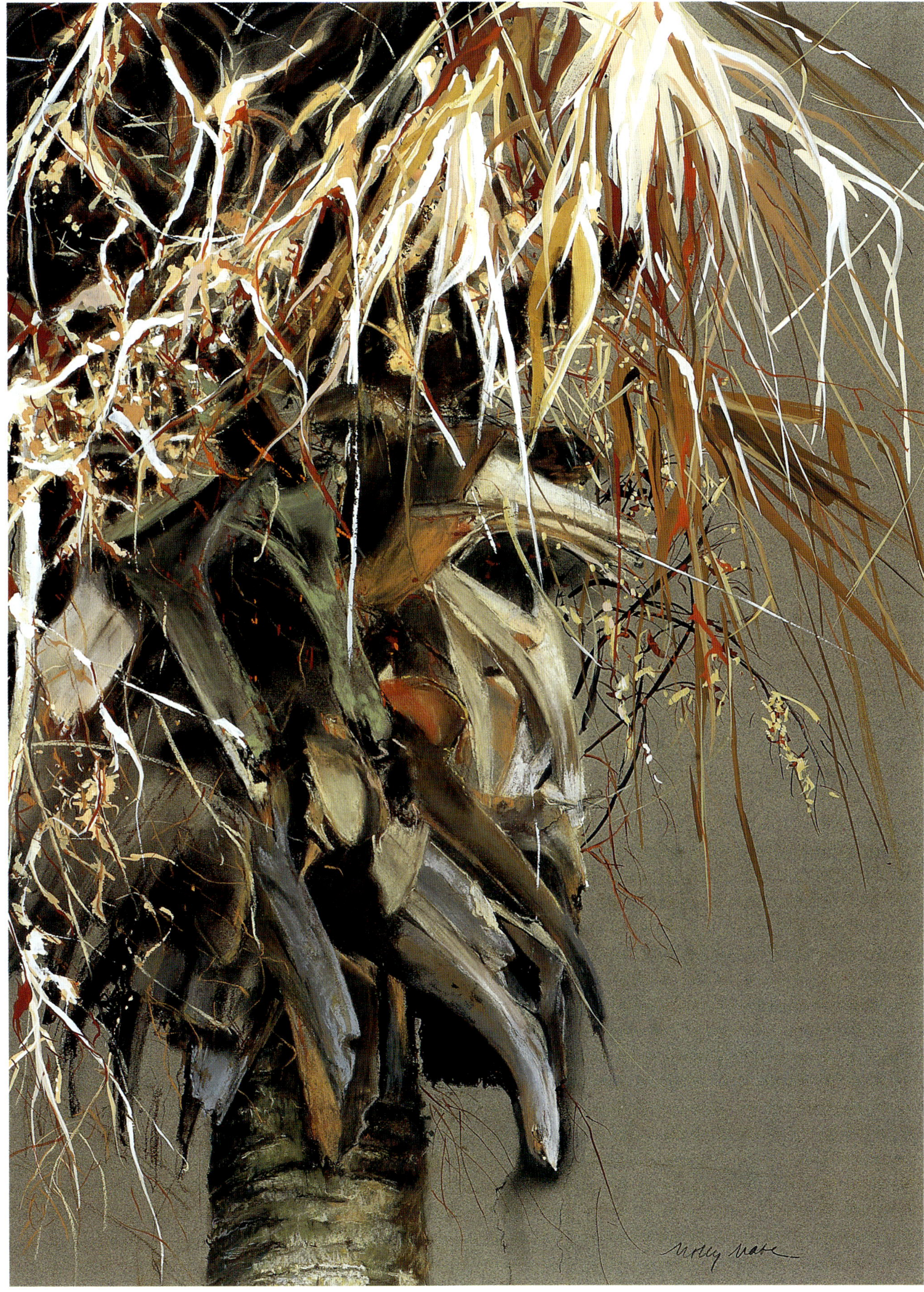

Bruce Marsh

St. Johns Study

1991, Oil on canvas, 8" x 18"

Bruce L. Marsh was born in Englewood, California, a suburb of Los Angeles, on November 24, 1937. After finishing high school, he attended the University of California at Santa Barbara, receiving a bachelor's of arts degree in 1959. From 1960 to 1963, Marsh served in the U.S. Army, followed by graduate studies in painting at the University of California at Los Angeles. In 1965, Marsh received a master's of arts degree from California State College in Long Beach. It was also in 1965 that Bruce Marsh moved to Florida, taking a position as an instructor at St. Petersburg Junior College. In 1969, he became professor of visual arts at the University of South Florida in Tampa, where he continues to teach and paint. Marsh served as a visiting professor at the Florida State University Study Center in Florence, Italy, in 1983. From 1986 to 1989, he developed a computer laboratory and imaging curriculum for the department of art at the University of South Florida, winning a research grant to develop digital prints in 1993.

Marsh exhibits widely and has enjoyed more than 50 exhibitions since 1965, including The Florida Gulf Coast Art Center, Belleair, Florida; The Tampa Museum of Art, Tampa, Florida; The Museum of Fine Art, St. Petersburg, Florida; The University of South Florida, Tampa, Florida; The Dunedin Fine Arts Center, Dunedin, Florida; The Ormond Memorial Art Museum, Ormond Beach, Florida; The Valdosta Art Center, Valdosta, Georgia; The Society of the Four Arts, Palm Beach, Florida; The Polk Museum of Art, Lakeland, Florida; The Jacksonville Museum of Art, Jacksonville, Florida; The Hollywood Art and Culture Center, Hollywood, Florida; The New Orleans Museum of Art (Isaac Delgado), New Orleans, Louisiana; and the University Art Museum, The University of California, Santa Barbara, California.

Marsh's work is included in significant private and public collections, including The National Gallery of Art, Washington, D.C.; The John and Mable Ringling Museum of Art, Sarasota, Florida; The Museum of Fine Art, St. Petersburg, Florida; The Polk Museum of Art, Lakeland, Florida; and the New Orleans Museum of Art, New Orleans, Louisiana. Bruce Marsh has been the recipient of two Individual Artists Fellowships from the Division of Cultural Affairs, the Department of State, Florida.

Bruce Marsh continues to produce significant bodies of work in printmaking, drawing, photography, computer media, and painting. A central interest in his work is "the process of perception and experience of sight," the way we process what we see and reconstitute the world in our consciousness. His paintings are more about the act of seeing than about the particular subject depicted. In many ways, his paintings, like *St. Johns Study*, are attempts both to understand and demonstrate many of the mechanisms of vision.

St. Johns Study was completed in 1991 as one study for a set of four large oils for the Mayo Clinic in Jacksonville, Florida. *St. Johns Study* was made from a series of photographs taken in the fall of 1991, along the St. Johns River, south of Jacksonville in the vicinity of Orange Park, Florida. This painting was a synthesis of three photos. His goal was to impose a fairly severe left-right symmetry on a natural stretch of the river. In the study, Marsh neatly divides his painting into two related scenes separated by a dense thicket of the blue-green foliage. To the right, the river is brightly lit as flotsam gently drifts in a milky mauve river below a cloudy blue sky. Here, Marsh captures the transforming quality of light on this section of riverine landscape. To the left, shadows created by cypress and other woody plants like persimmon, red maple and river birch, create a darker, richer texture. The result is an artificially constructed view that augments natural colors and combines individual "exposures" of the act of viewing the river. All of this is designed to yield a composite image that summarizes the visual information. The image is also constructed to have a tranquil, emotional effect. Bilateral symmetry, strong horizontal lines, and cool, restful colors, for example, all contribute to this effect, demonstrating that the way we reconstitute the world in our consciousness also depends upon emotional filters.

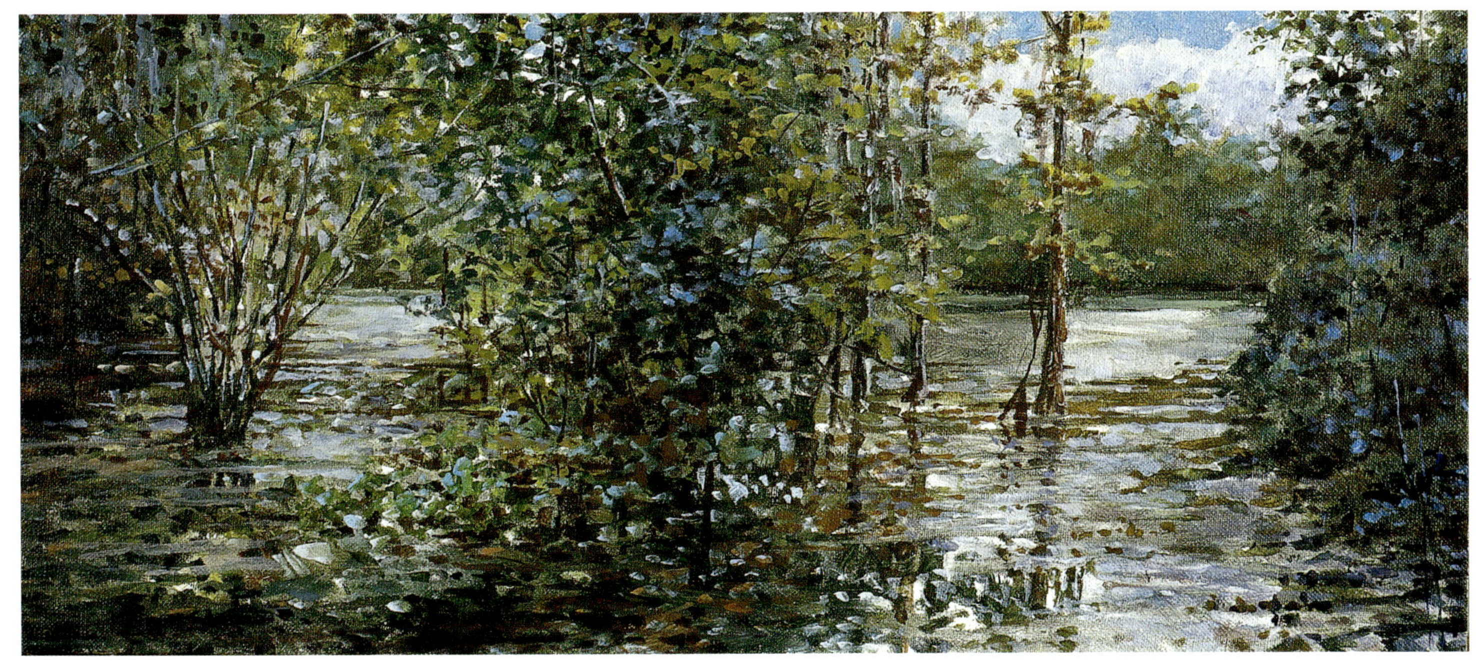

Joseph McFadden

St. Marks Morning

1993, Watercolor on paper, 14¾" x 20¾"

St. Marks Beach

1995, Oil on masonite, 12" x 16"

Joseph McFadden was born in Bridgeport, Connecticut, in 1949. Both of his parents were musicians and he grew up in an artistic family in a home full of books and music.

In 1972, he graduated from Florida State University in Tallahassee, Florida, with a bachelor's of arts degree in studio art. After spending two years in Boston, and two years in New York, following what he calls "the artist's life," he volunteered in the Peace Corps and, from 1979 to 1981, lived in the Republic of Korea where he developed an interest in oriental philosophy, literature and painting. Between 1981 and 1985, he lived in Seattle, Washington, as a commercial artist. In 1985, McFadden moved to St. Augustine, Florida, where he worked until 1990, when he discovered the Big Bend region of Northwest Florida, near Tallahassee, where he now lives. He is currently the director of instruction at the Florida Art Center in Havana, Florida.

McFadden is a versatile artist working in both oils and watercolor. In addition to landscapes, he paints still lifes, portraits, and humorous self portraits in the guise of saints. He is winner of numerous regional and national competitions, including the Texas Watercolor Society, the Georgia Watercolor Society, and the Florida Watercolor Society. When he works in watercolor, he uses only red, yellow and blue, plus sepia. He prefers round brushes, beginning with large ones and ending each work with small ones. His oil palette usually contains only 12 colors applied with hog-hair filbert brushes.

Each landscape painting is begun outdoors, on site, but finished in the studio. McFadden often uses photographs to jog his memory as he creates his own personal visions of the Florida landscape.

McFadden identifies several important influences on his perception of the landscape. From 19th century luminist painters, he developed an interest in rendering the effect of diffused light. In North Florida, the light is "cruel and harsh, different than in South Florida, and a special challenge to paint." In Korea, McFadden was impressed with "the artists' attention to detail and the serenity and spirituality of their landscapes." Many of McFadden's landscapes have a minimalist quality where the background and middle ground are blurred or eliminated in order to concentrate attention on one section of the painting. The blurring also produces a sense of mystery and an ethereal quality. McFadden is also part of a group of Northwest Florida painters (including Sally Boswell, Rosemary Gibson, John Stanford, and C.D. Smith) who have been exploring the landscape of the St. Marks Wildlife Refuge. They each regularly study one another's works, and their representations of the unique qualities of North Florida have evolved under this influence and relationship.

McFadden's *St. Marks Morning* is a watercolor on hand-made linen paper from 1993. "Although I had photos and loose pencil sketches from which to work, I relied primarily on my visual memory to produce the ethereal quality of this piece." McFadden selected early morning, around 6:30 a.m., on a winter day facing east as the context for the work where extreme atmospheric conditions reference an emotional state. "Early morning is a magical time of day for me. I tried to convey this through the loose handling of brushwork, and the economical use of detail. The light changes rapidly. As the mist clears, the landscape becomes more identifiable. I tried to catch that brief period of the serene glow of a misty sunrise." McFadden has selected an isolated stretch of Florida scrub in the St. Marks Wildlife Refuge near the Gulf of Mexico. To the right, a lone palm in comparatively sharp focus frames the composition as bright, golden light permeates and blurs the rest of the scene defining the moment captured by McFadden in this sunburst of light. "Others may go for the stereotypical beautiful scene, the perfectly balanced composition. I see the irregularities."

In his oil on masonite panel of 1995 titled *St. Marks Beach,* McFadden uses local color to define and describe a spring morning on a stretch of beach in the isolated Wildlife Refuge, which is accessible only by boat. "Visually, the painting is about the blinding, white sand surrounded by cool, earth colors. I exaggerated the foreground shadows to offer the viewer a sense of relief from the heat." In this oil, bold broad brushstrokes capture the high contrast in value and texture as McFadden presents the rich green of vegetation, the deep blue of a Florida sky, and the hot, white sand and strong North Florida light, softened only by the dramatic purple shadows of an unseen palm.

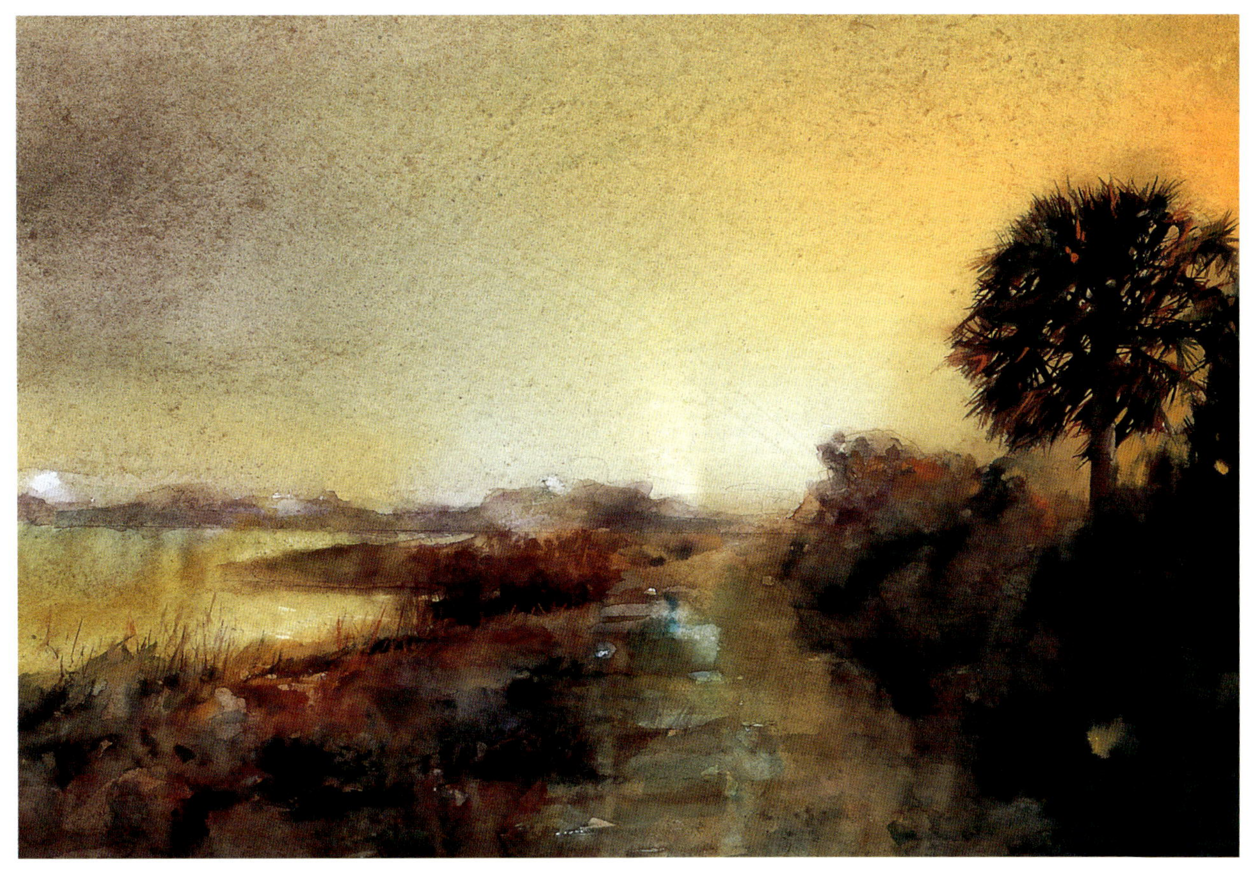

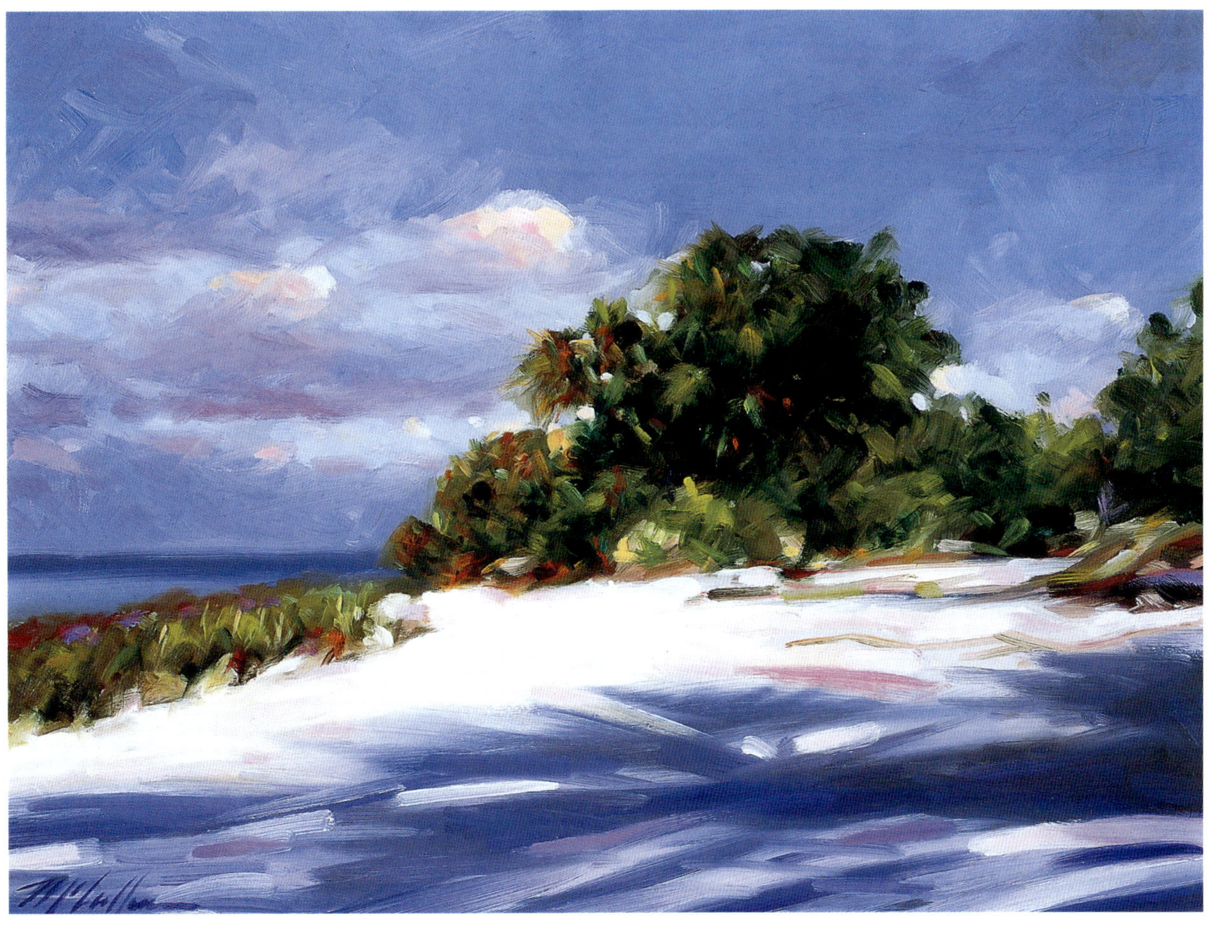

Ken Muenzenmayer

Deliverance
1992, Acrylic on canvas, 36" x 36"

Peace of Wild Things
1993, Acrylic on canvas, 21¾" x 36"

Ken Muenzenmayer was born near Cleveland, Ohio, on June 10, 1950. He attended Avon Lake High School where he was able to squeeze two periods of art training daily into his schedule from the seventh grade through graduation. Muenzenmayer always knew he wanted to paint and, after graduation from high school, he enrolled in the Ringling School of Art and Design, in Sarasota, Florida. After studying for a time at Ringling, he returned to Ohio and earned a bachelor's of fine arts degree at Kent State University, Kent, Ohio. In 1973, he returned to Sarasota, Florida, where he worked in order to travel for more than a year, painting on location throughout the United States. After this trip, he returned to Ohio and worked as a commercial artist. In 1977, he began to do serious work in acrylics. In 1984, he moved to Vermont, where he painted until 1987, when he moved to Sebastian, Florida, north of Vero Beach, on the east coast of the state. Muenzenmayer lived and worked in the Vero Beach area until 1990 when he married the artist Karen Vernon and moved to Texas. The Muenzenmayers often return to Florida for visits with friends, as well as to paint and exhibit at major art festivals. Muenzenmayer exhibits widely from Mono Bay, California, to Naples, Florida. His work received a recent award at the Laguna Gloria Museum, Austin, Texas. His paintings are included in the collections of Walt Disney World, Inc., Orlando, Florida; and Southwestern Bell, Dallas, Texas.

For Ken Muenzenmayer, "the Florida landscape is extremely subtle. It requires you to look closely." Muenzenmayer likes to visit potential locations, often photographing areas as visual reminders of the scene. He paints in the studio, often reinterpreting and reinventing his subject as he proceeds. The principal focus of his work is color and the edges of light and shadow. He paints tranquil places that restore one's sense of harmony with the world with a richness of color surface unusual in the acrylic medium. These may be isolated parts of nature with no trace of human presence or a landscape filled with houses. Many of his paintings have an architectural subject but these are also shown at special times of day or from certain angles of view that reveal each as a refuge. His Florida is not an Eden or a location threatened with destruction. It is a place of unique character no better and no worse than any other place where deliverance can be found along a man-made road or in a stretch of wild marsh.

Deliverance is a 1992 acrylic on canvas painting. The location is on Live Oak Drive off State Road 510 on Pine Island in the Indian River between Wabasso and Wabasso Beach, near Vero Beach, Florida. "The integrity and grace of these large live oaks, combined with the gravity of the Spanish moss in contrast with the horizontal patterns of the shadows cast by the noonday sun on the crushed shell road, intrigued me." Muenzenmayer has devoted the bottom two-thirds of the acrylic painting to sunlight as it is filtered through the branches of unseen trees. Pools of purple shadow boldly zig-zag along the white shell road viewed against a dramatic background of dark pine and oak. Overhead, delicate Spanish moss captures a tint of the golden glow generated by the overhead sun. The canopied road is a typical Florida scene.

In *Peace of Wild Things*, an acrylic painting of 1993, Muenzenmayer has selected a stretch of Florida marsh along the upper St. Johns River viewed from a pullover off State Road 520 between County Road 419 and Interstate 95 near Cocoa, Florida, on the east coast of the state.

The spacious wetland is rendered boldly in strokes of gold and green as waves of sawgrass fill the lower half of the painting. Distant stands of green pine and cypress crowd the horizon below a clear, blue Florida sky in this celebration of Florida's freshwater marshes so characteristic of Northeast Florida along the St. Johns, which flows north to Jacksonville and was a favorite subject of 19th century artists who visited the state and travelled up river by a steamboat.

"Both of these paintings were done during a time that I began paying more attention to the actual preparation of the painting surface by applying my primer in cross-hatched layers of gesso, allowing a weave of texture to exist upon which I began to layer color. I was experimenting with patterns of light and color. I feel that both paintings speak for the subtle balance that is so important in maintaining a healthy ecosystem so important to the quality of life in Florida."

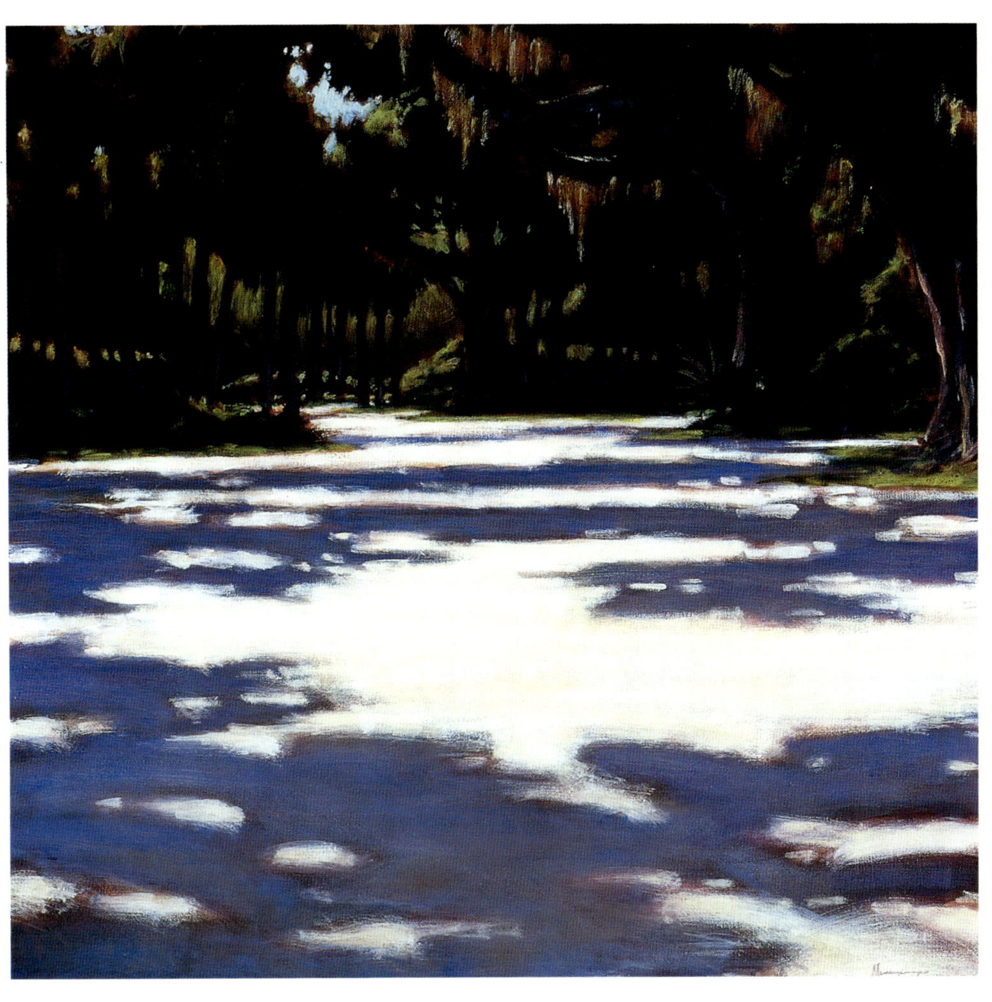

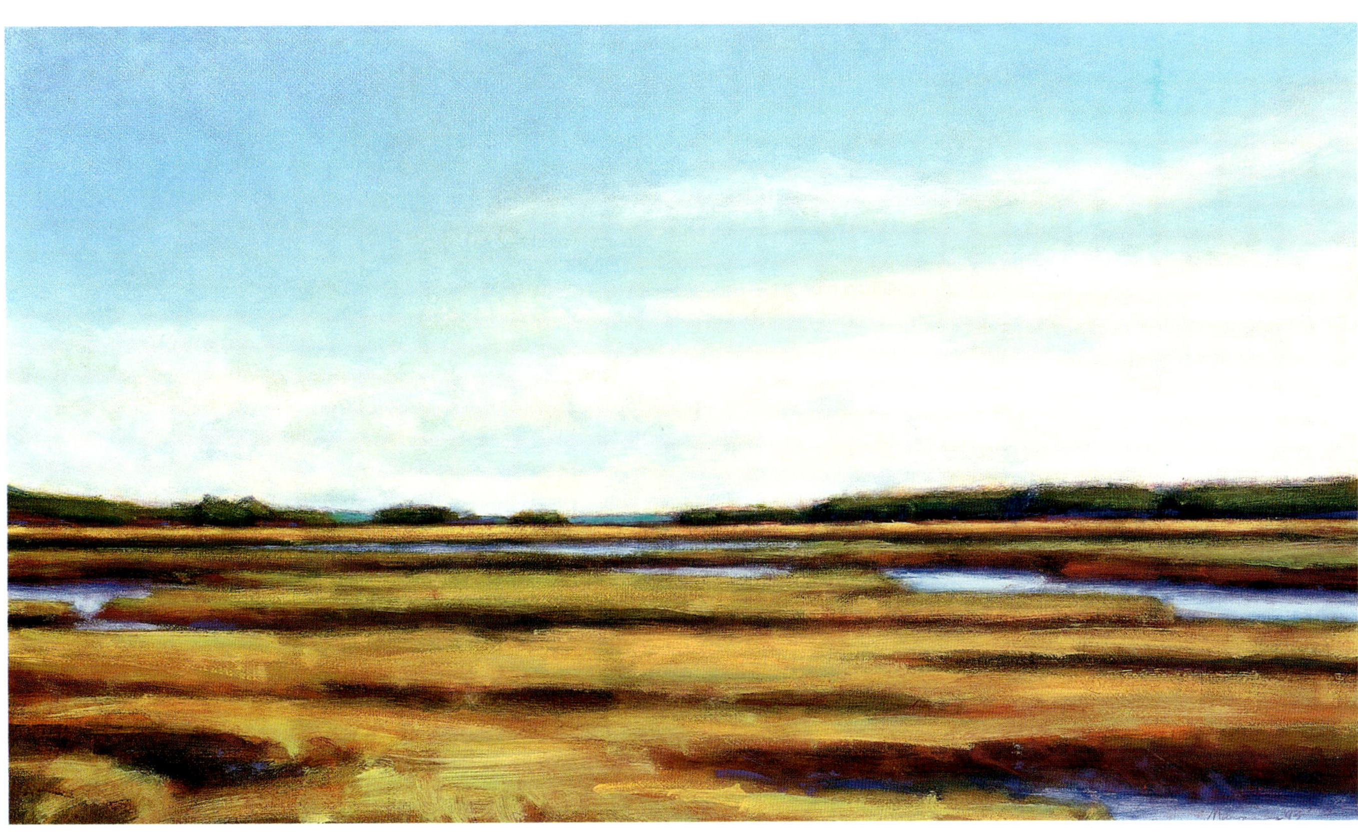

DONALD POWERS

CAPE SAN BLAS
1995, OIL ON MASONITE, 24¼" X 36"

Born in Madison, Tennessee, in 1950, Donald Powers attended schools there. He then attended Tennessee Technological University, Cookeville, Tennessee, where he studied painting. From 1973 to 1978, he worked as an artist, then as art director at the Tennessee State Museum, Nashville, Tennessee, where he completed a series of historical paintings for the Tennessee Bicentennial. In 1979 and 1980, he enjoyed his first solo exhibitions at East Tennessee State University, Knoxville, Tennessee and the Fine Arts Gallery at the University of the South, Sewanee, Tennessee. In 1980, he worked with muralist Frank Fowler at Lookout Mountain, while exhibiting at the Hunter Museum of American Art, Chattanooga, Tennessee; the Butler Institute of American Art, Youngstown, Ohio, and the Harmon Meek Gallery, Naples, Florida. Powers has continued to exhibit widely, including group and solo exhibitions at the Columbus Museum of Art, Columbus, Ohio; the Albrecht Art Museum at the College of William and Mary, Williamsburg, Virginia, the Minnesota Museum of Art, St. Paul, Minnesota; The Southeast Center for Contemporary Art, Winston-Salem, North Carolina; The Kalamazoo Art Institute, Kalamazoo, Michigan; Oklahoma Art Center, Tulsa, Oklahoma; The Riverside Art Museum, Los Angeles, California; The Museum of the Southwest, Midland, Texas; The Middleburg College Museum of Art, Middleburg, Vermont; and The Maryland Institute and College of Art, Baltimore, Maryland. His work is included in several corporate and public collections including Southeastern Assets Management Corporation, Memphis, Tennessee; Emory University, Atlanta, Georgia; The Hunter Museum of Art, Athens, Georgia; The National Portrait Gallery, Washington, D.C.; and The Museum of Modern Art, Haifa, Israel.

Powers' work was featured in *The Artist as Native: Reinventing Regionalism.*There he describes landscape painting as a way to express a passion for places that he has felt strongly about and for places that he knows well enough to be able to share his native understanding and love.

Cape San Blas, 1995, is an oil on masonite panel of a narrow hook of land that extends into the Gulf of Mexico in the northwestern panhandle of Florida. Powers first visited the location in 1980 when it was an isolated stretch of broken shells and populated only by sea birds. Powers selected this location because it still "has a sense of remoteness and wildness." The scene is late summer when tropical heat has toasted the wetland grasses to different shades of gold. Colors are subdued, yet the heavy, moisture-filled, blue-purple sky holds the potential of the storms and hurricanes that can literally transform the landscape. "It is this impending sense of possibility for a sudden radical change that interests me." In the realistic oil painting, Powers places white cattle egrets in the fore- and midground. A single cabbage palm, reflected in the still waters of the marsh, establishes both proportion and perspective in this accurately rendered yet painterly salute to the subtle moods and potential changes found within the Florida landscape.

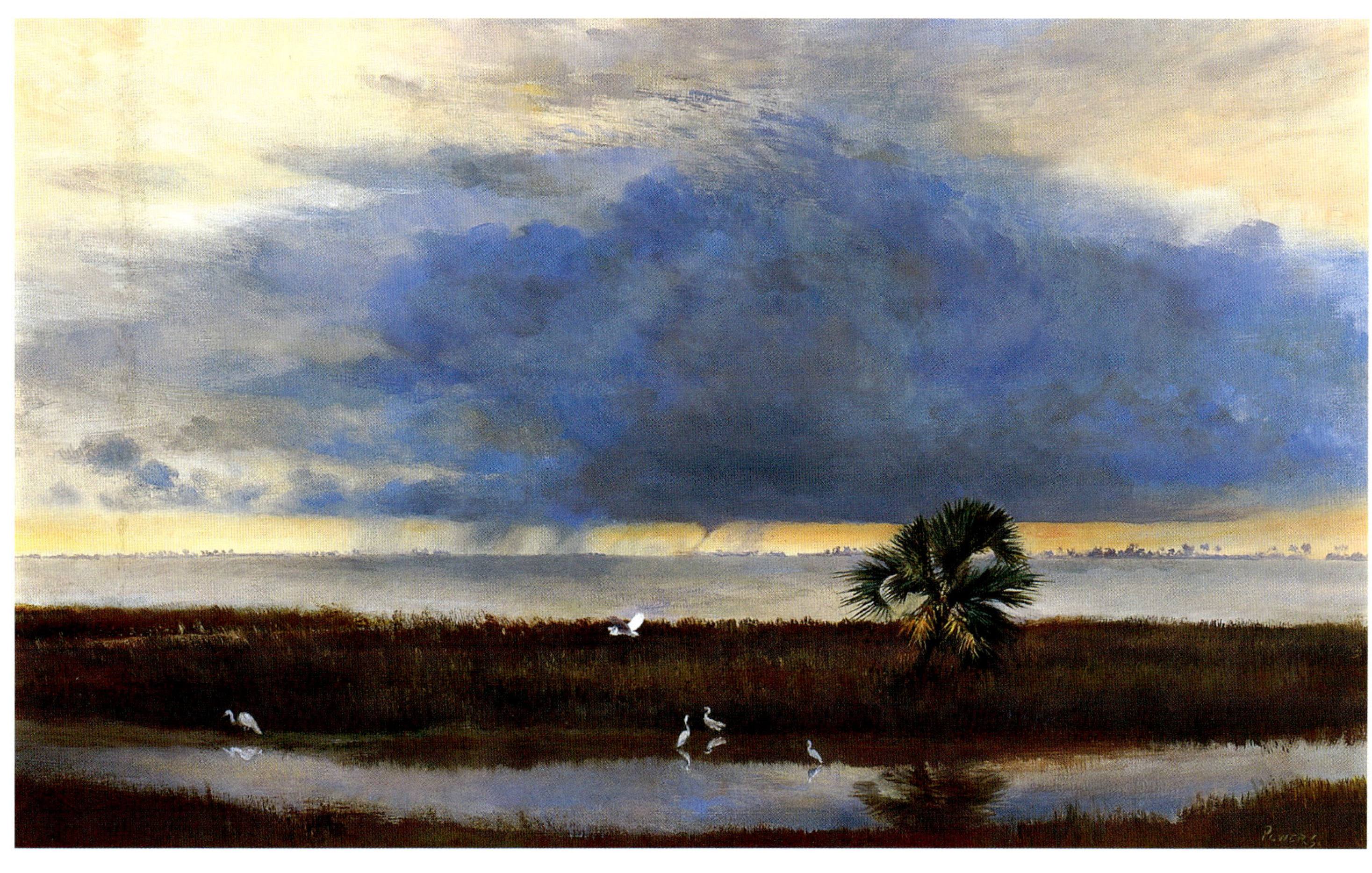

Gene Allen Roberds

Murphy's Creek

1993, Oil on canvas, 7⅞" x 14"

Gene Roberds was born in Colecamp, Missouri, in 1935. At the age of two, his family moved to Southern Illinois, where he spent his childhood and received his early education. At the age of four, he received his first set of paints. Roberds began his formal training in art in college where he studied the basics. In 1957, he received a bachelor's of science degree from Eastern Illinois State College. In 1959, shy one course needed to complete his master's of fine arts degree at the University of Illinois, Roberds came to Florida where he taught art at Fletcher High School in Jacksonville Beach while he finished his degree, commuting to the University of Florida in Gainesville. In 1961, Roberds became an instructor in the department of art at Murray State College in Murray, Kentucky, where he worked until 1964. He then became assistant professor of art at the Minneapolis School of Art in Minneapolis, Minnesota, until 1968, when he returned to Jacksonville, Florida, as assistant professor at Jacksonville University. In 1971, he opened the Roberds Studio in St. Augustine. In 1975, he became an adjunct professor at the University of North Florida in Jacksonville until 1976. In 1978, he joined the faculty of the Florida School of the Arts, Palatka, Florida, where he worked until his retirement in June 1997. He continues to work from his studio and home in Satsuma, Florida.

Roberds has exhibited widely, including exhibitions at the Butler Institute of American Art, Youngstown, Ohio; the Library of Congress, Washington, D.C.; The Knoxville Art Center, Knoxville, Tennessee; The Walker Art Center, Minneapolis, Minnesota; Time-Life Gallery, New York, New York; The Fort Hayes State University Art Gallery, Hayes, Kansas; and the Jacksonville Museum of Contemporary Art, Jacksonville, Florida. His work is included in the permanent collections of the Barnett Banks in Tampa and Jacksonville, Florida; Saint Johns River Community College, Orange Park, Florida; The Fifth District Court of Appeals, Daytona Beach, Florida; and The Atlantic Center for the Arts, New Smyrna Beach, Florida.

Most of Gene Roberds' oil paintings begin as small watercolor sketches done on site. For years, he worked in a boat "able to reach remote wilderness areas away from civilization and bothersome onlookers." He calls his work "a little impressionistic, a little expressionistic, but mostly fabrications of abstract brushstroke, patterning, calligraphy, and color; an ordered arrangement of abstract parts that results in a composition that is conceived abstractly and should be understood in that realm." For Roberds, "subject matter is only an excuse or reason to start a painting." His goal is to create a work that satisfies his personal involvement in the "abstract structure of composition" and, at the same time, can be read in a representational way.

Murphy's Creek, 1993, is one of the few oil paintings that Roberds completed while on location. For more than two years Roberds tried to paint small oils on location with the idea of recreating them in larger format in the studio. He now only works on site in watercolor making *Murphy's Creek* a rare survivor of a period in his development. The location is off U.S. 17, north of Crescent City and south of Palatka, Florida. Murphy's Creek is a small estuary of the St. Johns River, connecting it to Crescent Lake. Roberds captures the strong reflections of oak, pine and cypress in the glassy creek below a clear blue sky. Roberds' palette is bright as he creates both forest and water in painterly calligraphy where bold, individual strokes of color suggest both movement and form as they float above this jewel-like landscape. While not an environmentalist, Roberds is concerned about the future of Florida. "I feel strongly about the documentary aspect of painting these areas that may not be there much longer."

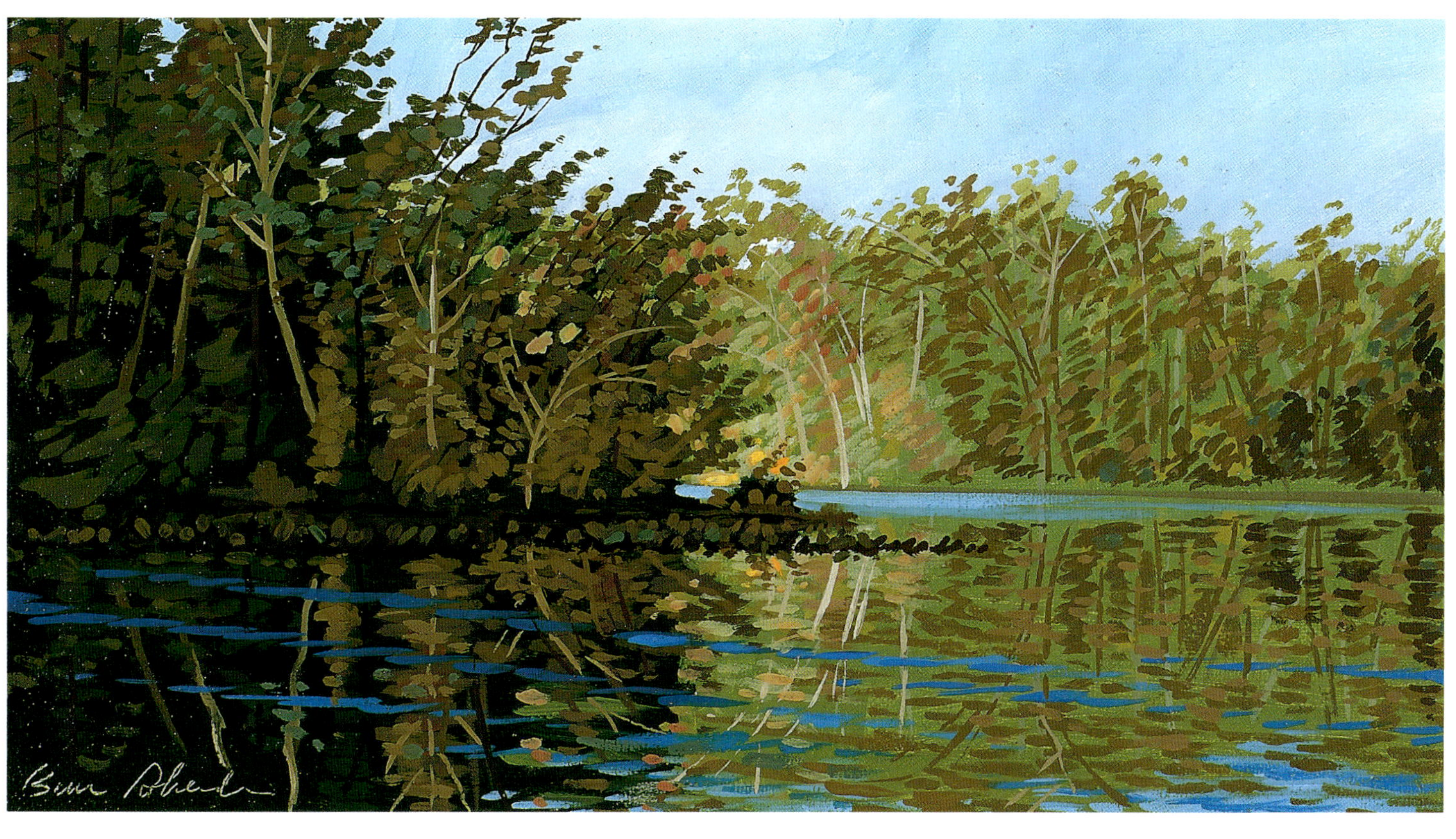

JERRY ROSE

STORAGE SHED - PARADISE CAY

1992, WATERCOLOR ON PAPER, 11½" X 15⅝"

Jerry Rose was born in Akron, Ohio, on March 30, 1948. He attended Ohio University from 1966 to 1968, where he began to study fine art. In 1968, he transferred to the University of Cincinnati where he studied graphics until 1972. He then moved to Massachusetts to study sculpture, which led him to boatbuilding, a serious hobby he still enjoys today.

A signature member of both the International Society of Marine Painters and the Florida Watercolor Society, Rose exhibits widely at commercial galleries from the Bahamas to Maine and at cultural institutions including The Florida Watercolor Society Annual Exhibitions and the Martin County Cultural Center in Stuart, Florida. Rose continues to work from his studio in Palm City, Florida.

Rose has painted the Florida landscape for more than 10 years. He particularly enjoys discovering traces of early settlers, like shell mounds, cisterns, sour orange trees and coconut palms. "I am drawn to the places where the touch of man's hand has been light, and the power and unpredictability of nature can still be felt."

The 1991 watercolor on paper, *Storage Shed - Paradise Cay*, depicts a wooden structure with a tin roof in the yard of a small, isolated fish camp located on a mangrove island, or cay, just west of Everglades City in Collier County, Southwest Florida, in Everglades National Park. The cay is a small, offshore island in the Ten Thousand Islands. Similar fish camps, used by locals as well as sportsmen from out of the area, dot the islands. They are little known but are typical bits of Floridiana found along the west coast of the state. In Southwest Florida, fish camps have a long history. Spanish commercial fishermen from Cuba fished these waters from the beginning of the 17th century until 1896 and the Spanish-American War. After 1896, local United States fishermen had the area to themselves and established their own camps.

Rose has caught the isolated, ramshackle nature of one of these camps. The shack has a tenuous relationship with its setting. It seems about to be overwhelmed by an indefinite wall of dark green vegetation accented by several old palm trees—the Florida artist's icon for wild, untamed nature. Overhead, a sliver of cloudy, blue sky is barely seen as Rose focuses on the dense, mosquito-filled landscape where buildings are on pilings to avoid the frequent standing water and the snakes.

Rose painted the watercolor on site on Thanksgiving morning in 1992. He describes it as a "pure watercolor painted with successive glazes, with some additional drybrush and gouache." Generally, he likes to paint on site taking plenty of time to "slowly absorb the sense of place," but "the mosquitoes and snakes caused me to paint quickly and deliberately." The work is very much in the tradition of Florida watercolors from the turn of the century by Winslow Homer and John Singer Sargeant. Rose is especially interested in capturing scenes of coastal fishermen and boats in Florida and the Bahamas. In Florida, this aspect of traditional culture is rapidly disappearing, making *Storage Shed - Paradise Cay* a telling prophecy of the future.

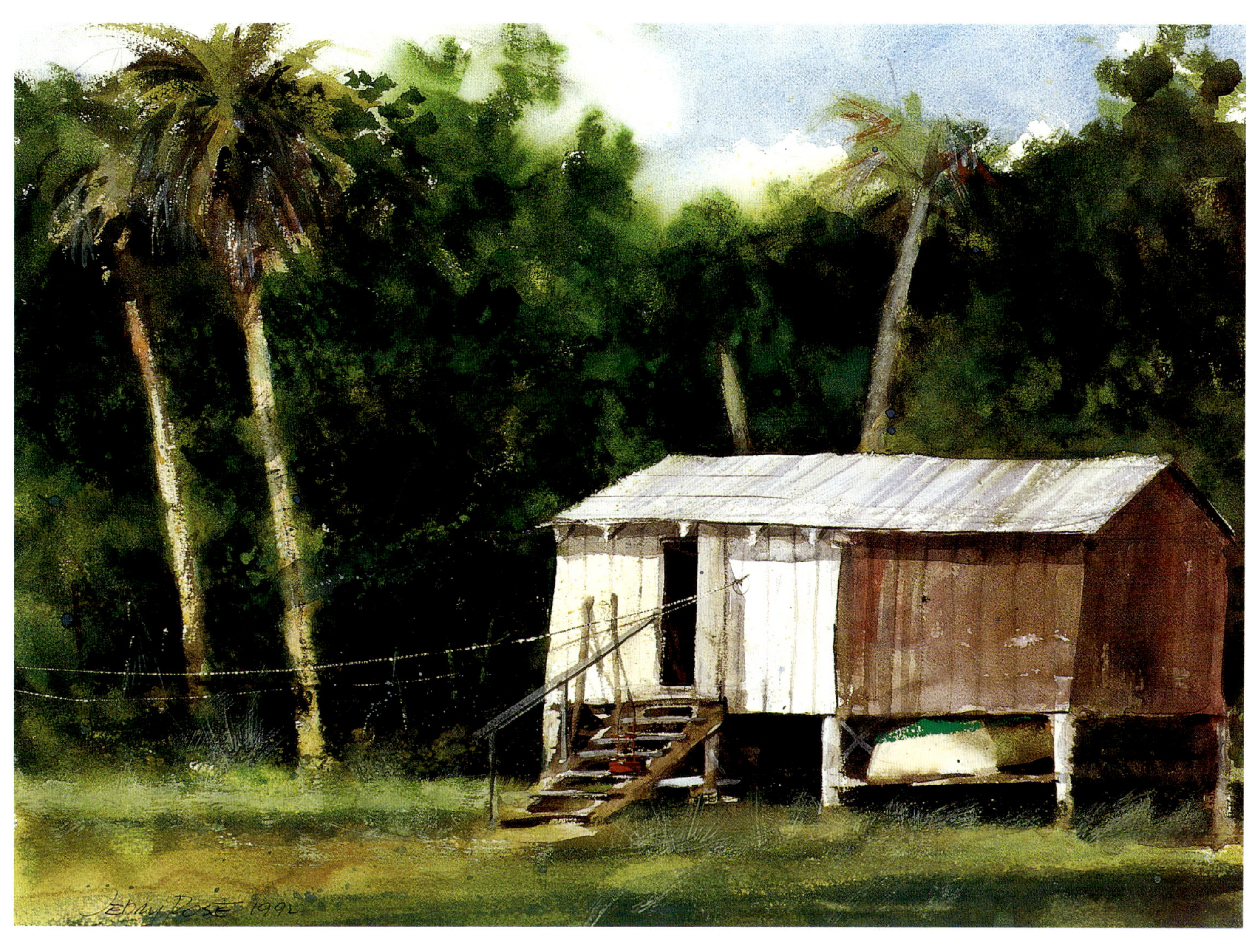

Craig Rubadoux

Playa de Plata
1988, Oil on paper, 25" x 30"

Born in Rochester, New York, in 1937, Craig Rubadoux received his early education there. In 1945, the family moved to Sarasota, Florida, where he completed his education. After finishing high school in Sarasota, he attended the Ringling School of Art on a one-year scholarship. This experience convinced Rubadoux to pursue a career in art. In the 1950s, Rubadoux accompanied artist-friend Ben Stahl and his family to Spain. After a two-and-a-half-year stay, Rubadoux returned to the United States where he painted in and around Westport, Connecticut. In 1962, Rubadoux returned to Florida. From 1969 to 1972, he was an adjunct professor of art at the University of Florida in Gainesville, the University of South Florida in Tampa, and Florida International University in Boca Raton. In both 1978 and 1980, Rubadoux received Individual Artist Fellowships from the state of Florida. In 1981, he received fellowships from the Ossabaw Foundation and from Alfred University. From 1985 through 1990, he served as lecturer at the Arts Center, St. Petersburg, Florida, and as a visiting artist at the Ringling School of Art in Sarasota. He continues to travel and work from his studios in Bradenton, Florida, and Rose Bay, Nova Scotia, Canada.

Rubadoux exhibits widely. Exhibitions have included the John and Mable Ringling Museum of Art, Sarasota, Florida; The Brevard Museum of Art and Science, Inc., Melbourne, Florida; The Florida Gulf Coast Art Center, Belleair, Florida; The George D. and Harriet W. Cornell Fine Arts Museum, Winter Park, Florida; The Museum of Arts and Sciences, Daytona Beach, Florida; The Art Center, St. Petersburg, Florida; The Art and Culture Center, Hollywood, Florida; The Tampa Museum of Art, Tampa, Florida; The Museum of Art, Fort Lauderdale, Florida; The Polk Museum of Art, Lakeland, Florida; and the Museum of Fine Arts, St. Petersburg, Florida. His work is included in many public and private collections, including the Soloman R. Guggenheim Museum of Art, New York, New York; The High Museum of Art, Atlanta, Georgia; The Ringling Museum of Art, Sarasota, Florida; The Museum of Fine Arts, St. Petersburg, Florida; The Museum of Art, Fort Lauderdale, Florida; and the State of Florida.

While Craig Rubadoux has been known to paint on wood, clay, tile, table tops, chairs and almost any surface that can hold an image, the majority of his work is on canvas or paper. His paintings are intensely personal glimpses into particular emotions, and he frequently speaks of his work as a journal. His interest in landscapes became more than casual in the 1980s when the sanctity of his studio on the Braden River was threatened by nearby development. He began to paint landscapes with a sense of urgency, expressing his love of Florida, which, to him, "means home, safety, beauty—especially the parts man hasn't gotten around to harming." In the words of critic Marcia Corbino, his "palms and pines seem to rear out of the ground...signalling confidence and joy. Non-referential radical color pulsates and sprawls in passionate strokes. Compositions are inventive, complicated with unexpected conceptions of space. Each painting is a world alive—a primeval paradise."

Playa de Plata is a 1988 oil on gessoed paper. It is a "dream location" based on a stand of three Washingtonian palms that existed near the artist's former home in Sarasota. Rubadoux created the landscape, which represents "serenity of place," from his imagination in his studio.

The work is a very abstract rendering of the basic elements of a landscape—sky, horizon, water, beach, grass, trees, all organized into horizontal bands of color. Three tall palms rear out of the ground expressing the confidence of nature and the joy of the artist at seeing them, symbolizing his love for life. A stormy, gray sky and blue beach grasses are energized by many short brushstrokes. The storm descends on a smoother, calmer pink horizon, blue band of water, and gray beach. In the distance, slivers of green suggest other land. This is a very personal, cerebral image of a Florida landscape, which also stands for a more universal image of nature and its importance to human beings.

Rubadoux's style is very different from that of most other Florida landscape painters. It has many similarities with Milton Avery's landscapes, which are stripped to essentials, with an emphasis on color relationships and flatness. And, like Avery, Rubadoux seems interested in the essence rather than the facts of nature. For both artists, their subject is their own intensely personal conception of the world and their own feelings and responses to that world. In this respect, Rubadoux—and perhaps a few others, like C.D. Smith and Trish Thompson, with their own unique styles but concentrating the burden of expression in their paintings on color—are the antithesis of the "environmental realists" whose regional fascination results in images that are particular and literal, rather than metaphorical and general.

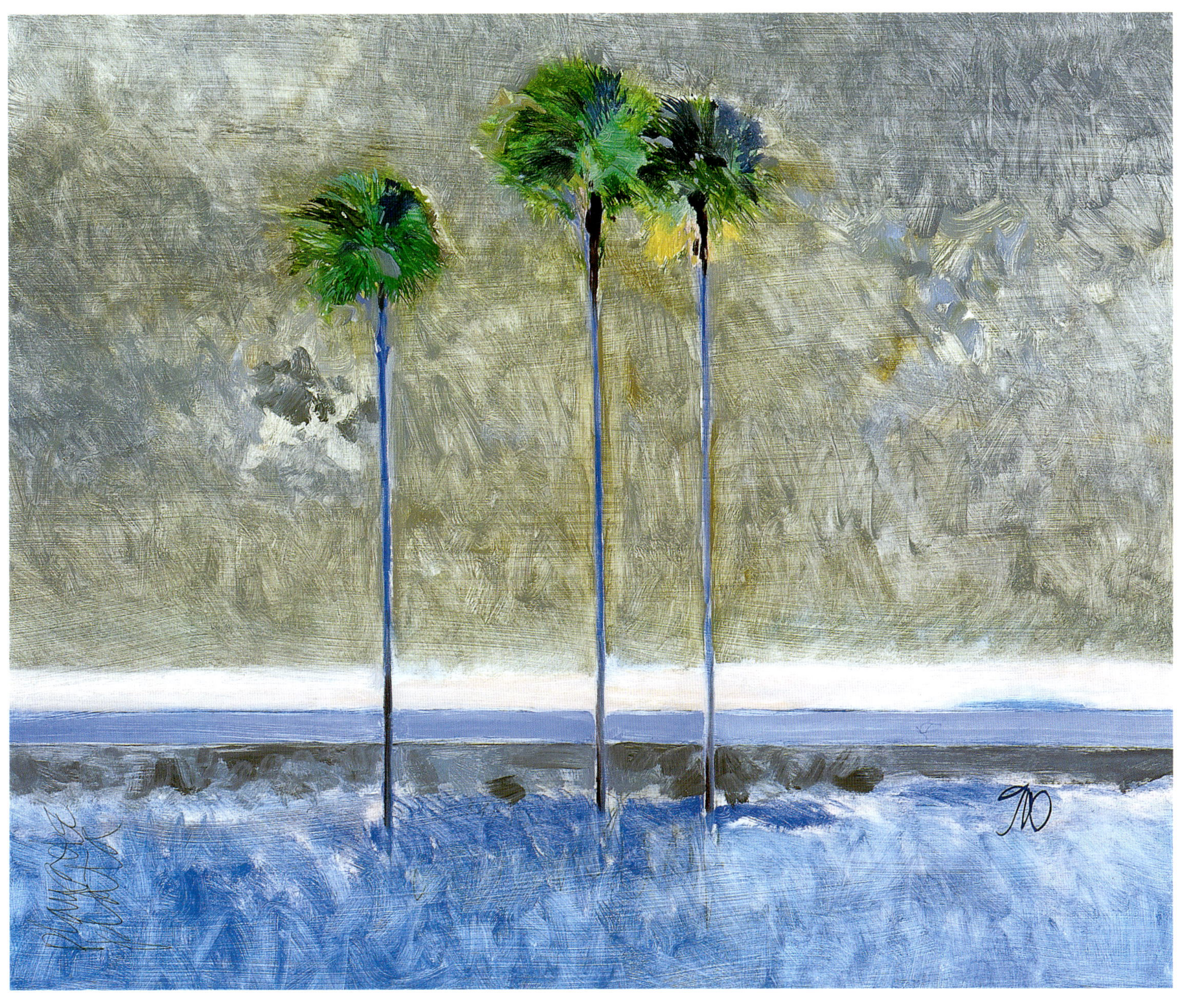

C.D. Smith

St. Marks #8

1992, Watercolor on paper, 21" x 28"

Born in Ocala, Florida, in 1944, C.D. Smith was raised near Brooksville, north of Tampa on the west coast of the state. He went on to Florida State University in Tallahassee where he spent four years exploring different aspects of studio art. After Tallahassee, Smith spent nearly a year in Washington, D.C., where he studied and copied the masters at the National Gallery of Art and other Washington museums. Rembrandt, Titian, Lorrain, Cezanne, Van Gogh and Turner were some of the artists that influenced him at this time. He returned to Florida, taking a variety of jobs that would allow him to paint. He also decided to re-study drawing at this time and spent nearly 10 years perfecting his skills in draughtsmanship. Having developed an allergy to solvents, he shifted his interest to watercolor as his medium of choice.

Always interested more in painting than selling, Smith continued to work privately "developing his skills; just painting good paintings." C.D. Smith exhibits his work sparingly. He has enjoyed exhibitions at The Florida State University Art Gallery, Tallahassee, Florida; The Banks Haley Museum, Albany, Georgia; and The Museum of Florida History, near his home in Tallahassee, Florida.

Smith likes to begin his watercolors on site. He often moves into the studio where he works and re-works each piece, taking from six months to more than three years to complete a watercolor. Often, a sunset or a moody afternoon piece becomes a dazzling sunrise. Visual memory is important to Smith as he recreates his ideas on paper. He is interested in capturing "poetic imagery and getting the feel of his subject."

Smith uses 100 percent textured linen paper that he custom orders from a Montreal, Canada, supplier. He cross orders his paints and currently is exploring single pigments from more than 15 national and international suppliers. Smith likes to work with large sable brushes as he directs his technical skills toward an abstract approach to subject matter. "Landscapes and seascapes are merely motifs, a poetic framework that may, with luck and hard work, be pushed toward a more universal and meaningful vision. My position is essentially that of a cipher, interpreting the profound beauty and spiritual significance of nature."

St. Marks #8, a watercolor on paper completed in 1992, was inspired by visits to the St. Marks National Wildlife Refuge in Wakulla County in the panhandle of Florida. Smith often works there because "it still has a quality of remote and unspoiled beauty." The highly abstract watercolor captures an atmospheric scene where bright golds and yellows define and describe land and light; the sun is barely seen at the horizon above a hazy stand of grasses. The heat of the scene is undercut by the deep blue of water as it balances the composition and helps intensify the complementary colors of the tonalist watercolor.

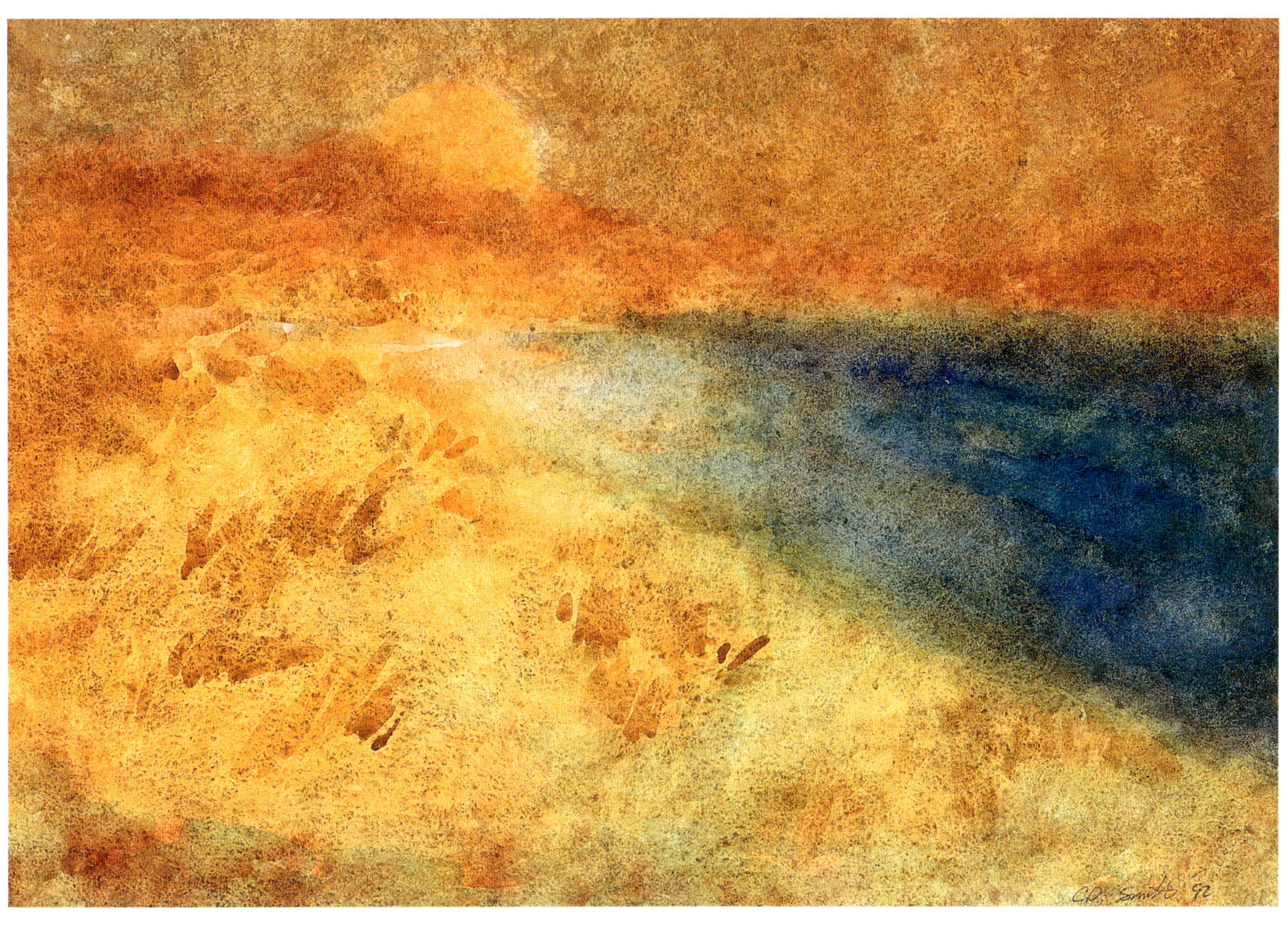

Clifford Smith

Study for Everglades River
1994, Oil on paper, 10" x 12¾"

Clifford Smith was born in Passaic, New Jersey in 1951. He earned a bachelor's of science degree at Southern Connecticut State College in New Haven in 1973, and a master's of fine arts at Pratt Institute, Brooklyn, New York in 1979. After his master's degree, he spent a year studying at the University of Massachusetts in Amherst, Massachusetts.

Smith exhibits widely and has enjoyed exhibitions at New England College, Henniker, New Hampshire; The Greenville Museum of Art, Inc., Greenville, North Carolina; Fairleigh Dickinson University, Teaneck, New Jersey; The New Hampshire Institute of Art, Manchester, New Hampshire; University Gallery at the University of Florida, Gainesville; The Pensacola Museum of Art, Florida; The Center for the Arts, Vero Beach, Florida; The State Capitol Building, Tallahassee, Florida; The Art and Culture Center of Hollywood, Florida; The Henry Morrison Flagler Museum, Palm Beach, Florida; Gregg Gallery, The American College, Bryn Mawr, Pennsylvania; Ben Shahn Galleries, William Patterson College, Wayne, New Jersey; The Muscarelle Art Museum, College of William and Mary, Williamsburg, Virginia; The Minnesota Museum of Art, St. Paul, Minnesota; The Museum of Science and Industry, Los Angeles, California; and The Canton Art Institute, Canton, Ohio.

Smith's work is included in more than 25 corporate collections including The American Stock Exchange, New York, New York; and The Bank of Boston, Boston, Massachusetts. His work is also in the permanent collections of The Center for the Arts, Vero Beach, Florida; Fairleigh Dickinson University, Teaneck, New Jersey; The New Hampshire Historical Society, Concord, New Hampshire; and Yale University, New Haven, Connecticut. Smith continues to paint from his studio and home in Henniker, New Hampshire.

The *Study for Everglades Rive*r, is an oil on gessoed, acid-free Reeves BFK paper completed in 1994 as part of a project titled, *Expedition: Everglades - River of Grass*; a large, traveling exhibition of the work of eight contemporary artists who depicted the Florida Everglades engaged in a struggle for its survival, organized by the Sherry French Gallery of New York. Smith executed 20 oil paintings and studies during his involvement with the project. "I was impressed by the expansive land, the atmosphere and the color."

Study for Everglades River is a loosely painted view of the tranquil river as it gently flows, filled with aquatic vegetation, through dense forests of pine, oak, cypress and palm. The sky is clear with bright, overhead light causing reflections in the river. Smith has limited his palette and broadened his brushstroke emphasizing the dark greens and yellows of the swampy terrain.

The location of *Study for Everglades River* is within the Big Cypress National Reserve off Route 41 near Everglades City in South Florida. Smith used on-site drawings and photographs for reference during the completion of the work back in his studio. "I've been painting the landscape for more than two decades. I am concerned about our relationship with the environment because nature demands our attention. We, as a nation, both socially and physically impact the landscape. Decisions to respect or disrespect the land are made by individuals and groups, which affect the relationship of man and the environment."

Smith describes himself as a committed realist: "Many in the art world frown on realism because it's been around forever. But, the landscape evolves; it continues to change; historically, culturally, socially. That's why I feel realism has a place." Many of Smith's paintings, like the current example, are views of places to which everyone has access; not wilderness, but places close at hand. Even though the scene appears unspoiled, it is a romanticized view of a world that does not really exist anymore. Just outside the frame is evidence of human presence, giving rise to the question of how long the scene will remain as it is. A larger consideration in his work is the interaction of the natural environment and human use of it. In his paintings, Smith does not make judgmental statements, but tries to convey to the viewer the essence of a place, a feeling of "what it's like to be there" and a sense of what its future may be in today's fast-changing environment.

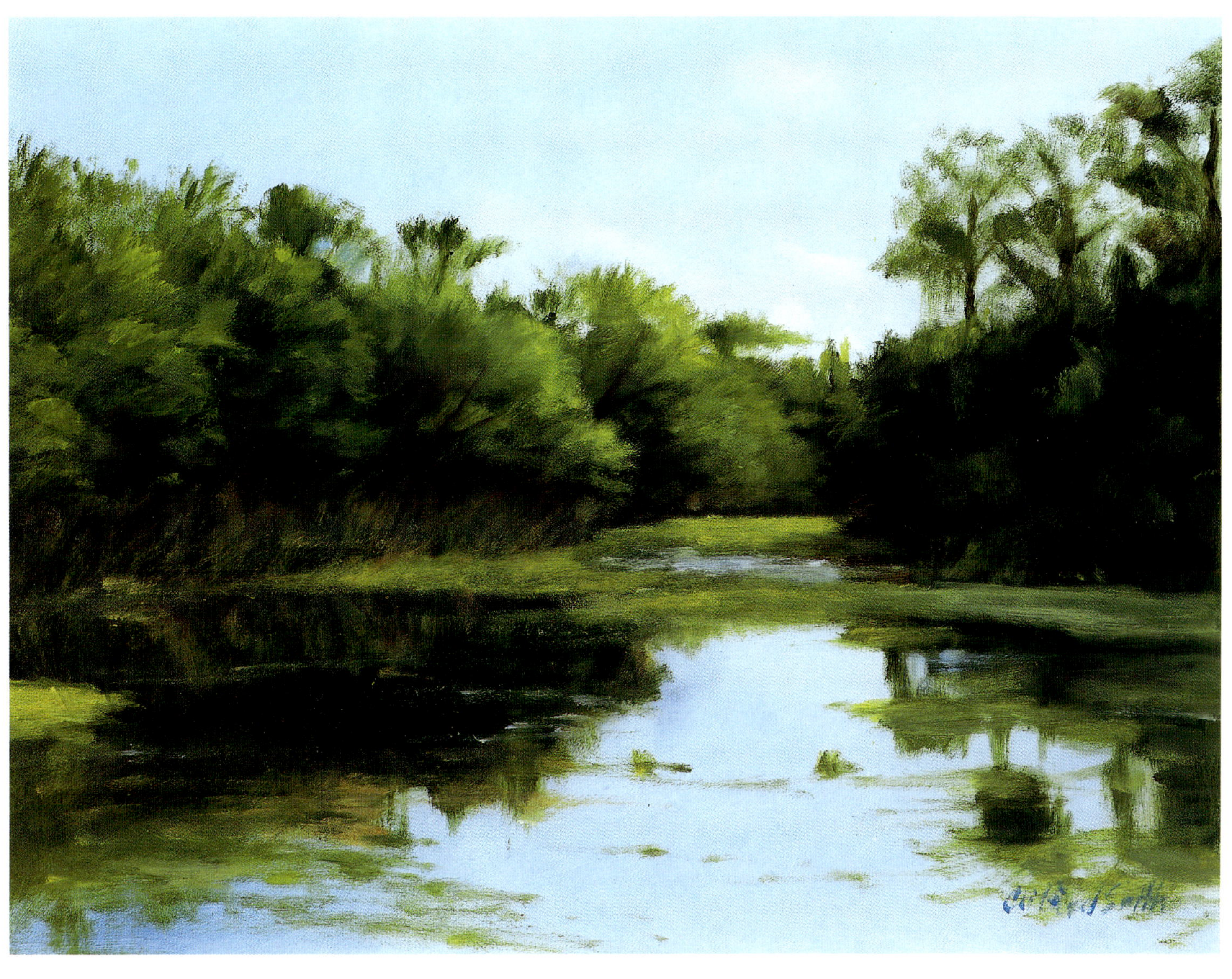

DOROTHEA E. SMITH

MOON ON SOUTHERN WATERS

1994, PASTEL ON PAPER, 6¾" X 9½"

EARLY MORNING, INDIAN PASS

1995, PASTEL ON PAPER, 6¾" X 10"

Dorothea E. Smith was born in Rockford, Iowa, on January 31, 1919. Soon after, the family moved to Mason City, Iowa, where she received her early education. In 1928, Smith attended Pasadena College in California where she majored in studio art. She has also studied at The Art Barn School of Art, Salt Lake City, Utah; The Walker Art Center in Minneapolis, Minnesota; The Alhambra Art School, Alhambra, California; Purdue University, West Lafayette, Indiana; and at The Weaver's Guild in St. Paul, Minnesota.

In 1982, she first visited the panhandle region of Northwest Florida. She was impressed with the "picturesque and unusual quality of the area, and the constant change reflected in the Florida landscape." Since 1985, the Smiths have spent six months of each year in Port St. Joe, Florida, on the Gulf Coast of the panhandle near Apalachicola, Florida.

Dorothea E. Smith has exhibited widely with exhibitions at Pasadena College, Pasadena, California; The Tweed Gallery, Duluth, Minnesota; The Walker Art Center, Minneapolis, Minnesota; The University of Iowa, Iowa City, Iowa; Hanover College, Hanover, Indiana; St. Lawrence University, Canton, New York; Purdue University, West Lafayette, Indiana; Olivette College, Olivette, Michigan; The Herron Art Institute, Indianapolis, Indiana; The Fort Wayne Museum of Art, Fort Wayne, Indiana; The Lafayette Art Center, Lafayette, Indiana; and The Paul Whitney Larson Gallery, The University of Minnesota, St. Paul, Minnesota. Her work is included in more than 50 public and private collections in the United States. She continues to work from studios in Port St. Joe, Florida, and St. Paul, Minnesota.

Moon on Southern Waters is a pastel on paper from 1994. The tonalist pastel captures a full moon above an indistinct, dark land mass and brilliant orange sea. The horizon is rendered in a deep purple in this romantically conceived "magical scene, slow and quiet, where shimmering light makes me want to express nature at its best." In *Early Morning, Indian Pass*, a soft impressionist pastel on paper from 1995, Smith is more descriptive. Here, soft pastels describe a watery scene of pine and marsh. White wading birds accent the blue of the water. Above, the sunrise fills the sky with pinks and golds as a pair of marsh birds fly toward the horizon in this vision of the Florida landscape as an extension of the Eden motif in American landscape art.

Smith's pastels reflect a unique view of Florida. They are not so much representations of places as they are mood pieces conveyed by the use of a tonalist palette. Especially noteworthy are her depictions of the Gulf of Mexico at nighttime under moonlight in nonreferential colors that evoke a feeling of other worldliness and tranquility.

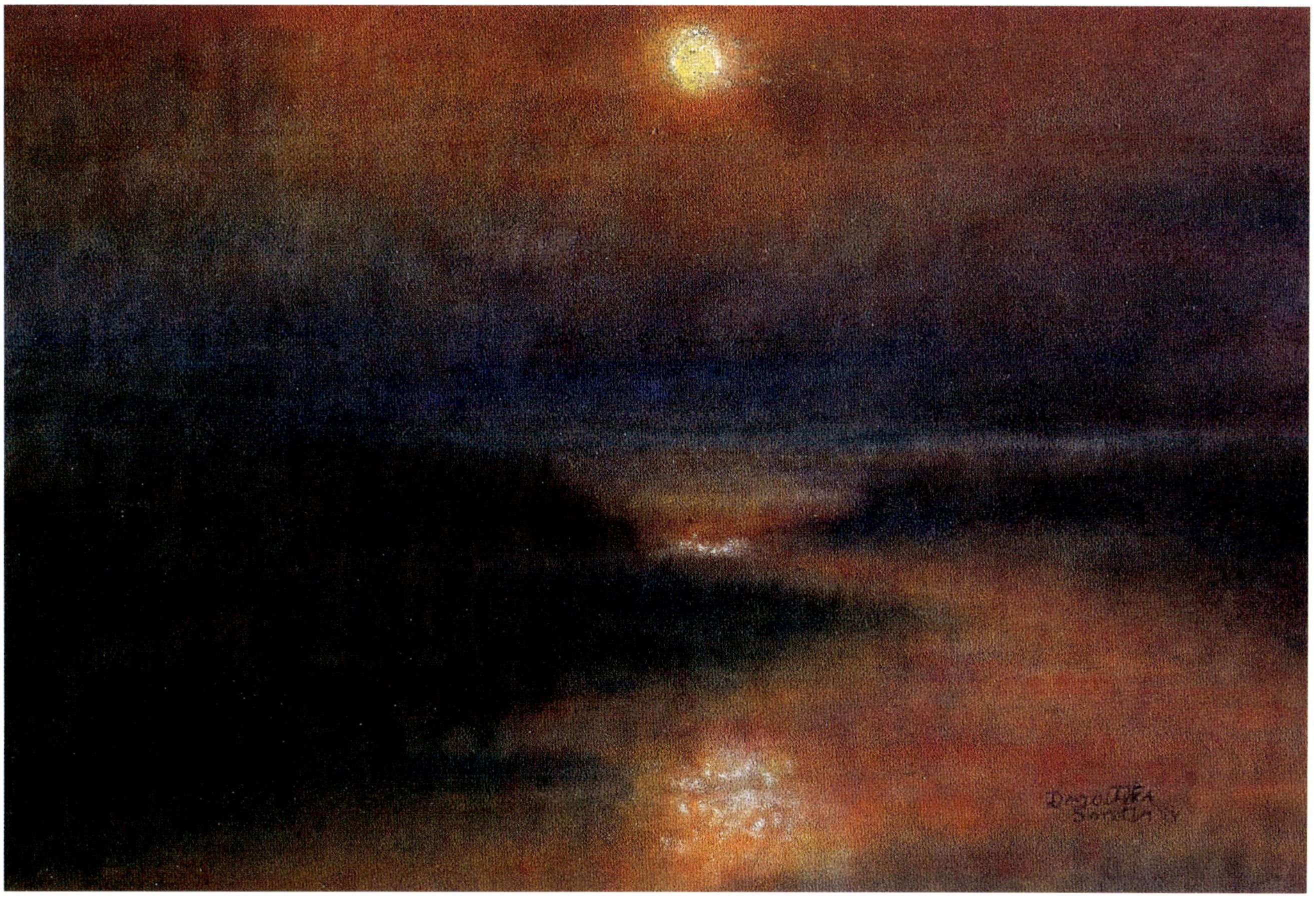

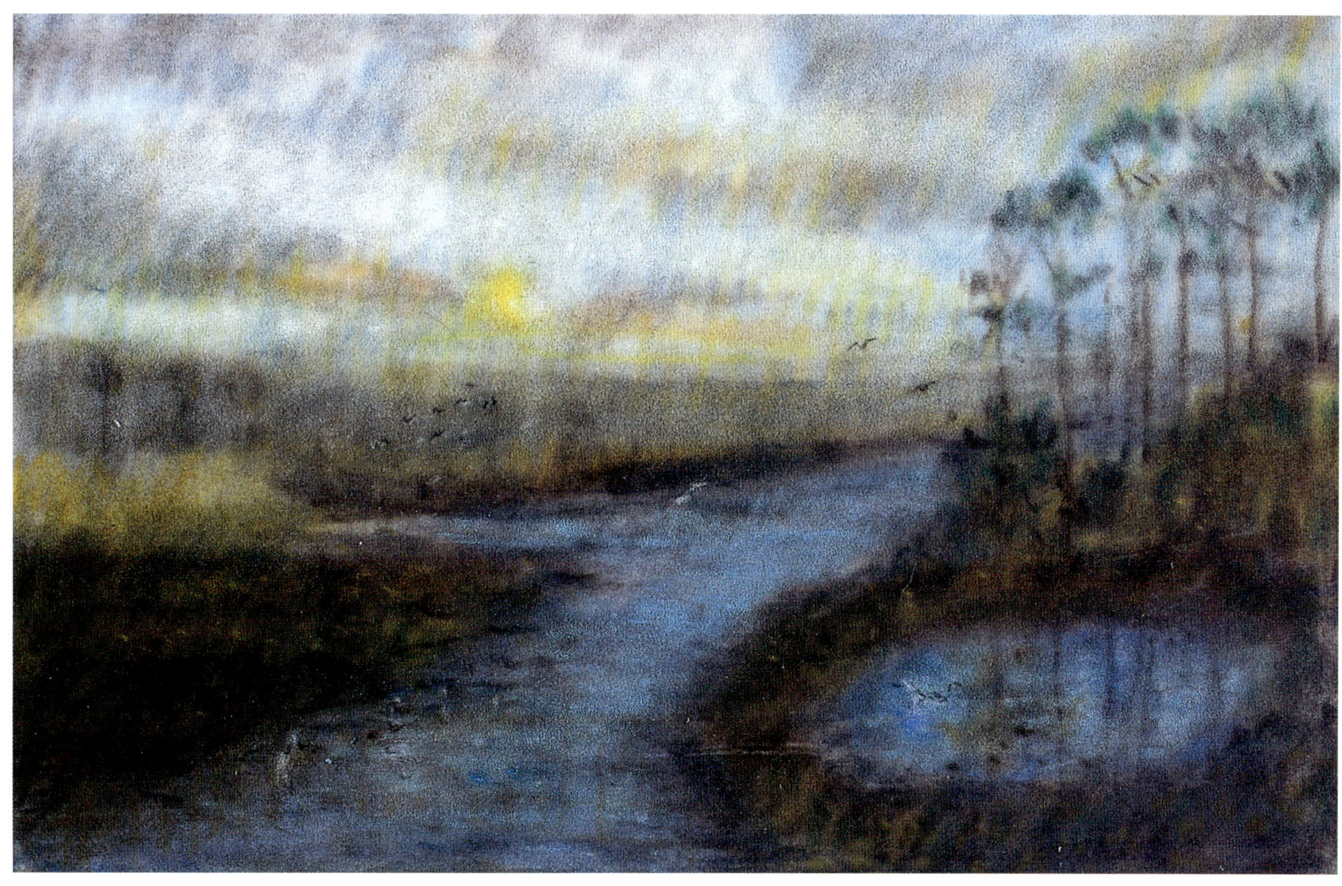

JOHN STANFORD

EVENING BALES
1993, OIL ON PAPER, 8¾" X 13½"

UNTITLED LANDSCAPE
1994, OIL ON PAPER, 15" X 22"

Impressionist painter John Stanford was born in West Palm Beach, Florida, in January 1947. He was raised in Orlando, where he completed his secondary schooling. Stanford then went on to junior college where a studio art course with Ralph Bagley changed his life. Bagley had studied at Michigan's Flint Institute of Art and was a full-time artist. "He gave me insight into what painting was about and what the life of an artist was like," recalls Stanford. After junior college, Stanford attended Florida State University where he received a bachelor's of arts degree in 1972. "When I first began to paint landscapes in college, I was heavily influenced by 19th century landscapists; both European and American. I loved the immediacy of the Barbizon painters, who, for the first time, took canvas and brush outdoors to confront nature directly."

After graduation from Florida State University, Stanford worked as a computer operator in a bank for eight years until he attended an evening art class where he met internationally known artist Richard Schmid who had recently moved to Tallahassee. "I felt as if God had moved in right next door to me," Stanford recalls. Schmid was an established realist painter showing in New York at the Grand Central Art Galleries. From Schmid, Stanford learned skillful brushwork, the alla prima technique, and wet-in-wet painting.

Stanford approaches his work on two levels. "Intensive observation explains a landscape in its physical terms. This is always a process of discovery. On a completely different level, I am reacting to color, edges, values, shapes and the painting surface to produce an emotional effect. I often begin with a tentative idea that involves a great deal of working and reworking, always reacting to what is put down, until something begins to click for me. My paintings reveal as much about myself as they do about the scenes portrayed."

Stanford's basic method begins with a charcoal sketch on canvas or paper that he develops into a basic painting on location. "In most of my paintings, I usually start with dark transparent paint to indicate the major dark areas. I thin this mixture to a wash to indicate the other large value planes. With this 'road map' of the major areas of my painting established, I begin with the sky and paint from the background forward always working wet edge against wet edge. I am very much interested in surface quality and try to leave a little 'record' of each stage of the painting. The variety, the thickness and thinness, the light and dark, the hard and soft, the transparent and opaque, and the lushness of color are what I find exciting."

After a trip to Taos, New Mexico, in 1990 that developed into a year-long stay, Stanford and his wife, painter Sally Boswell, decided to remain out West. It was in Missouri that Stanford met regionalist Gary Bowling, who introduced Stanford to oil on paper. In 1993, the Stanfords returned to Tallahassee, Florida.

He is one of a group of North Florida painters, including Sally Boswell, Rosemary Gibson, Joe McFadden and C.D. Smith, who have chosen the St. Marks Wildlife Preserve in Wakulla County as a source for a growing body of important Florida landscape art.

Stanford exhibits widely and has enjoyed exhibitions at the Springfield Museum of Art, Springfield, Missouri; The Florida State University Gallery and Museum, Tallahassee, Florida; and The LeMoyne Art Foundation, Tallahassee, Florida. His work is in the permanent collection of the Barnett Banks of Florida, Tallahassee; the SouthTrust Bank of Birmingham, Alabama; and the Southern Bell Collection, Jacksonville, Florida.

Stanford believes that there is a subtle transition for most artists when they stop looking for "things" and begin to see shapes, values and color. This different way of seeing the world is when the ordinary becomes the extraordinary. oil on paper *Evening Bales*, 1993, is an "ordinary" moment that became extraordinary. "I saw these large bales at the end of the day and was struck with the softness of the forms in the late afternoon light and the shapes of the bales against the distant trees. There was a feeling at once of monumentality and softness. I am lucky to live in an area of Florida where I am very close to small farms and can enjoy the beauty of open fields and ponds. This was among the first of my paintings to use paper as a support. I love the way the paint works with this surface and I find it very sympathetic to the way I paint." In *Evening Bales*, Stanford captures a field of large hay bales in the afternoon sun against a stand of dark green trees. The mellow yellows of the bales and the dramatic chiaroscuro of falling light help transform the scene into an important moment in the Florida landscape.

Untitled Landscape is an oil on paper completed in 1994. This is one of several paintings that evolved in Stanford's studio and is a composite of many areas along the Gulf Coast. The painting is concerned with color and the sense of late afternoon light on the marsh in Florida. "When I first began to paint the coastal areas I spent several frustrating years coming to grips with scenes that provided no real landmarks, few verticals and almost no foreground; the expansiveness, the incredible, subtle color and the anxiety of this open, wild space. Putting it down with paint is another matter."

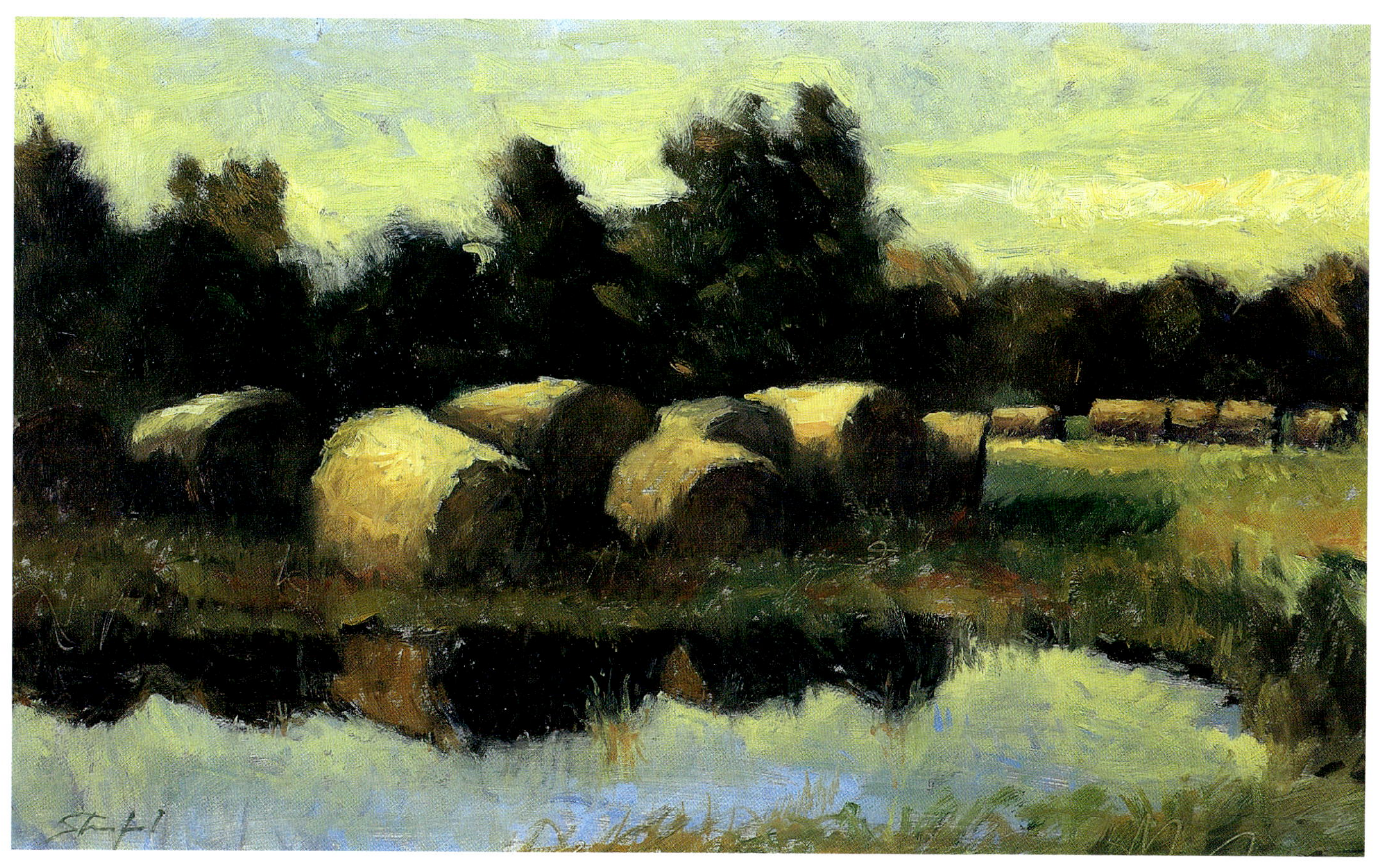

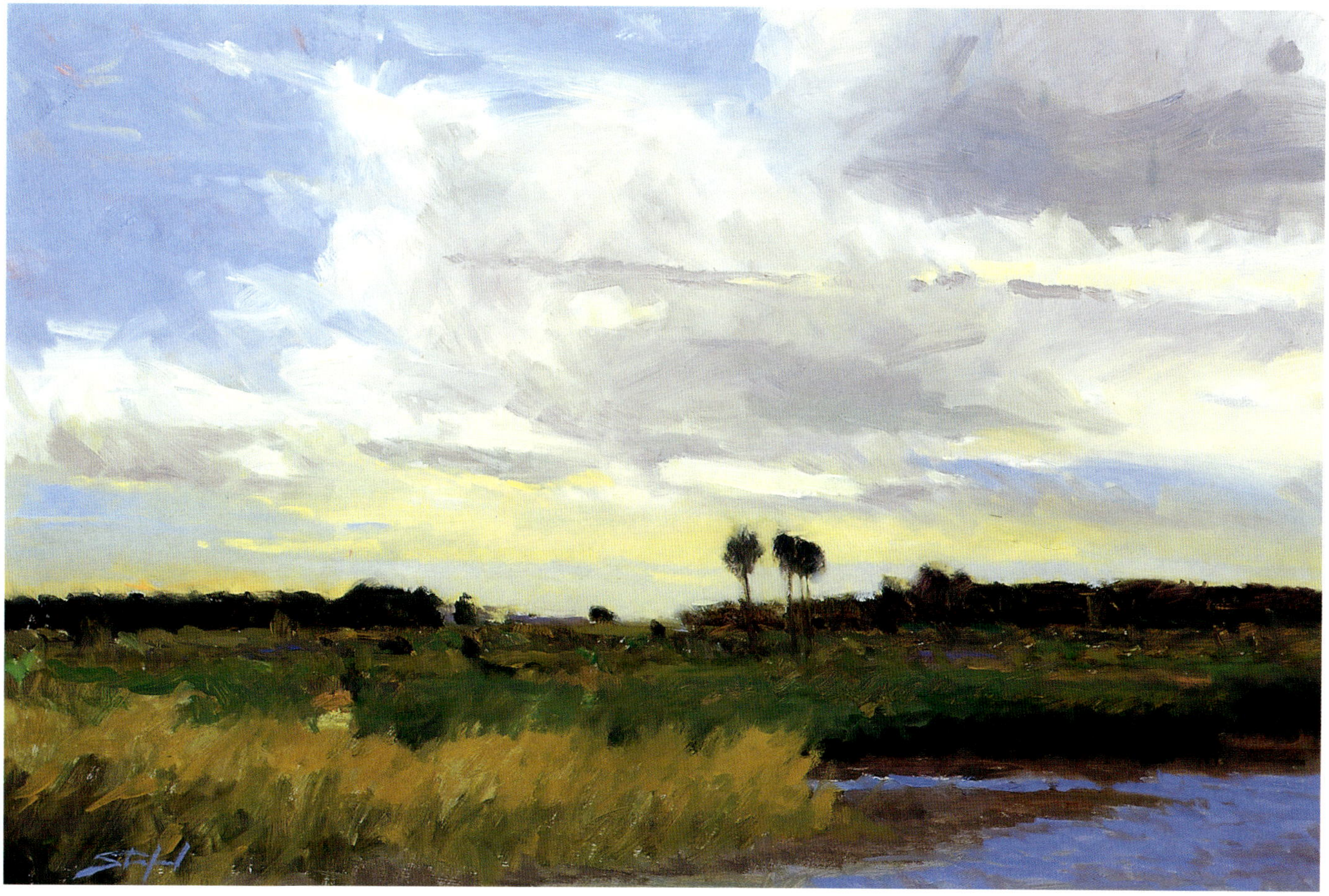

Joseph W. Taylor

Bulow Hammock
1995, Oil on wood panel, 10" x 8"

Joseph W. (Joe) Taylor was born in Indianapolis, Indiana, in 1940. In 1942, the Taylor family moved to St. Augustine, Florida, on the northeastern coast. Taylor was a precocious child and began to draw at an early age, copying animals and figures from photographers and illustrations in books, newspapers and magazines. In elementary school, he started to paint and continued through high school. He even took his paints with him during a tour of duty in the U.S. Navy. After his military service, Taylor worked for Lockheed Aircraft Company, but continued to perfect his developing painting style. At the age of 29, he left Lockheed and enrolled in college, graduating from Valdosta State University, Valdosta, Georgia, with a bachelor's of fine arts degree at the age of 33. Taylor then left the South and moved to New York, where he studied at the Art Students League with Everett Raymond Kinstler, Moses Soyer, David E. Leffel, Robert Phillips and Robert Brackman.

In 1976, Taylor left New York to open a studio in Ocala, Florida, in the center of the state, south of Gainesville. In Ocala, he studied landscape painting with Joyce Ballantine Brand. In 1980, Taylor traveled to Miami to visit colleagues at the Robinson Gallery. During this visit, he met impressionist painter Franz Josef Bolinger, an important senior South Florida landscape artist and link to the great landscape tradition in Florida of the last century. Bolinger and Taylor developed a deep friendship and travelled the state together, painting in Key West, Miami and Jacksonville. Bolinger was a major influence on Taylor's developing sensitivity toward the Florida landscape. Bolinger also instilled in Taylor his unique perspective as an independent and self-reliant individualist totally committed to art and not to the marketplace. In 1987, Taylor moved back to St. Augustine where he continues to work from his gallery on Aviles Street in the old city.

Taylor's oil on wood panel, *Bulow Hammock*, 1995, was completed on site at Bulow State Park, north of Daytona Beach, south of Flagler Beach and State Road 100, and east of Interstate 95 in southern Flagler County. The ruins of the Sugar Mill, burned by Indians in the Second Seminole War (1835-1842), lie in a dense, tropical hammock of live oaks and palmettos, where sunlight filters through the canopy of mature trees and brush. Taylor loosely paints a forest of slender trees in the foreground where bark, foliage and leaf litter explain the tropical scene. The background of the painting is filled with a soft, dappled tone as the jungle is backlit by sunlight filtering through the hammock. Similar in many ways to the work of William Glackens (1870-1938) who painted Florida 50 years earlier, Taylor provides both an accurate and poetic look into the primeval landscape in Northeast Florida by placing the viewer directly within the hammock where sight, sound and smell suggested in the painting help convey the integrity of this unique part of the Florida landscape.

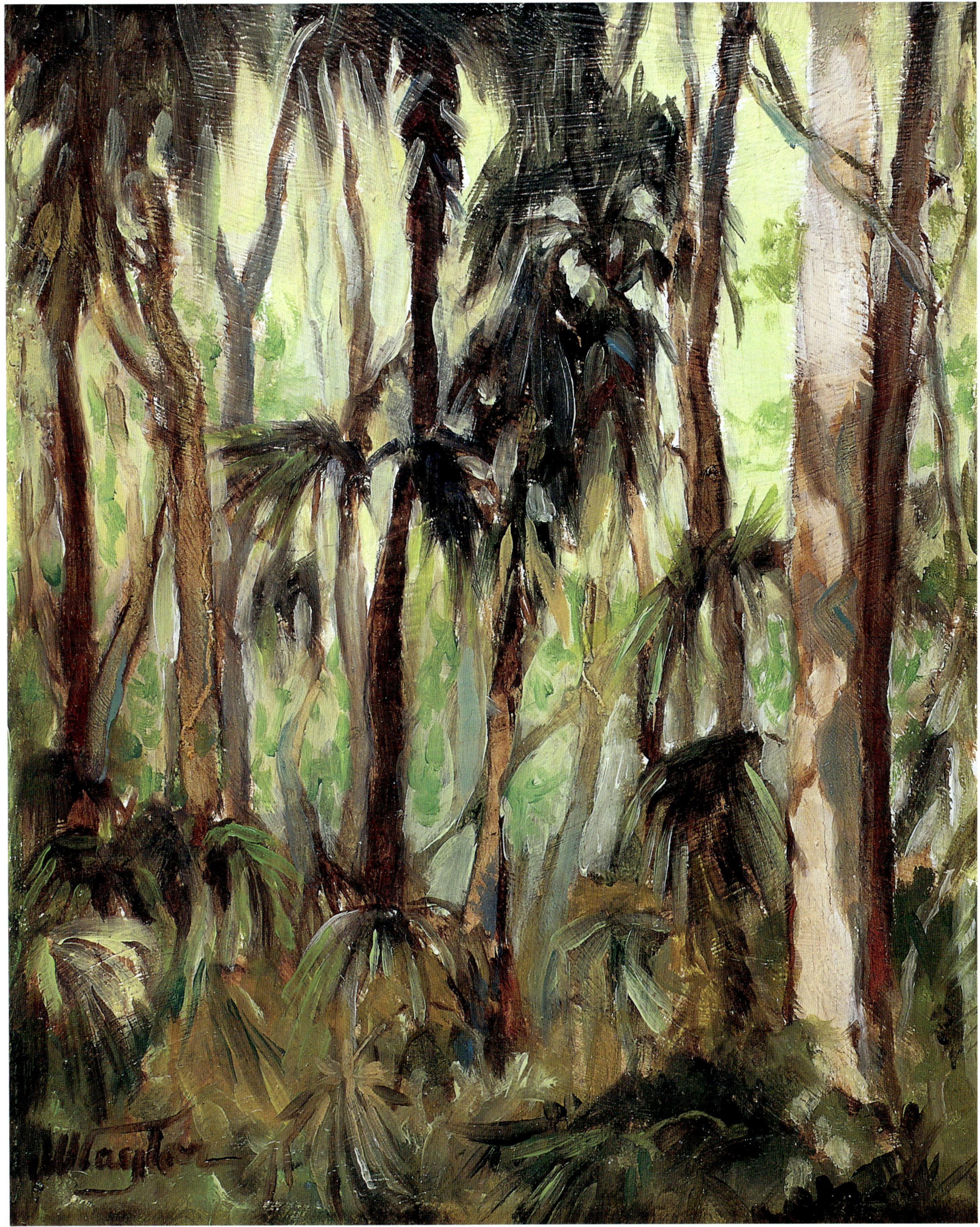

Patricia Kelly Thompson

Landscape Fresco III

1995, Mixed media, 17⅝" x 17⅝"

Trish Thompson was born in Panama City, Florida, on April 12, 1947. She received her early education in Panama City schools taking her first art lessons at the age of five. After high school graduation in 1965, she attended Gulf Coast Community College in Panama City, where she received an associate's of arts degree in studio art. In 1967 and 1968, she attended the Florida State University Overseas Study Program in Florence, Italy, where she studied both studio art and art history. In 1968, Thompson received a bachelor's of arts degree in painting and advertising design and, in 1971, she received a master's of arts degree in art education and constructive design from Florida State University, Tallahassee, Florida. In 1990, she began a Ph.D. in art education also from Florida State.

In addition in her painting, Thompson has enjoyed a distinguished career in the arts in Florida. She has taught art in the Leon County School system from elementary to high school. She was an art specialist at the Maclay Preparatory School in Tallahassee, and an art instructor at New Smyrna Beach High School in Volusia County, Florida. She served as curator of education at the Museum of Arts and Sciences in Daytona Beach, and was selected Museum Educator of the Year by the State of Florida Museum Education Association. Since 1995, she has been an assistant professor in the cultural arts department of Daytona Beach Community College in Daytona Beach. She lives and maintains a studio in New Smyrna Beach, near the Indian River.

Trish Thompson exhibits widely and has enjoyed exhibitions at The Gallery of Art, Panama City, Florida; Harris House of Atlantic Center for the Art, New Smyrna Beach, Florida; the 22nd Floor Gallery, The Capitol, Tallahassee, Florida; the School of Architecture Gallery, Florida A&M University, Tallahassee, Florida; The University of Central Florida Art Gallery, Orlando, Florida; Daytona Beach Community College Fine Arts Gallery, Daytona Beach, Florida; Mount Dora Center for The Arts, Mount Dora, Florida; The Art League, Daytona Beach, Florida; the Thomas Center, Gainesville, Florida; The Museum of Florida History, Tallahassee, Florida; Valencia Community College, Orlando, Florida; The Maitland Art Center, Maitland, Florida; The Museum of Arts and Sciences, Daytona Beach, Florida; Ormond Memorial Art Museum, Ormond Beach, Florida; Seminole Community College, Sanford, Florida; Dunedin Fine Arts Center, Dunedin, Florida; The New Orleans Museum of Art, New Orleans, Louisiana; the Mobile Art Gallery, Mobile, Alabama; DeLand Museum of Art, DeLand, Florida; and the Pensacola Art Center, Pensacola, Florida.

Thompson's work is included in private and public collections including: The Riverside National Bank, New Smyrna Beach, Florida; Acme Glass Corporation, Sarasota, Florida; Express Communications, Orlando, Florida; The Art In Public Places Collection of Volusia County, Florida at the Daytona Beach International Airport; The New Orleans Museum of Art, New Orleans, Louisiana; and the Museum of Arts and Sciences, Daytona Beach, Florida.

Thompson's mixed media painting, *Landscape Fresco III*, 1995, is composed of acrylic paint, gesso and joint compound applied in layers on a mahogany panel. And, while the title of the work mentions "landscape," Thompson is involved in more than a traditional rendering of a topographical place in time. "I have always been drawn to work that implies place. As my work became more non-objective, more process intensive, I wanted to leave signs of the process but still refer to a mood or a location. After experimenting for a year with a mixture of materials, I was uncertain about any subject matter other than the process itself. After a visit to Seattle, Washington, I discovered the ephemeral quality of the fog and air. The Seattle palette was born. I returned to Florida and to the Indian River near my studio in New Smyrna Beach. I watched it in fog and rain. This painting is one of the riverscapes from that period." The actual location of the scene is a dock on Riverside Drive in New Smyrna Beach, Florida, facing east. The fresco part of Thompson's title refers to an ancient Greco-Roman technique of painting on wet plaster. Thompson's use of this process begins with layers of wet plaster on paint that are sanded and scraped until a desired surface is created. This painting was the third in a series, hence the addition of the Roman numeral III in the title.

In the mixed media work, Thompson suggests a landscape where cool grays and blues imply a river view seen against a dark land mass across the river. Above it all, Thompson paints the suggestion of a sky, clouds and a setting sun. In reality, however, Thompson isn't creating an accurate topographical scene. Instead, the large square in the upper right of the painting reminds the viewer that he is looking at a flat object covered with texture and subtle color. In doing so, Thompson creates an exciting tension between the painted object itself, and the painting it becomes in the mind of the viewer who seeks to understand the object as a snapshot of reality. Instead, Thompson's Florida landscape is an elegantly painted flat piece of wood that allows each viewer, through the process of perception, to personally create a referential Florida landscape of the mind.

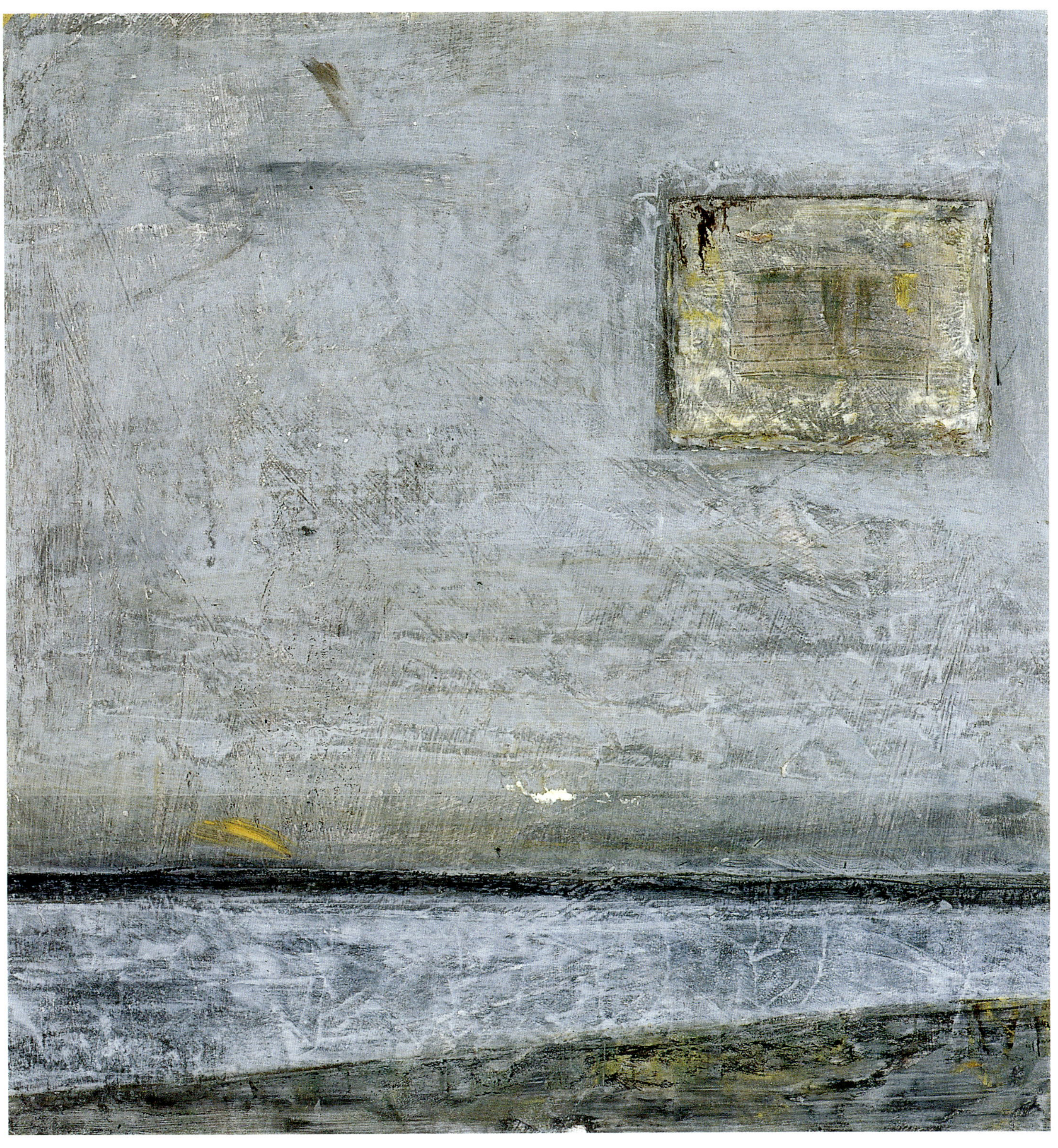

JEAN WAGNER TROEMEL

MATANZAS BAY

1993, ALKYD OIL ON CANVAS, 7¾" x 9¾"

Jean Wagner Troemel was born in 1921 in Alma, Michigan. She spent her early childhood in Florida, attending schools in the Palm Beaches. After high school, she attended the National Cathedral School for Girls in Washington, D.C. She attended the Art Students League and the National Academy of Design in New York City in 1940 studying with George Bridgman, Henry Dumont, Sidney Dickinson and Henry Rittenberg. Troemel also studied privately with M.A. Rasko in New York. She also attended The Norton School of Art in West Palm Beach, Florida and the University of New Mexico, Albuquerque, where she studied with Santa Fe painter Randall Davey.

Jean Troemel came to Florida in 1923 at age 2, settling with her family in West Palm Beach. Her father was influential in the founding of the Norton Museum and School of Art. Troemel began painting as a child. Her first teacher was Eric Geski in 1930. Later in Palm Beach, she studied with Nunzio Vayana, an important force in the development of art in the Palm Beaches. Troemel specializes in portraits and the landscape. She exhibits widely and has shown her work at the University of Florida, Gainesville, Florida; The John and Mable Ringling Museum of Art, Sarasota, Florida; The Sarasota Art Association, Sarasota, Florida; The Norton Museum of Art, West Palm Beach, Florida; The Society of the Four Arts, Palm Beach, Florida; Florida Southern College, Lakeland, Florida; The Jacksonville Art Museum, Jacksonville, Florida; Stetson University, DeLand, Florida; The New Mexico Art Museum, Santa Fe, New Mexico; The Denver Art Museum, Denver, Colorado; The Birmingham Museum of Art, Birmingham, Alabama; The Dallas Art Museum, Dallas, Texas; The St. Augustine Art Association, St. Augustine, Florida; and Flagler College, St. Augustine, Florida. Her work is included in numerous public and private collections including The Sarasota Art Association, Sarasota, Florida; North Florida Community College, Jacksonville, Florida; The Palm Beach Art League, Palm Beach, Florida; The Lightner Museum, St. Augustine, Florida; and the Museum of Arts and Sciences, Daytona Beach, Florida. Jean Wagner Troemel is a Fellow of the Royal Society of Arts in London, England, and a member of the American Portrait Society and the Florida Artists Group Inc. She continues to live and work in St. Augustine where she is the founding director of the Professional Artists of St. Augustine (P.A.S.T.A.) Gallery, located on Charlotte Street in the old city.

Troemel's alkyd oil on canvas, *Matanzas Bay*, was completed in the spring of 1993. The scene selected by Troemel reminded her of a yearly stopover in St. Augustine as her family traveled from Michigan to Palm Beach. "St. Augustine and the fort, the ancient cemetery, the Plaza, the gigantic Ponce de Leon Hotel, and the beautiful Matanzas Bay with rocking boats was my favorite stop in Florida."

After living in the city of St. Augustine for 29 years, the view of the bay seen through narrow streets still holds a fascination for Troemel. "Its changing colors and tones from early morning to sunset, the moored sailboats, brilliant in bright light, but silhouetted at dusk, cause me to paint to communicate to others my joy and excitement in seeing those special effects, as in this particular Matanzas Bay painting. I chose the area of the bay that opens to the sea suggesting that possibility of adventure as well as the security of an anchorage."

Very much in the romantic tradition of earlier St. Augustine painters, Troemel's brightly lit oil captures a number of sailboats at anchor in the right half of the canvas. To the left, two large sailboats help define scale and establish an interesting series of reflections in the richly painted and highly reflective bay water. Overhead, a bright blue sky is filled with billowy, pink clouds in this loose and painterly impressionist masterwork of Matanzas Bay at the city of St. Augustine.

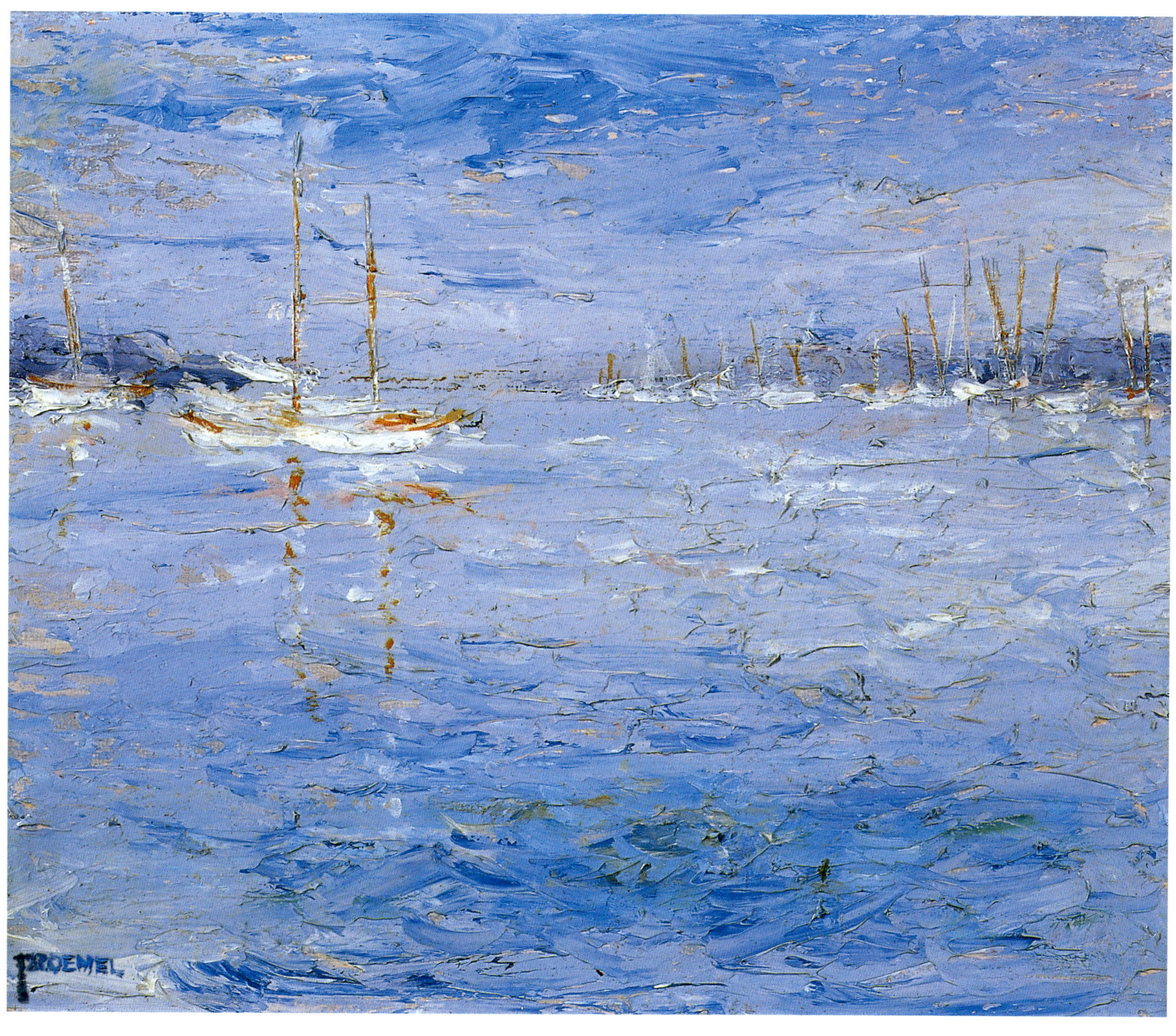

DEBBY WEST

WANDERING SPIRIT

1994, ACRYLIC ON CANVAS, 14" X 18"

Debby West was born in St. Paul, Minnesota, on December 19, 1952. In 1960, she moved to Florida where she attended elementary through high school. She remembers "memorizing crayons at the age of four but didn't really study art until college." She attended Florida Community College, Jacksonville, receiving an associate's of arts degree in 1976. In 1977, she attend the South Florida Art Institute, Hollywood. She returned to Jacksonville and studied the humanities at the University of North Florida until 1996.

Debby West became interested in fine art in 1972 after an influential trip to Europe. Basically self taught, she began to paint seriously in 1978. West describes herself as a visual person with an "introverted, spiritual personality." During her college studies, she was influenced by the painting of the 19th century French master Paul Cezanne and the 20th century Russian innovator Wassily Kandinsky. Today, she appreciates and studies the landscapes of American colorist Wolf Kahn.

West has shown her work twice at the University Gallery of the University of North Florida, Jacksonville. She has also exhibited at The Jacksonville Museum of Contemporary Art, and at Florida Community College, both in Jacksonville.

West's *Wandering Spirit* is an acrylic on canvas painting completed in May 1994. West was impressed by a recent visit to the Ichetucknee River near Gainesville, Florida. The river was "turbulent, yet, relaxed. I felt that way emotionally, at the time, having moved to Ponte Vedra, Florida, less than a year before that. The boat is a recurring theme in my paintings—a metaphor for my soul or spirit, it is usually the same shape and seen from above. I frequently picture scenes from an overhead view. *Wandering Spirit* contains a light turquoise color I refer to as healing green, which I believe has an ability to calm and heal."

In *Wandering Spirit*, West presents the viewer with an abstract and simplified aerial view of a small rowboat on a blue-green body of water. Palm tops and other topographical bits of the landscape are pictured from above, creating a geometrically oriented look down into a decorative surface. The boat and river are "reminiscent of a glorious ride down the Ichetucknee River, the image portrays a journey that clearly isn't over." The Ichetucknee is a popular destination for "tubers" who enjoy floating for miles down the river. It is a clear, cool, spring-fed stream between Gainesville and Lake City in North Central Florida. It flows into the Santa Fe River, that, in turn, feeds the Suwannee River. This painting is a modern statement of the ability of the Florida landscape to restore the soul. Even though the style is contemporary, the subject is one familiar to artists and writers since they began coming to Florida. One is reminded of Ralph Waldo Emerson's reflections upon leaving Florida after a successful rest/cure.

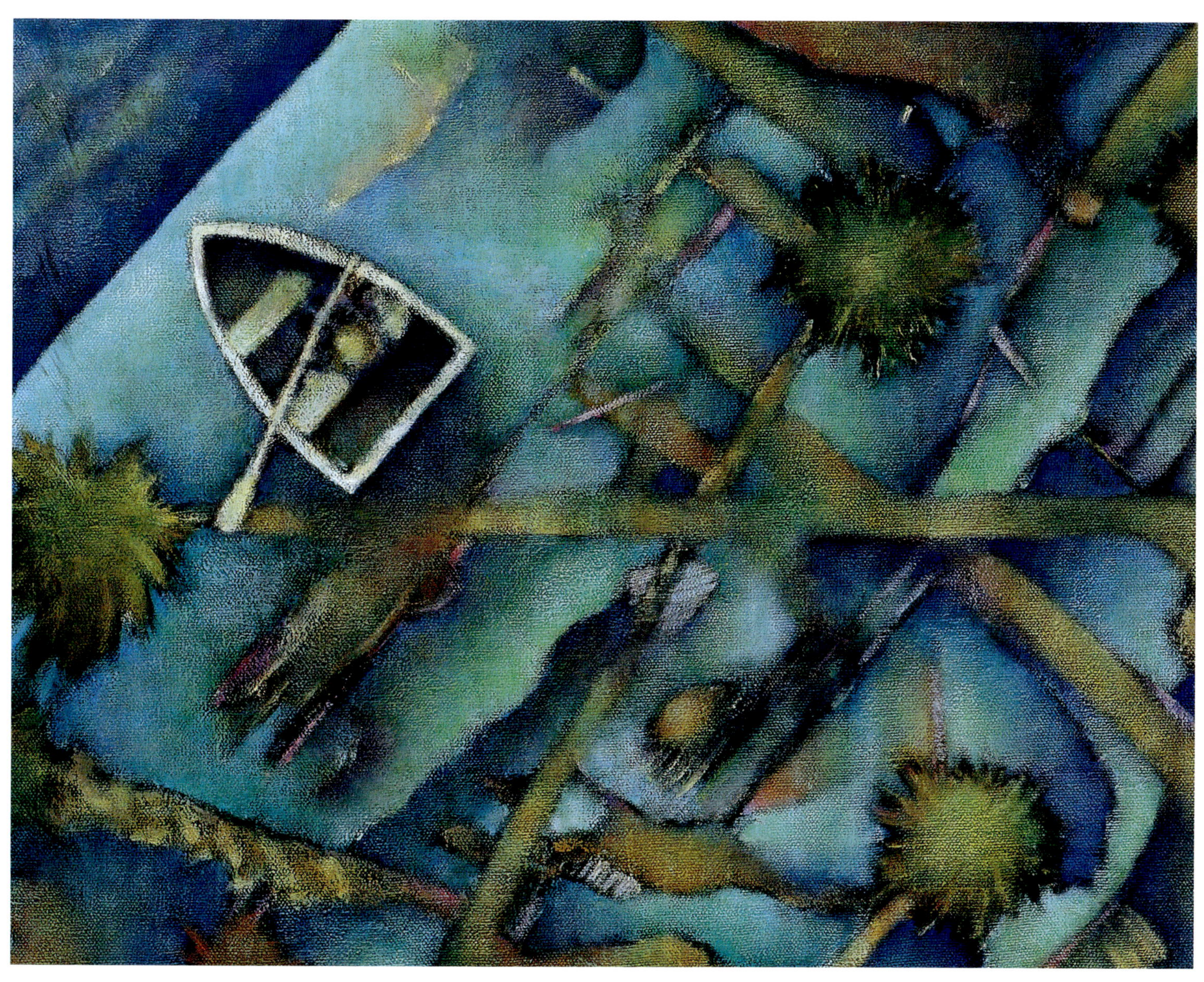

Ruth Olson Wickey

Sewall's Point
1995, Oil on rag board, 20½" x 29"

Ruth Olson Wickey was born in Trenton, New Jersey on November 3, 1938. In 1960, she received a bachelor's of arts degree from Rider College in Trenton. After college, she studied at the Art Students League in New York, followed by additional post-graduate study in fine art at Kean College in Union, New Jersey, and additional study with New York University's Jochen Seidel in Morristown, New Jersey.

Wickey exhibits widely and has many awards. She has participated in more than 75 exhibitions, including The Museum of Florida History, Tallahassee, Florida; The New Jersey Center for Visual Arts, Summit, New Jersey; The Unitarian Fellowship Galleries, Morristown, New Jersey; The National Arts Club, New York, New York; The National Academy of Design, New York, New York; The Jersey City Museum, Jersey City, New Jersey; The Morris Museum, Morristown, New Jersey; The Hunterdon Art Center, Clinton, New Jersey; The Fort Lauderdale Museum of Art, Fort Lauderdale, Florida; The Lowe Art Museum, University of Miami, Coral Gables, Florida; The Milwaukee Art Museum, Milwaukee, Wisconsin; the Pennsylvania State University, State College, Pennsylvania; and the New Jersey Biennial at the Newark Museum of Art, Newark, New Jersey.

Wickey's work is included in public and private collections, as well, including Prudential Insurance Company, Roseland, New Jersey; Dean Witter, New York, New York; The Morris Museum, Morristown, New Jersey; The Kenosha Public Museum, Kenosha, Wisconsin; and The City of Aurora, Illinois Public Arts Commission.

Philosophical in her approach to art, Ruth Olson Wickey believes that it takes "20 years to make a good painter. The real work involves experiencing life with all of its difficulties and pleasures, and the struggle to form one's own world view. An artist may have a mature technique, but she needs also to make decisions about style, subject matter, social comment, materials and media." Wickey decided 10 years ago to explore the United States by visiting national parks and monuments that she recorded in hundreds of photographs. Back in her studio, she began to analyze the photos to determine how she would paint them. Several years ago, she developed a method for integrating abstraction with the literal landscape.

In 1994, Wickey moved to Florida. Her first project was to explore the state and photograph it. "I love the subtle landscapes in the Everglades, the beaches, the orange groves. I settled in Jensen Beach—it is quiet, old Florida—on the Indian River. The view from my front door is of cabbage palms, the river and Hutchinson Island beyond."

Wickey begins a painting with a light pencil drawing. She prefers to work on acid free 100 percent rag board coated with generous layers of gesso to prime and seal the board. After her drawing on the board is finished, she uses washes of thin oil paint to establish the color relationships and the darkest and lightest values. She proceeds to build up layers of paint until she reaches a plateau where the photograph is put away and a second process begins. "I put the photograph away and, with great concentration and intensity, begin the process of trying to capture the essence of the place I am painting. This takes time and I often work on several paintings at the same time, in various stages of completion, so that I can be fresh for each one. I strive for clarity and heightened reality in my work. The result is sort of impressionism up close and a photographic quality at a distance when the eye is able to mix the colors. I like impasto painting and use a variety of tools to achieve my goal including brushes, knives, my fingers—anything that will yield the desired result."

Sewall's Point is an oil on rag board painting completed in 1995. The scene captured by Wickey is based on her visits to a piece of property on the St. Lucie River. "I walked down to the river and, turning around, looked back to see lagoons, and ponds reflecting the light trunks of beautifully carved coconut palms, and a row of royal palms behind them. It was very special and I returned many times to photograph the place, which was known as Lot 13. The paintings I have done of this wonderful place became the series I call *Sewall's Point*, and it will be ongoing, as I never tire of visiting Lot 13." Wickey places the viewer close to the dense, tropical jungle rendered in bright yellows and greens. The foreground is a still body of black water reflecting the elegant palms of the midground. Areas of a deep blue Florida sky can be seen behind the lush tropical foliage of *Sewall's Point*. Wickey's brushstroke is fluid, loose and painterly in this bright mid-day study of a unique location within the Florida landscape.

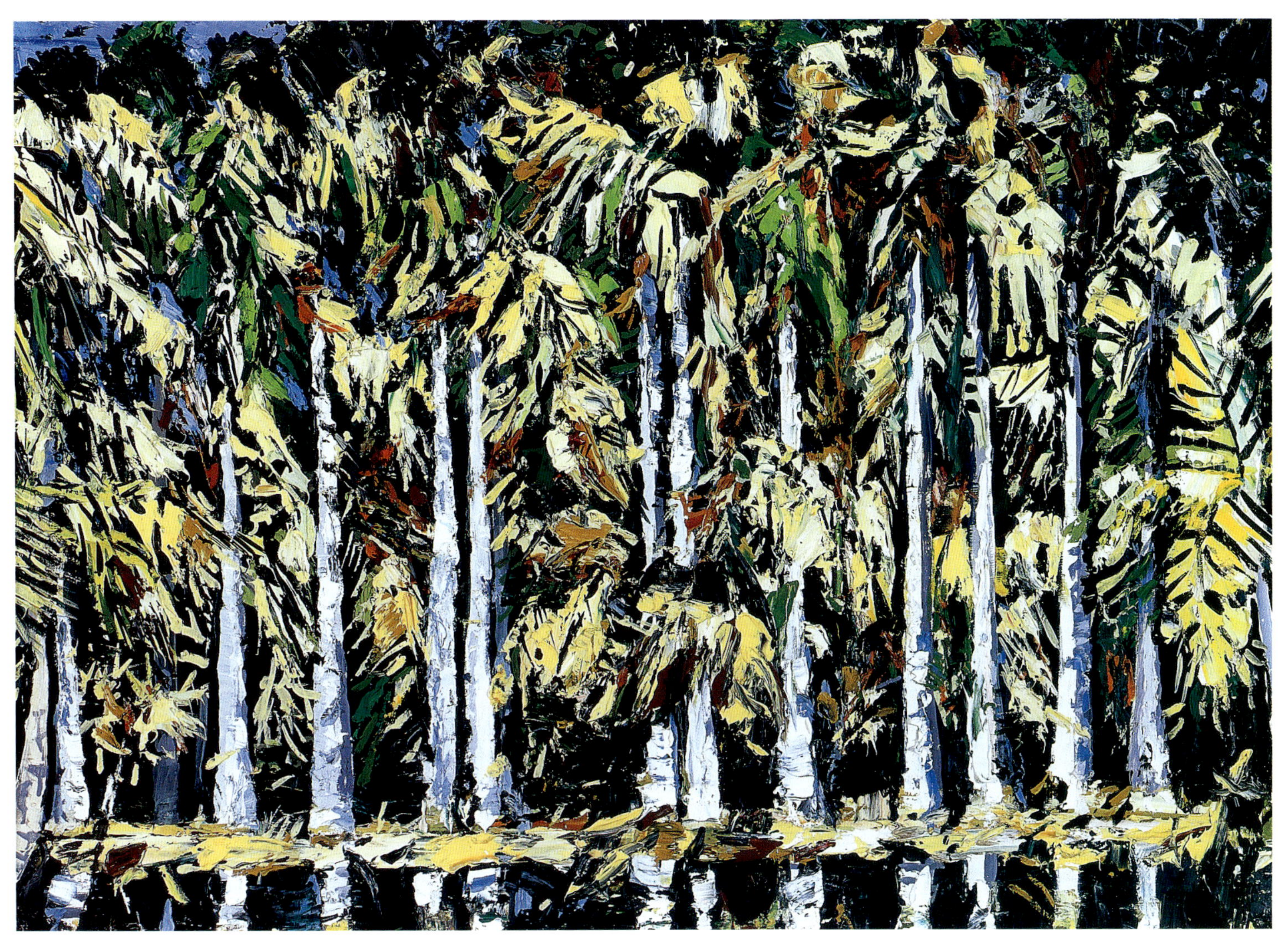

List of Plates

Listed Alphabetically by Artist

Bibliography

The following sources were consulted in the preparation of
Coast to Coast: The Contemporary Landscape in Florida

General

Chambers, Bruce W. *Art and Artists of The South: The Robert P. Coggins Collection.* University of South Carolina Press, Columbia. 1984.

Delehanty, Randolph. *Art in the American South: Works from the Ogden Collection.* Louisiana State University Press, Baton Rouge. 1996.

Fernald, Edward A. and Elizabeth D. Purdum. *Atlas of Florida.* University Press of Florida, Gainesville. 1992.

Gannon, Michael. *Florida: A Short History of Florida.* University Press of Florida, Gainesville. 1993.

Griffin, Patricia C. "Ralph Waldo Emerson in St. Augustine." *El Escribano: The St. Augustine Journal of History*, Vol. 32, pp. 113-34. St. Augustine Historical Society, St. Augustine. 1995.

Grootkerk, Paul. *Art in the American South, 1733-1989: Selections from the Roger Houston Ogden Collection.* University Art Museum, University of Southwestern Louisiana, Lafayette. 1993.

Jahoda, Gloria. *The Other Florida.* Charles Scribner's Sons, New York. 1967.

Jones, Jane Anderson and Maurice J. O'Sullivan (editors). *Florida in Poetry: A History of the Imagination.* Pineapple Press, Inc., Sarasota. 1995.

Libby, Gary R. (editor). *Celebrating Florida: Works of Art from the Vickers Collection.* The Museum of Arts and Sciences, Daytona Beach. 1995.

McCarthy, Kevin (editor). *The Book Lover's Guide To Florida.* Pineapple Press, Sarasota. 1992.

Pamer, Laurence. *Tropical Terrain: South Florida Landscapes.* Museum of Art, Fort Lauderdale. 1998.

Pennington, Estill Curtis. *Look Away: Reality and Sentiment in Southern Art.* A Saraland Press Book, Peachtree Publishers Ltd., Atlanta. 1989.

Phagan, Patricia, (editor). *The American Scene and the South: Paintings and Works on Paper, 1930-1946.* Georgia Museum of Art, University of Georgia, Athens. 1996.

Price, Marla. *Milton Avery: Works from the 1950s in the Collection of The Modern Art Museum of Fort Worth.* The Fort Worth Art Association, Fort Worth. 1990.

Rose, Barbara. *Twentieth Century American Painting.* Rizzoli International Publications, Inc., New York. 1986.

Rowe, Anne E. *The Idea of Florida in the American Literary Imagination.* Louisiana State University Press, Baton Rouge. 1986.

Severens, Martha R. *Greenville County Museum of Art The Southern Collection.* Hudson Hills Press, New York. 1995.

Specific Artists

George Atkinson
Gerrit, Henry. "George Atkinson." *ARTnews*, p. 140, November. 1992.

Kinsey, Joni L. *Plain Pictures: Images of the American Prairie.* Smithsonian Institution Press, Washington, D.C. 1996.

Eleanor Blair
Hodges, Steve. "Eleanor Blair: A Pragmatic Approach to Painting." *American Artist*, pp. 34-39. January. 1981.

John Briggs
Anonymous. *Four Paintings by John Briggs at the James Laurence King Federal Justice Center, Miami, Florida.* Exhibit brochure. n.d.

French, Sherry. "Expedition: Everglades - River of Grass." *ARTnews*, pp. 149-50, April. 1995.

James Couper
Martinez, Juan. "Some Thoughts on Landscape Painting in the Late Twentieth Century and on the Art of James Couper." The Art Museum of Florida International University, Miami. 1993.

Emmett Fritz
Edwards, Page. Personal correspondence to George W. Percy, Tallahassee, Florida, September 12. St. Augustine Historical Society, St. Augustine. 1997.

Miller, Chris. Personal correspondence to Page Edwards, St. Augustine Historical Society, St. Augustine, Florida, November 15. 1997.

Rene Guerin
Guerin, Rene. *Painting Plein Aire When You Travel.* Ms. Fort Pierce, Florida. n.d.

Rachel Hartley
Bénézit, E. *Dictionnaire Des Peintres Sculpteurs, Dessinateurs Et Graveurs.* p. 603. 1951.

Falk. *Who Was Who in American Art.* p. 266.

Opitz, Glenn B., ed. *Mantle Fielding's: Dictionary of American Painters Sculptors & Engravers.* p. 406. 1984.

Pocock, Andrew. Personal correspondence to George W. Percy, Tallahassee, Florida, October 10. Fort Lauderdale. 1994.

Pocock, Andrew. Personal correspondence to George W. Percy, Tallahassee, Florida, August 6. Fort Lauderdale. 1997.

John David Hawver
Blazier, Wendy M. "Introduction" in *Earthly Delights: South Florida Artists Look At Landscape.* The Art and Culture Center of Hollywood, Hollywood, Florida. 1987.

Sanders, Vicki and Barbara Young. "Introduction" in *John David Hawver Sea-Saw-Scene: Paintings and Pastels.* The Art and Culture Center of Hollywood, Hollywood, Florida. 1997.

Artemis Skevakis Jegart Housewright
Bosch, Gulnar K. Notes to accompany Artemis Jegart Painting Exhibition, January 3-February 9, 1961, Washington Federal Savings and Loan Association of Miami Beach. 1961.

Jahoda, Gloria. Notes to accompany *The Other Florida* exhibition, March 13-April 30, 1968, The Lewis State Bank Gallery, Tallahassee, Florida. 1968.

William James
Feliciano, Kristina. "Eliminating the Obvious and Exaggerating the Essential." *American Artist*, pp. 38-43. April. 1997.

Robert Larsen
Corbino, Marcia. "An Interview with Robert Larsen." *American Artist*, Vol. 48, Issue 509, pp. 53-55, 86. December. 1984.

Corbino, Marcia. *Robert Larsen Exhibition* brochure, Corbino Galleries, Sarasota, April 5-19, 1996.

Hilton Leech
Astorino, Frank. "Hilton Leech - The Man, The Studio, The Legend." *Attitudes Magazine.* December. 1994.

Roland, Katherine L. Personal correspondence to George W. Percy, Tallahassee. December 29. Sarasota. 1997.

Treacy, Eleanor. "Hilton Leech Experiments with Mixed Media." *American Artist*, pp. 25-28, 80. May. 1953.

Tod Lindenmuth
Bénézit, E. *Dictionnaire Des Peintres Sculpteurs, Dessinateurs Et Graveurs.* pp. 587. 1951.

Falk. *Who Was Who in American Art.* p. 373. 1985.

Fisk, Ann. Personal correspondence to George W. Percy, Tallahassee, Florida, November 14. Rockport, Massachusetts. 1997.

Fisk, Ann. Personal telephone conversation with George W. Percy, Tallahassee, Florida, November 21. Rockport, Massachusetts. 1997.

Fisk, Ann. Personal correspondence to Page Edwards, Executive Director, St. Augustine Historical Society, St. Augustine, Florida, November 27. Rockport, Massachusetts. 1997.

Opitz, Glenn B., (editor). *Mantle Fielding's: Dictionary of American Painters, Sculptors & Engravers.* p. 569. 1984.

Molly Mabe
Mabe, Molly. "The Voice." Tallahassee, Florida. 1997.

Zimmer, William. Molly Mabe brochure. Tallahassee. n.d.

Joe McFadden
Safran, Verna. "Painting Without a Formula," *American Artist*, Vol. 59, Issue 633, pp. 50-55. April. 1995.

Don Powers
Gussow, Alan. *The Artist As Native: Reinventing Regionalism.* Pomegranate Artbooks, San Francisco. 1993.

Craig Rubadoux
Anonymous. "Craig Rubadoux Works on Paper, 1962-1984." Notes accompanying exhibition at The John and Mable Ringling Museum of Art, Sarasota, Florida. n.d.

Corbino, Marcia. "Craig Rubadoux." Notes accompanying exhibition at Corbino Galleries, March 10-24, 1989. Sarasota, Florida. 1989.

John Stanford
Safran, Verna. "Finding Drama in the Ordinary." *American Artist*, Vol. 59, Issue 633, pp. 34-37, 72-74. April. 1995.

Publications at The Museum of Arts and Sciences are also sponsored in part by
the National Endowment for the Arts, the Institute of Museum and Library Services;
the State of Florida, Department of State, The Division of Historical Resources,
Division of Cultural Affairs; and the Florida Arts Council.